THE EPQ
JOURNAL

THE EPQ
JOURNAL

A COLLECTION OF ESSAYS CRAFTED BY STUDENTS LIKE YOU

Lubavitch Senior Girls School
Supervised by Dr N. Loewenthal

The EPQ Journal:
A Collection of Thought Provoking Essays
Copyright © 2023 by Lubavitch Senior Girls School

For information contact:
http://www.chabadlearninginstitute.com

Book and Cover design by Y. Gruber
Proofreading: You know who you are. Thanks ;)
ISBN: 9798396467347
Imprint: Independently published

First Edition: June 2023
Volume One

Dedicated to the Lubavitcher Rebbe,
who's guidance and teachings are embedded into so
many of our essays, just as they are woven into the
fabric of our lives .

CONTENTS

Contents.. 2

The Rebbe's Letter 4

Foreword 6

Introduction 9

Comparing the Development of Medicine in the West and
China up Until 1900 12

What Distinctive Demands Does Chabad Chassidism Make on
it's Followers Compared with Other Branches of the Chassidic
Movement?.. 34

What is the Jewish View on Music? 57

Investigating the Interaction Between Greek Philosophy and
Jewish Thought, Rejection or Adaption? 66

Why We Do What We Do, When We Know What We Know 86

How and Why Should I Leave my Cult? 107

What Makes Life Meaningful?................................ 126

How does Jewish Law View Debates Concerning Life, Death
and Related Medical Issues?.................................. 144

How Does Religion Affect Your Happiness? 167

How Did the Holocaust Affect Jewish Children? 191

Investigating the Place of Traditional Judaism in USSR...... 218

Can the Modern State of Israel and Traditional Judaism Coexist? **239**

How A Leader can Build Effective Leadership? **261**

What Will Life be like in the Messianic Era? **284**

How are the Concepts of Masculinity and Femininity Discussed in Traditional Jewish Thought? **303**

What was Spinoza's relationship with Judaism? **322**

THE REBBE'S LETTER

By the Grace of G-d
28th Sivan, 5738
Brooklyn, N. Y.

The Editor
Lubavitch Senior Girls School Magazine
London N.16 5RP, England

Blessings and Greetings:

I was pleased to receive a copy of the magazine and "a thing at the right time is very good," for it arrived at this time between the Festival of Matan Torah and the Chag HaGeulo of my father-in-law of saintly memory. As has been pointed out before, the Giving of the Torah at Sinai and the Chag HaGeulo have a special relationship in many respects. One point is that the Giving of the Torah marked the beginning of the Chinuch of our people as a "Kingdom of Priests and a Holy Nation," with emphasis on the doing, namely the fulfillment of the Mitzvoth in the daily life and conduct of every Jew. And the Chag HaGeulo reminds us, and shows us the way of how one is to implement this in actual practise, even under such adverse circumstances as my father-in-law of saintly memory had to face in that country at that time. It also reminds us that when a Jew is determined to uphold the Torah and Mitzvoth and to spread it to the fullest extent of his ability, he is bound to triumph over all obstacles and hindrances. The above is particularly relevant to young people, boys as well as girls, who are in the process of advancement in their Torah Chinuch. In addition, there is the promise of Yogato u'Motzoso, namely that when the proper effort is made, the results and achievements by far exceed all expectations. The magazine makes a very favourable impression, both in its form as well as content, and all who have been associated with preparing and publishing it certainly deserve a great deal of credit. With prayerful wishes for Hatzlocho in going from strength to strength in all matters of goodness and holiness, Torah and Mizvoth and,

With the blessing of Chag HaGeulo,

(the Rebbe's signature)

FOREWORD

Dr. Naftali Loewenthal

Lubavitch Senior Girls' School is a Chabad school, with a high level of study and attainment, both in Kodesh subjects and in the general academic curriculum. Over the decades, it has produced scores of Shluchos, women who, together with their husbands and families, dedicate their lives to inspiring other Jews about Yiddishkeit, traditional Judaism. The LSGS alumna also include many wonderful teachers who have been significant role models to their pupils, whether teaching here in LSGS or in other schools. Further, LSGS has educated hundreds of girls, now women, who actively promote meaningful Jewish life in their homes and local communities, as well as those who also achieve various kinds of fame and distinction.

In order to develop this sense of purpose, confidence and internalised wisdom in LSGS pupils, an important ingredient in the education of each girl is her sense of personal empowerment. There are many aspects of a Chabad-Lubavitch upbringing and education, especially at LSGS, which promote this aspect of each individual.

A recent development in the academic curriculum, which has precisely this function, is the emergence of the Extended Project Qualification, EPQ (for Year 12), worth half an A level, or Higher Project Qualification (for Year 11), administered by the Assessment and Qualifications Alliance (AQA).

This qualification seeks to promote autonomy. It is a research qualification in which the students select the subject themselves. As the EPQ website states: '[The students] can take inspiration from something touched on in class or something personal and unrelated to their studies…'

It might be a topic relating to a student's family, or something she has always wanted to explore, or something she has recently heard of and now wants to investigate. Independently, taking responsibility herself, she then researches the topic. There is input from staff and a variety of levels of guidance. But the autonomy and responsibility are hers.

After some months of independent research the student produces a written report (5000 words for the EPQ, 2000 for the HPQ), and also presents a Power Point lecture on her subject to a comparatively wide audience of teachers, parents, her peers, and other classes in the school.

In addition, the student has to keep a careful log, explaining her individual route towards the specific topic for research, how she defined the final title and research question for her project, and also expressing her personal reflections on the whole process.

In this collective journey, the classroom atmosphere during our weekly lessons, in which the students advised and encouraged each other, is a very noteworthy aspect of the course.

LSGS caters to a wide spectrum of pupils, with diverse interests and personalities. Some of that diversity can be discerned from this book. In each case, I believe, the process of research, writing, presentation, and reflection aided that student discover and realise more of her boundless potential. The Rebbe's inspiration on the spiritual significance of every aspect of life when perceived through the lens of Torah has been, for me personally, a very strong impetus in my understanding of the goals of this course. Not every student refers to Jewish teaching in her project; nonetheless, I believe the Rebbe's inspiration underlies every essay in this book.

I feel privileged to have been able to act as Supervisor for the substantial pieces of work collected here. I am very grateful to Mrs Risa Gruber, the Centre Co-ordinator for this subject and Head of Sixth Form studies, who initiated and manages the course; gratitude is also due to Mrs Helen Freeman, the Head Teacher, and Rabbi Shmuel Lew, the Principal of the School, for their encouragement and support of this subject over the years. Most of all I am grateful to the pupils themselves, who have devotedly worked on researching and completing these fascinating essays.

Warm thanks to Yehudis Gruber, who first suggested the compilation of this book at the beginning of this school year. More recently, when Draizy Raskin shared the letter from the Rebbe relating to her request for a Brocha for success for her EPQ (see her Introduction), Yehudis and many others thought this meant the plan should indeed go ahead. Supported by her friends in the Sixth Form, Yehudis enthusiastically edited and published the book. May she and her fellow students whose work is featured here have much success in the future, in all aspects of life, material and spiritual.

חזק חזק ונתחזק!!

INTRODUCTION

Draizy Raskin

I decided to do my EPQ on the Messianic era. It was not easy as there is no concrete evidence (yet!) to support my findings. There is also a lot of controversy surrounding the topic and I really wanted to present the ideas in the best way possible. It was nerve-racking task and I often found myself at loss as to which would be the correct direction to present.

It was four days before the day I had to present, and I was specially stressed. I realised I has to redraft the entire essay and was working ridiculous hours into the night (or morning?!). One of my friends who was interested in my EPQ and who constantly encouraged me on my EPQ journey, contacted me then. She wrote: *"Hi Draizy! I'm going to the Ohel soon, Bezh. What's your full name and your mother's name? I'll daven for you."*

Feeling encouraged, I sent her my full Hebrew name and asked her if she could ask the Rebbe, who's resting site is by the Ohel where my friend would be going, for a *Bracha* that the presentation and EPQ goes well. Just four hours later, she sent me a picture of the following letter:

By the Grace of G-d
28th Sivan, 5738
Brooklyn, N. Y.

Miss –

London, England
Blessings and Greeting:

Enclosed is a copy of my letter to the editor of the Lubavitch Senior Girls School Magazine, which speaks for itself.

It is specially sent to you because I have been informed that you had quite a substantial part in the work, which the publication of the publication entailed. Needless to say, it is a great *Zechus* for you and may G-d grant that, as has been mentioned in the enclosure, you should be blessed with *Hatzlocho* in both your own advancement as well as in spreading Yiddishkeit in an ever growing measure, in accordance with the saying of our Sages "One who has 100, desires 200," etc., meaning that every achievement in the past naturally stimulates the desire for a greater achievement in the future and, indeed, is in itself a springboard for such advancements.

With blessing
(the Rebbe's signature)

I was blown away. The Rebbe's *bracha* came at a time when I needed it most. I took this as a *bracha* that EPQ would go well and felt it was speaking directly to me as it mentioned "*Lubavitch Senior Girls School*" which is the school I attend and referenced to "*a substantial amount of work.*" My concerns were calmed. Since then, I've gotten positive responses from people who I thought would have found the themes covered in EPQ to be contentious, fulfilling the Rebbe's *bracha*.

The presentation day arrived. I and two of my classmates presented our EPQ's to a roomful of people. The air was electric. Everyone came out of the room feeling uplifted and inspired.

The room emptied and soon only the EPQ students and a handful of others were left.

A friend, who had done an EPQ the year previously, came and pulled me into a hug, "It was amazing," she said, "You guys need to publish!"

Dr Loewenthal, who guides the EPQ students, overheard the comment and smiled at us both, "Especially after the letter from the Rebbe that Draizy received." He turned to me, "Draizy, did you tell her the story of your Rebbe letter?"

I told her. It seemed as an impetus to do something more with my essay, to take it to the world. We decided to collect all the EPQ essays written by students in our school over the past few years and publish them.

That is the story of the book in your hands. I hope you enjoy our findings as much as we enjoyed researching them

CHAPTER ONE

COMPARING THE DEVELOPMENT OF MEDICINE IN THE WEST AND CHINA UP UNTIL 1900

Esther Safarti

In this dissertation, I will be exploring the development of medicine in the West and China and how they interact. Clearly today, Traditional Chinese Medicine (TCM) in China is not the central medical practice as it once used to be and the West ignored alternative medicine for a while. I want to understand what influenced China to westernise itself, learn of the introduction of TCM to the West and its appliance in modern day life.

Included in my piece is the way science and medicine were understood by the West and China, in addition to the therapeutic practices that were established as a result. The conclusion will consider the relationship between the West and China as it can be a topic of further research in itself. However, I believe, just as Western medicine has integrated into China and its medical legal requirement, so too Chinese alternative medicine will eventually be an expected part of Western medical training and practice. My data was obtained in a range of different ways such as books, websites, articles and interviews.

Before the Common Era
West BCE

Before the Common Era, there are texts that refer to medicine however; they make no mention how it was practiced. For example, the Bible suggests medical training in Exodus 21:18-19, obliging on to pay a doctor and Exodus 1:15 where the midwifery of Shifra and Puah is mentioned. The Western medical tradition dates back to the ancient Greeks. The Greeks and Romans established various methods to treating health-related issues: they tried preventing disease in communities, storing of medical works and most importantly treating the ill by the bedside.

The Father of the medical world was none other than Hippocrates (460-370 BCE). Little is known of his life. Among the many stances found in Hippocrates' theories on medicine, the one approach that attracted so many healers was its holistic view; treating the whole person which took into account the mental and social factors in addition to symptoms and disease. Magic and religion played a large part in the ancient medical world. There were healing Temples (early 'hospitals') dedicated to the god of

Medicine, Asclepius, at every place where the Greek sphere of influence had reached. Although there was a large amount of religious influence on the Greek culture, the Hippocratic treatise suggested that diseases were presumably due to natural causes, he never used anything besides his naked eye and focused more on foretelling the course of a disease than on identifying or diagnosing it, aiding the body in its natural process of self-healing rather than offering other therapies.

Some of Hippocrates' ideas came from Persia, India and others say from Babylon and Egypt too - countries that were medically more developed. Many mistakenly thought that embalmment was the stimulation for anatomical study, although due to the embalmment the Egyptians discovered and learnt about illnesses that the deceased has suffered, such as gout.

For centuries to follow the abandonment of Hippocrates' fundamental hygiene rules increased the danger of surgery to the extent that it had to be reduced to a minimum, treatments were confined to amputations during the Middle Ages, as hygiene practises were deemed superstitions. Later on, through improving the cleanliness of the sewer system and water in the cities, the communal health greatly improved and there was less experience of disease.

China BCE

Before 2597 BCE, "Chinese Medicine began with a myth." They say that there were two emperors, The Yellow Emperor and the Red Emperor. The Red Emperor occupied himself with the work of herbalism to attain remedies to prescribe to the sick. His collective data acquired over the years are included in his treatise the Classic of Herbal Medicine *(Shen'noug Bencaojing)* written during the Warring States Period in the Chou dynasty. The Yellow Emperor on the other hand, invented most things that are known in China today, for instance mathematical scales. Contrary to the Red Emperor, he focused more on the mechanism of the body and its anatomy and the results are written in his work, the Classic of Internal Medicine (*Huangdi Neijing*) which is one of the most influential writings in TCM.

Shang: 1766-1122 BCE

During the Shang dynasty, many turned to Shamans to consult ancestors the hope of achieving insight regarding their troubles, including health issues. There are many excavated evidence suggesting divination was common in the Shang dynasty in addition to their belief in demonology.

BCE - Zhou 1100-221

During the Zhou dynasty, alchemy was a popular practice, which over the years developed into chemistry. Alchemy is about creating elixirs to prolong life as the thought of death haunted many, in the process, the quest for the elixir did shine light on medication. Tsou Yen (305-240 BCE) was a Chinese philosopher, best known for developing the Five Element theory. It is difficult to say that this concept is originally his, as there were many other magicians and alchemists that supported the idea[7].

The Warring States period (475 BCE – 221 CE) was an era of division in China with various kingdoms fighting to rule until the Qin dynasty conquered all and brought peace. In this period A Hundred Schools of Thought movement arose, it consisted of many complete works of older discoveries such as the Huangdi Neijing (the Yellow Emperors Classic of Internal Medicine) which relies on key concepts; *qi, ying, yang* and *wu xing*. One of the main principles in Chinese medicine is the relative properties; *Yin* and *Yang*. Physiology of Chinese medicine states that human life and the body's existence is as a result of the balance between these two forces and energies (*Qi*), *Yin* being the inner, negative, while the *Yang* stands for outer, positive. *Qi* is the air and our energy. Lastly, *Wu Xing* are the five elements wood, fire, earth, metal and water. It is said that these five elements are linked to nature and man, for instance, heating metal produces steam, which condenses into water, and water represents humidity and the kidneys. The Huangdi Neijing focuses mainly on preventative procedures, for example acupuncture, moxibustion, massage, drugs and phytotherapy. According to the Huangdi Niejing, surgery was a last resort and not a common procedure, rather the restoration of balance to the body was a preferred therapy.

Phytotherapy is a treatment that uses plants. This includes moxibustion, a burning of moxa (dried leaves) on or near the surface of a person's skin to act as a counter-irritant. Herbs do not deal with the issue; instead, they are nutrients that promote the body's health and strength so that in due course the body could heal itself.

Acupuncture is a practice that aims to restore balance in the body via inserting needles in specific points on the body. Additionally, dietetic therapies was a standard exercise prescribed by physicians and remains in use today.

1ST- 14TH Century
West 0-1300

The humoral doctrine was part of the Hippocratic's medical theory; nevertheless, it was his student Galen (131-200 AD) that pieced together the rare mentions of the humoral concept. The four humours (blood, black bile, yellow bile and phlegm) founded a challenging agenda for understanding health and disease. Hippocratics believed that balance of the humours is what determines the health of an individual and the excretion of any of the liquids was the healing power of nature (*vix medicatrix naturae*). Following this idea, bloodletting was a method of therapy, which was viewed by many as barbaric due to the extent doctors allowed the bloodletting to go on for.

Galen carried out surgical dissections and vivisections, becoming the first to correlate a patient's symptoms and *signs* found on the examined body, whether alive or dead, consequently he was powerful and greatly respected. However, some have the opinion that performing vivisection on animals was useless. Not only did it not provide him teachings regarding the human body, but it also caused havoc for fifteen centuries because of the medical world actually following his false findings. Due to his monotheistic beliefs, the Catholic Church decreed that his scientific findings and theories were the only correct ones and if anyone contradicted his doctrine, they were made to recant on the rack of the Holy inquisition. In my opinion, this suggests that instead of admiration towards Galen during his lifetime, people followed his teachings out of fear, subsequently suffering because of his ignorant mistakes.

Autopsies were not an accepted practice until Galen. Similarly, today there are still many social, moral and religious opposition to this procedure, yet we cannot deny that a substantial amount of our medical knowledge is because of the internal study of the deceased.

In general, autopsies were performed to determine cause of death, evaluate diagnostic and treatment routines (which exposes mistakes and bad habits) and learn about the evolution and mechanism of disease. This is one way the medical world began to develop; as Dr Alan Schiller (a chairman of pathology at Mount Sinai School of Medicine in New York) says: "Neglecting the autopsy, is anathema to the whole practice of medicine."

By introducing diagnostics, the door to classification also opened. Many other practitioners would perform autopsies in public demonstrations during the winter. The first open dissection in Bologna in about 1315 was conducted by Mondino de' Liuzzi (1270-1329), who also wrote the first modern anatomy book, aided by Galen's anatomical study and Hippocrates' concepts.

Institutions such as religious establishments, hospitals and universities were central places for the discovery of medicine. From the late 11th century, doctors trained in medical schools such as Salerno (in Italy), Bologna (founded 1180), Paris (1200), Oxford (1200) and Salamanca (1218). Eventually, by the 15th century there was over 50 universities in Europe, which clearly marks the acceptance of a systematic medical institutions and practices.

China 0-1300
Han 221 BCE – 220 CE

Between 206 BCE and 220 AD, the Han dynasty dominated China with Emperor Wu as their leader. Emperor Wu was haunted by the thought of death just like the majority of Chinese leaders, paying large sums to physicians, alchemists and herbalist to find a method of prolonging life.

The two most celebrated physicians were Zhang Zhongjing and Hua Tuo. Zhang Zhongjing's work Treatise on Cold Injuries was published in 220 (end of Han Dynasty) and is the first known treatise on drug and herbal medicine, many of which are still in use today. Hua Tuo (141-208 CE) on the other hand was the pioneer of Chinese surgery and was extremely skilled in internal and external medicine. He performed the first known laparotomy, i.e. a surgical incision in the abdomen for diagnosis and in preparations for major surgery.

The Han Dynasty gave birth to one of the most acclaimed books in CM; the Shen'nong Bencaojing on essential herbs *(bencao)*. There are the 120 superior drugs, non – toxic, with an invigorating effect and used in tonics to repel illness (e.g. ephedra) and the 125 toxic drugs (e.g. croton), both of which were then classified into the Four Spirits (cold, hot, warm and cold) or the Five Tastes (sour, sweet, hot, bitter, and salty). This treatise focuses on the herbal aspect of medicine, describing the medical plants and how they are prepared.

Chinese Middle Ages 220-589

During this period, China was mainly Buddhist. Buddhism spread from India due to the traveling of Monks and vice versa; Indian Monks journeyed to China. The arrival of

Indian Monks brought about the influence of their culture, including mathematics, astronomy and medicine.

A common practice during this time was alchemy. It is said that alchemy prompted the development of pharmaceutical science that began in the Chinese Middle ages. A noted alchemist Ge Hong (283–341) was inspired to take upon himself this practice by the desire to prolong human life.

An additional circumstantial contributor to the development of medicine in both China and the West was the occurrence of conflict, for war required the treatment of victims. Subsequently, surgical practices improved and books on surgery were written. To become a physician, it was necessary to shadow a practicing doctor and learn on the job. This was the norm until Qin Chengdu, proposed to create a medical school in the year 443, whereas the West established their first medical school in the 9th century at Salerno in southern Italy, namely the Schola Medica Salernitana.

During the third century, Wang Shuhe compiled the Pulse of Classic *(Maijing)* which until today is an essential part of diagnostic methods. The treatise named The ABC of Acupuncture and Moxibustion *(Zhenjiu Jiayijing)* was written by Huangfu Mi (215-282). It is known to be the earliest summary of the detailed method of acupuncture and moxibustion, which many referred to when studying these complex therapies.

Gong Qingxuan merited the sobriquet The Surgeon. Traditional Chinese surgeons would use stone slivers *(bian)* to create incisions. Gong recorded the surgeries he performed in a work called Liu Juanzi Guiyifang, the oldest

Chinese treatise on surgery that provides significant insight regarding invasive procedures and cures used up to the 5th century.

It is clear that until now, physicians simply expanded on the traditional theories and did not totally deviate from them to experiment and discover new grounds, as was the practice in the West.

Tang Dynasty 581-907

The Tang Empire is well known for its significant achievements in Chinese history. During this time, aetiology (cause of disease or condition) and semiology (studying symptoms and signs and learning of their use and interpreting them) were the focal point in the development of medicine, pharmaceutical practices and published works.

It seems that by now, demonology and ancestral vengeance plots were being disregarded and instead, scientific and natural reasoning to illness was being sought. Sun Simiao (581-682) shared this mindset, as he stressed that the cause of cholera (an infectious and often fatal bacterial disease of the small intestine) should be found rather than continue the practice of blaming spirits.

Hospitals were established to treat leprosy and apply preventative methods for common illnesses such as rabies, smallpox and typhoid. Pharmaceutical growth was demonstrated in the vast *bencao* (herbal medicine) collections written by physicians, often in the form of manuals on growing and gathering the specific plants.

Knowledge was shared among the Eastern countries, namely Japan, Korea, Vietnam, India and Persia. While Vietnamese herbs were used in phytotherapy, Korean works were exported to China and Arab countries. They introduced new incense, as they too learnt from China, specifically the art of pulsing. There are some that say that exchange of information and goods between the West and China began in the Tang dynasty[20].

Song Dynasty 690-1279

The medical industry in the Song dynasty increased the amount of written and published books, particularly about internal and herbal medicine. Additionally, this was the time forensic science was establishmed. Xiyuan Jilu, by Song Ci (1186-1249) recommended ways to perform autopsies and provides information regarding physiology, pathology and pharmacology.

Chen Yan of the twelfth century introduced in his work on pathology a new approach to aetiology; the three causes. There are three kinds of pathogens, the endogenous emotional cause, exogenous environmental characteristics and one that is neither endogenous nor exogenous e.g. animal bite or inflicted wounds. Any of the three pathogenic characteristics could create an imbalance between the Yin and Yang or the Qi and blood.

There is evidence that suggests a man named Zhao was the first to use the method of inoculation, a process where a small amount of virus is injected into the body either through nostrils or incisions made to the body, while others say it began in the Qing dynasty (1614- 1819). Applying this method, they discovered the potential to heal smallpox via 'vaccine.' As pathogens and disease were spreading, the importance of hygiene was noticed, especially in urban locations, kept up by road sweepers and soil collectors.

The Song dynasty had a variety of possible prescriptions such as pills, powders and ointments, consisting of various materials including minerals, plants, animal products and pearls.

Jin & Yuan Dynasty 1115-1368

Zhang Congsheng (1500-1228) said, "The prescription of former times could not completely cure the illness of today." This is clear proof that these military physicians were forming a new approach to medicine. Congsheng is known for the 'three methods', namely sweating, vomiting and purging. One can understand that by this period, Chinese physicians began to notice the necessity to discover anew, especially since works of antiquity did not offer therapies for diseases spreading in those years.

14th – 19th Century
West 1300-1800

During the Renaissance there was one person who began to discover Galen's errors; Vesalius (1514 - 1564). Vesalius pioneered the exit from the medical darkness of the Middle Ages. He always performed dissections himself, which aided him in creating anatomical charts for his students to refer to during their studies. As surgery and anatomy were not deemed as important as other medical branches, Vesalius aimed to enhance its reputation and prove its worth and usefulness, especially in terms of understanding the anatomy and medicine. He began discovering Galen's errors when he stole the corpses of executed men and dissected them. However, Vesalius was unable to present his work for it contradicted Galen and consequently he would have been burnt alive as punishment for heresy.

A century after Vesalius released his treatise, William Harvey published his work in 1628, on the blood circulation. During 2650 BCE, the Chinese were the first to comment, that blood flows in a circle and is controlled by the heart, whilst Leonardo de Vinci's renowned studies of human anatomy, taught him a great amount about blood and the organs.

There are many honourable mentions of people that assisted in the development of the medical world, such as Thomas Willis (1621-75), Giovanni Maria Lancisi (1654-1720) and Herman Boerhaave (1668-1738). While Willis discovered the arteries at the base of the brain that are now called the 'circle of Willis,' Lancisi wrote documents on neurology, developed the 'stamping out' method to remove the cattle plague in Europe and contributed to early work on malaria. Boerhaave emphasised bedside and clinical training and argued that medicine should be based upon physical science and mathematics.

By the 17 century, anatomists rarely turned to books written by the ancients, i.e. Galen.

China preceded the West on many occasions when it came to anatomy, but with regard to technology and pharmacy, the West were more educated. A Swiss mastermind, Paracelsus (1493-1541) whose overall emphasis was on chemistry and alchemy, led the Chemical Movement. Some say Arabian countries introduced alchemy and pharmaceutical practices to the West, with Paracelsus leading its growth and development. In addition to the many theories and views Paracelsus expressed, the idea that disease has an external existence to the body (some say this was the beginning of the germ theory) and contradicted the magic-religious beliefs held by some. This caused controversy.

Thomas Sydenham, known by the sobriquet 'English Hippocrates' (1624-89) worked on many aspects of medicine such as diagnostics which then led to the formation of remedies. Sydenham's way of viewing medicine proved to be a turning point in clinical thinking by encouraging classification of disease, just as one would classify plants.

The Enlightenment was characterised by abundant optimism, it was a period that gave birth to great thinkers and became a turning point in medicine; marking a shift from antiquity to modernity, from philosophy to experimentation. The belief that everything could be broken down into science by experiments and observations was a pivotal change in how medicine was perceived and practiced.

While Galen used autopsies to correlate symptoms and signs, Giovanni Morgagni (1682- 1771) introduced the practice of using pathology to understand disease, linking the symptoms to signs displayed on the body, granting him the label 'Father of Modern Pathology.' Furthermore, his work encouraged being educated in medical practice over classical works.

Inoculation practices from China spread to Arabian countries such as Egypt and Turkey. The first person to introduce it to the West was Lady Mary Wortley Montagu in 1717, albeit it was Edward Jenner (1749-1815) who developed the 'modern' vaccination known to us today.

China 1300-1800
Ming Dynasty 1368-1644

Yang Jizhou (1522-1620) compiled The Great Success of Acupuncture and Moxibustion (Zhenjiu Dacheng) which was printed until the nineteenth century. This work was a complete piece and comprised of the collective data acquired until the fifteenth century, in addition to Yang's own experiences and appliance of acupuncture.

Ask any Traditional Chinese doctor about Li Shizhen and they would respond with acknowledgment. Li Shizhen (1518-1593) wished to create a material free of past mistakes that he detected in the 800 works he read in over thirty years. Li introduced the notion that the brain was the central source of vital energy. Lastly and most importantly, his practicing days as a physician was focused on preventative rather than actual cures.

The West's introduction to China began in the Ming dynasty. The Italian Jesuit, a Roman Catholic order of priests, sent Matteo Ricci (1552-1610) to China with the purpose of establishing a Jesuit order. He came with spiritual, cultural and scientific knowledge with hope of proselytizing Christianity. Nevertheless, China rejected the religion and kept the scientific knowledge. In the History of the Christian Expedition to the Kingdom of China, the Jesuit notes that "China is rich in medical herbs which are known elsewhere only as importations." This suggests there was exportation of Chinese herbs between China and the West for already many years and it explains why some say that the starting point at which the West and Chinese exchanged information is unknown, especially since there are similar therapies in the early years, such as the cupping technique which is evident in TCM and in early Greece. One notion that truly stunned the Jesuit was the ability for anyone to attempt at curing illness in China, regardless of his or her level of skill.

Qing Dynasty 1614-1819

During the former dynasty, encyclopaedia volumes grew rapidly and continued to do so. Works included many chapters on the history of Chinese medicine. The Qing dynasty was a burgeoning written period in which books of all sorts were printed and published, especially refined works and commentators on traditional pieces like Huangdi Neijing and the Shanganlun. The Shanganlun (Treatise on Cold Injuries) was a truly celebrated work in the Qing period, as was its author, Zhang Zhongjing, who was the source of inspiration for many writers. Another new and important publication was Errors Corrected from the Forest of Physicians (Yilin Gaicuo) by Wang Qingren (1768-1831), important because it was written via the aid of observed corpses that were dropped in cemeteries.

Inoculation was very popular during this period, especially in relation to small pox, known in China as 'heavenly flowers'. Although they did not manage to perfect this method, its ideas were spread to Europe, which was later introduced as a vaccine in the West by Edward Jenner in 1796. There is evidence that suggests Russia sent a representative to study the cure for smallpox, whereas others say China invented the vaccine, which was exported to other nations, as mentioned previously.

Some say that China underwent Western modernization in the 1800's. It began when missionary doctors and other doctors from the West travelled to the Qing Empire. Another Jesuit, Dominique Parrenin (1665-1741) failed in his attempt to introduce Western scientific knowledge, despite Emperor Kangxi's interest in the quinine paste. His continuous communication with the West included sharing information on Chinese medicine, proving the West's commendation, acceptance and even practice of these therapies.

19TH – 20TH century
West 1800-1900

At the beginning of the nineteenth century, herbal medicine was considered old fashioned, and disregarded in favour of the new and growing pharmaceutical medicine. However, in 1847, the American Medical Association was founded partly due to the growing revival of interest in herbal and alternative medicine.

Although hygiene improved slightly by the nineteenth century, there were still many issues that had not yet been dealt with, especially in hospitals. After Leeuwenhoek discovered germs (unicellular organism), Lazaro Spallanzani (1729-1799) performed many experiments with heat and demonstrated that germs are killed via high temperature. Following on from Spallanzani's results, Louis Pasteur (1822-1895) took his discovery of the effect of heat on bacteria further by determining the minimum temperature and time necessary to kill a germ, whereas Robert Koch (1843-1910) was the first to cultivate bacteria. Together, Pasteur and Koch introduced the germ theory, proving the existence of bacteria in our environment, subsequently encouraging improvement in hygiene, especially in surgical procedures

With the availably of microscopy and other technologies, anatomy and microanatomy was nearly fully understood. "The microscope and the burgeoning chemical procedures could restore the post-mortem examination to its place of importance," is the opinion held by J.H. Bennet (1812-1875), a clinical teacher in Edinburgh. Honourable mentions of great figures in the medical world in this time are Charles Darwin (1809-1882) for his theory of evolution, Gregor Johann Mendel (1822-1884) on genetics theory and Claude Bernard (1813-1878) physiological work.

Karl Rokitansky (1804-1878) led the pathology institute in Allgemeine Krankenhaus medical school in Vienna. He believed in using the naked eye rather than technology when it came to studying the anatomy, inspired by Giovanni Morgagni's appliance of pathological findings, he stressed the importance of correlating symptoms and disease to the *anatomical* appearance. Rokitansky would work backwards. Upon completing an examination, he would retract the steps of what occurred to the body. Some say, due to rarely studying disease with microscopy, his theories on disease were incorrect. Microscopy was made available for medical use by Anthony Leeuwenhoek (1632-1723), a dry goods shop owner, whose a hobby of creating powerful lenses, led him to being the first to see a unicellular organism.

Unlike Rokitansky, Rudolph Virchow (1821-1902) was one of the many pioneers in the movement to include microscopy into the system of studying disease. He stressed the importance of physicians practicing physiological pathology – studying the mechanism of disease, in addition to the regular pathological anatomy. Virchow would use microscopy to examine the microscopic cellular structure of pathogens, meriting him the nickname 'The First Modern Pathologist.' Pathology was a practice he was very fond of, and he believed it was underrated. Consequently, he wanted to develop its status and make it a science in itself.

Although there was a pathological boom, obtaining the bodies were not always done in an ethical, moral or legal manner. This is clearly demonstrated by the infamous Burke and Hare case in Edinburgh, where sixteen people were murdered in 1828 in order to sell the bodies to pathological establishments. Even by the end of the nineteenth century, where bodies were procured more easily, it was not enough and illegal acquirement took place, i.e. grave robbing.

During this period, there were many diseases spreading among people, especially in the urban, populated areas. This was due to travel and animals. As travel was made more accessible, doctors and physicians journeyed to other countries in hope of learning of their medical advancements. Unknowingly, some were infected by a pathogen and upon returning, it spread among the people, leading to many deaths, for instance yellow fever. Animals were used to test disease and remedies, instead of human trials. While some possess a grateful attitude to what they helped to discover, others believe that due to animals having different physiology and obviously a different immune system, the results they provided proved to be of no help, often overlooking possible remedies because it did not induce a recovery in the animals.

China's Westernisation 1849-1911

The fall of the Qing Empire in 1849 after the Opium War, brought about the 1842-4 treatise signed with Britain, France and the US, which enabled trade, the establishment of clinics and influenced Chinese doctors. The first Chinese man to go abroad to learn medicine, was Cantonese Huang Kuan (1828-79). When he returned, he practiced and taught Western medicine, inspiring his students and many others to travel to Europe and the US to study.

Yan Fu was a pioneer for the introduction and integration of Western medicine, translating many Western works and believed that the success of the West was not in their technologies but rather in their way of thinking. As he said: "in the field of scholarship, one prides oneself in China on being learned in the classics, while in the West priority is given to acquiring new knowledge." I infer from this, as I noted earlier, that China's attitude was not to experiment and discover new territory like the West, but rather to remain on the route set in antiquity.

Today

There are some that do not support TCM, either because they fear the consequences of error like poisoning or because they do not see its effects. As Health Secretary Jeremy Hunt in 2014 said: "What I've learnt is that the most important thing is to follow the scientific evidence and where there is good evidence for the impact of Chinese medicine then we should look at that but where there isn't we shouldn't spend NHS money on it."

On the other hand, many hold a positive opinion on TCM. I interviewed Mrs. Esther Samuels, who practices alternative medicine in New York, America. She commented that nowadays, Western and alternative practices are integrating, and even in hospitals, doctors sometimes perform acupuncture prior to a surgery as a form of anaesthetic and are incorporating the holistic approach of TCM into their own treatments. Especially in our generation, where there is more awareness of the importance of a healthy lifestyle, many prefer to turn to natural remedies than to conventional medicine. According to Mrs. Samuels, "if Chinese medicine was free, people would use it just as much." She also said that in the cities of China, there are as many Chinese doctors as Western, but in the countryside, there are more Chinese practitioners.

Even though TCM has not attained a legal status in many countries and the NHS does not fund alternative treatment, more TCM clinics and colleges have opened, and medical practices often prescribe it. In Australia too, TCM practitioners are registered officially on a Chinese Medicine Board.

In China, hospitals are run by the government which follow Western medical methods, although research proves that Chinese citizens prefer alternative medicine, "slower action and milder side effects and a greater focus on treating the underlying illness versus alleviating the symptoms." The undisputed founder of modern China learned in the Western ways and representative of the political group of reformers, Dr. San Yat-sen (1866-1925), otherwise known as Sun Zhongshan said: "if we do not learn what has been done better abroad, we will sink into backwardness."

Conclusion

In this written piece, I have attempted to evaluate what influenced major development in medical practice in both China and the West and consider how the two are related. Initially, I wanted to study the history up until the 18th century, but when I noticed that was the period in which West-Chinese interaction occurred, I extended the timeline I would be focusing on to enable comparison between the two. I did not manage to include the Chinese Communist Revolution of 1946–1950 as it was very vast and complex, being a possibly topic for an individual research paper.

My conclusion is that even though Western and Chinese medicine have different histories, understanding of medicine and science practices, they are now converging. One could not say which one had a greater influence as it is a matter of personal opinion and there are different practices and views in every country. However, I suspect that in the future it will be compulsory to study both Western and alternative medicine due to its beneficial contribution to the medical world.

ABOUT THE WRITER

Esther Sarfati is a graduate of Lubavitch Senior Girls School. She went on to study at Beis Chana seminary in Tzfat. She wrote her EPQ in 2016 out of her interest in Chinese medicine and conventional medicine, particularly on the historic pivot points that lead to their integration.

CHAPTER TWO

WHAT DISTINCTIVE DEMANDS DOES CHABAD CHASSIDISM MAKE ON IT'S FOLLOWERS COMPARED WITH OTHER BRANCHES OF THE CHASSIDIC MOVEMENT?

Chaya Citron

In my essay, I am going to explore the demands on a Chabad follower in comparison to the demands on followers of other paths of Chassidism. We will see that the distinguishing expectations of a Chabad follower is to internalise the ideas of Chassidism, so that his service of G-d becomes an emotional, soul connection and thus is able to communicate, embody and spread these ideas and way of life to others.

Section One

What was the direction in which one who joined Chabad Chassidism was headed towards? What is a Chabad Chassid expected to do that differs to what a Chassid of another branch is expected to do?

The Chassidic Movement

The founder of Chassidism was Rabbi Yisrael Ba'al Shem Tov. Chassidism is based on the mystical, esoteric dimension of the Torah, Kabbala. Kabbala had always existed, and been studied by select individuals, most notably the Arizal of Safed and his elite group. (Kabbala is like an anatomy of the various manifestations of G-dliness. Chassidism perceives the essence of G-d within everything: within the manifestations of G-dliness, all of creation, and all of the levels of interpretation of the Torah. In order to understand this, Chassidic teachings will often use the terms, names and locations as labelled in the anatomy of Kabbala.)

Rabbi Yisrael Ba'al Shem Tov now used the Chassidism that he knew to re-enliven Jews, to awaken them from the 'spiritual faint' in which they had fallen. The Chmelnitsky Massacres (1648-1649) had left physical destruction as well as embitterment and heartache. The revelation that Shabtai Tzvi - whom many, including great Rabbis, had believed to be *Moshiach* (the Messiah) - was an absolute fraud, crushed the Jews' spirits even further. Additionally, a chasm had developed between the scholarly and the unlearned masses, the former often looking down upon the latter. The Jews of Eastern Europe were largely disillusioned with their lives and their faith in the leadership.

Rabbi Yisrael Ba'al Shem Tov sought to heal and re-enliven them through the spirit and teachings of Chassidism. Since Chassidism is the essence of the Torah, perceiving the Divine essence of everything, Rabbi Yisrael Ba'al Shem Tov would show the people how in essence every Jew is indescribably holy. He would go around to villages and cities, visit the town square, and tell inspiring anecdotes, stories and parables of Chassidic teachings. It was common at the time for wandering preachers to go from village to village to speak to the Jews there. Most of them used fiery speeches about the punishments that awaited a Jew in Hell if he was not careful to keep each commandment exactly and perfectly. Rabbi Yisrael Ba'al Shem Tov, on the other hand, stressed how in addition to every human having been created in the image of G-d, every Jew is uniquely precious to G-d, no matter how simple or unlearned he might be.

Those who heard his teachings and became his followers soon were given the appellation '*di freilicher*' – the happy ones. No longer did they perceive themselves as the inferior masses, living a bleak life with strict demands, for which negligence would lead to burning in Hell. They were now shown how their soul and every action they did was important and special.

A deeper understanding of how Chassidism could uplift the Jew can be found in a talk of the Lubavitcher *Rebbe*, Rabbi Menachem Mendel Schneerson. There, he writes that (in the times of Rabbi Yisrael Ba'al Shem Tov's successor) when a paper with Chassidic thought was found rolling in a gutter, a parable was told to defend the revelation of such holy teachings. The parable is of a sick prince: The doctors told the king that his son's only hope for recovery was if the precious Jewel at the base of the crown would be crushed and mixed into a liquid, and hopefully a drop of that liquid would enter his mouth and heal him. Of course, the father agreed to crush the crown jewel in order to try to save his son. The Jews are called G-d's Children ('My son, my firstborn, Israel' Numbers 4:22). Chassidism, being the essence of Torah, is G-d's crown jewel. G-d wanted Chassidism to be revealed in order to save the Jews from their spiritual 'sickness'.

How does Chassidism revive the Jew spiritually? By reviving, we mean that their faith in G-d should be revived from its latent, concealed state. Chassidism is the essence of the Torah, revealing the essence of G-d within everything in the world, including the essence of the Jew, which is their soul. By revealing the essence of the soul, the Jew will reveal their latent faith in G-d.

Rabbi Yisrael Ba'al Shem Tov accomplished this enlivening of Judaism, by being not a mystic as many had been in the past, but a mystic *leader;* not an individual learning the esoteric parts of Torah, but a leader communicating the esoteric in order to transform the peoples' service of G-d to be with inspiration, excitement and vitality.

A mystic leader would be someone who knows Chassidism and through learning and applying its teachings has himself reached an exalted level of Divine Service. Now he seeks to communicate Chassidism to others – not to lofty people like himself – but to ordinary, simple people. We can group his possible 'strategy' into two parts:

1) Through his charisma and actions, he inspires people around him to want to join him and learn from him. This could be classified as emotional communication – the mystic leader affects their emotions.

2) By communicating these esoteric ideas of Chassidism that he knows in a way that these people can understand, they too can transform themselves on their own level using these teachings. This could be classified as intellectual communication – teaching intellectual concepts.

Under the category of emotional communication, Rabbi Yisrael Ba'al Shem Tov performed many miracles, often healing people or blessing barren women with children. He also used melody to touch the people. One song that he composed was the first stanza of the 'Three Stanza Melody.' The stories which he would often tell, are both emotional as they inspire, and intellectual, since they were used to give over the lofty concepts of Chassidism. However, the second type of communication was primarily reserved for Rabbi Yisrael Ba'al Shem Tov's 'Holy Brotherhood,' his very close disciples, who themselves were holy people of lofty souls. To them, he taught the extremely deep Chassidic teachings which lay behind the short inspirational messages he told to the masses.

Development of distinctive paths in Chassidism: Chabad and Chagas

After his passing, Rabbi Yisrael Ba'al Shem Tov was succeeded by his leading disciple, the Mezritcher Maggid. The Maggid continued to expand the reach of the Chassidic ideas and lifestyle. After the Maggid's passing in 1772, no one student took his place as the leader of the Chassidic Movement. Rather, each follower became a Chassidic leader in the area where he lived. Without central leadership, differences emerged. We want to explore how the resulting groups, under their respective leaders, carried on from their teacher, the Maggid, and Rabbi Yisrael Ba'al Shem Tov before him.

A leading disciple of the Maggid, Rabbi Shneur Zalman of Liadi, became one of the leaders in White Russia. After his colleagues Rabbi Menachem Mendel of Horodok and Rabbi Avraham of Kalisk emigrated to Israel, his leadership strengthened over the area.

As a Chassidic leader, Rabbi Shneur Zalman began to teach Chassidic teachings in a broader way than they had been taught in the past. His discourses increased in length and became more expansive and explanatory and 'consequently more accessible to rational thought.' He published the *Tanya*, one of the first published books of Chassidic teachings. The first section, called the Book of the Intermediate Man, guides the average person on how to achieve the level of a '*Beinoni*,' who is in perfect control of his thought, speech and action, so that he only uses them for what is correct according to G-d. Rabbi Shneur Zalman stressed that this is a level within the reach of every person, since we have the ability within our human nature for the 'mind to rule over the heart.' I.e: for our intellect to control emotions. Our emotions might be excited about and desire something inappropriate, but our mind understands that it is wrong and holds us back. This section also discusses how to attain love of G-d through contemplation.

The second section explains what to contemplate. In one sentence: the unity of the world with its source – G-d. To explain these concepts, the *Tanya* uses Kabbalistic terminology.

A further development in his approach happened after his imprisonment by the Russian government. Some '*misnagdim*' (Jews who opposed the new Chassidic movement) had slandered him, saying that he was changing Judaism and that he had sent money to Turkey, an enemy of Russia. (In truth, he was enhancing, not changing, Jewish life by revealing its essence, and he sent charity to the poor Jews in Israel, which was then, under the Ottoman Turkish Empire.) When he was in prison, his teachers, the Maggid of Mezritch and Rabbi Yisrael Ba'al Shem Tov, appeared to him from the next world. They told him that there had been a Heavenly decree against him for spreading the secrets of the Torah (i.e., Chassidism), and that is why it was decreed that he be sent to prison. He asked if he should stop teaching and spreading Chassidism. They told him that on the contrary, he should now spread it even more. In the words of his son Rabbi Dovber of Lubavitch, "The one [discourse] from before 'Peterburg' [in reference to the imprisonment, this is where Rabbi Shneur Zalman was held] not everyone can understand... The text which is from after 'Peterburg' one does understand." Because "after 'Peterburg,' the radiance [referring to esoteric ideas of Chassidus] was enclothed in the garment of intellect."

Therefore, Rabbi Shneur Zalman was thus teaching and explaining esoteric concepts of Chassidism in a very intellectual manner to a very broad audience. The Tanya was specifically aimed for the non-mystic, not specifically for his close students, but for the regular masses, and its publication meant that anyone had access to it. He gave discourses that could be understood by an intellectual, in contrast to his predecessors and contemporaries who largely taught ideas of Chassidism to the lofty and refined; while saying only short gems of inspiration and instruction to everyone else. In other words, they continued to teach to the masses what Rabbi Yisrael Ba'al Shem Tov had taught to the masses, while R' Shneur Zalman was making what Rabbi Yisrael Ba'al Shem Tov had taught to the Holy Brotherhood increasingly accessible and understandable to the masses.

Rabbi Avraham of Kalisk – now in Israel – became strongly opposed to Rabbi Shneur Zalman's techniques. He 'insisted that the matter of simple faith should be stressed over that of intellectual inquiry.' His approach towards the general Chassidic followers was that 'suffice for them faith in their leaders, and recognition of their own deficiencies,' as he wrote in a letter to R' Shneur Zalman. He said that 'too much oil in the lamp could, Heaven forfend, cause the flame to be extinguished-' too much lofty ideas could be misinterpreted and have a negative effect on a simple person's faith. Connecting to the mystic leader (their '*Rebbe*,') and hearing inspiration and direction from him, would bring them to emotional feeling in their service of G-d. An emotional, fiery, passionate service of G-d was his aim. R' Shneur Zalman felt that the emotion that is reached through the understanding and contemplation of an intellectual idea, is in fact on a higher level.

Rabbi Shneur Zalman's way became known as Chabad Chassidism. Chabad is an acronym of the three Hebrew letters that stand for *Chochma, Bina* and *Da'as*, the three soul powers of intellect. Those who continued to follow R' Avraham of

Kalisk, as well as those outside of White Russia--in Poland and elsewhere, became known as Chagas Chassidism. Chagas is an acronym for the soul's powers of emotion. Looking at the above two strategies of a mystic leader, Rabbi Shneur Zalman focused on intellectual communication while the mystic leaders of Chagas focused on emotional communication.

It should be pointed out, that we cannot say that Chabad is the path of intellect. In other words, the end goal of Rabbi Shneur Zalman was not intellect; the point was not to rationalise Judaism in the mind. Chabad Chassidic teachings, in fact, stress the importance of action, fulfilling G-d's will even if one does not understand it yet- and might never understand it. *'Kabalos Ol'* – accepting the yoke of heaven and obeying G-d's commands, must come *before* delving into the understanding of the command, provided by deep Chassidic teachings. But after this commitment to the action, after the fulfilment of G-d's Will, should come the intellect. Why isn't the basic fulfillment of the commandment enough?

Besides for the fact that Rabbi Shneur Zalman was naturally inclined to be more intellectual, there is a further reason for this path of Chabad. R' Shneur Zalman saw another thing that Chassidism could achieve, which he believed was another reason for the revelation of Chassidism.

He believed that Chassidism would prepare the world for the coming of *Moshiach* (the Messiah). In 1746, on the eve of the Jewish New Year, Rabbi Yisrael Ba'al Shem Tov made an ascent to the heavenly chamber of the Messiah and asked him, "When will you come, Master?" The reply was "When your teachings will become public and revealed in the world, and your wellsprings spread forth to the outside..."

The Messianic Era will be a time when "the world will be filled with the knowledge of Hashem, just as the water covers the sea" (Isaiah 11:9). Knowledge means an understanding of the essence of G-dliness. Thus, in order to prepare for the Messiah, knowledge of G-dliness had to be spread. Chassidism, as explained above, is exactly that: knowing the essence of G-d. When Chassidism would be spread out and be known by everyone - not only those 'inside' the elite circle of mystics, but by the 'outside,' by even the simple folk - the Messiah would come. The intellectual path as described above, of making the Chassidic teachings accessible to the rational mind of any person, could bring about this second aspect that Chassidism could achieve.

On the other hand, Chagas Chassidic groups believed that Rabbi Yisrael Ba'al Shem Tov 'wept' at the idea that the holy Chassidic teachings be taught to such people who are not of lofty soul or inner purity. It is clear that Rabbi Yisrael Ba'al Shem Tov wanted to spread the lifestyle of Chassidism, the emotional passionate faith in G-d, to everyone, but they say that he did not want the concepts and teachings of Chassidus to be taught to the 'outside.'

The Role of the Mystic Leader – Rebbe - in Chabad and Chagas Chassidism

Rabbi Shneur Zalman used intellectual communication as a Chassidic mystic leader, a *Rebbe*. He taught in an increasingly rational way so that a broader range of people could understand concepts of Chassidism, and, through contemplation of these intellectual concepts, reach a high emotional state as well. The mystic leaders (*Rebbes*) of Chagas used emotional communication to inspire and direct their followers to an emotional service of G-d. This is not an outcome of the differing ideas of Chabad and Chagas Chassidism, but an essential difference that helps define the two paths.

We know that Chassidism was supposed to reveal the essence of the Jew, to reveal a Jew's faith. The *Rebbe* is a G-dly man in touch with his essence (his soul, a part of G-d). So the *Rebbe* had the ability to reveal this in his followers too. There is a verse that says '*Tzaddik Be'emunaso Yichye* – literally: A righteous man lives by his faith.' (Habbakuk 2:4) According to Chagas Chassidism, they said that it should be read '*Yechaye*,' thus meaning a righteous man enlivens with his faith. For Chagas followers, the focus was on the *Rebbe*. They would regularly travel to their *Rebbe* to spend time in his presence, to hear inspiration from him. They would be uplifted by the singing and dancing, and the atmosphere of faith and holiness. The *Rebbe* would say short messages of inspiration especially at the '*tish*,' a special gathering of the *Rebbe* and his followers. Common topics covered at a *tish*, were how every Jew is holy, every Jew is a part of G-d, every Jew is beloved by G-d. These nuclear messages stimulated the followers, and, combined with the atmosphere and feeling of connection to their *Rebbe*, fuelled their spiritual tanks with emotional energy towards their Divine Service, until they could come back again.

Rabbi Shneur Zalman, however, disagreed with this approach. His approach was 'a righteous man lives with his faith.' He would model and teach how to live a life according to Chassidism through the intellectual teachings of Chassidism. But he wasn't 'making his followers live' – i.e.

revealing their faith, so that they are passionate in their Divine Service. This, they had to do themselves.

The following story illustrates the differing role of the *Rebbes* of Chagas and Rabbi Shneur Zalman of Chabad: A Chabad follower had a neighbour who was a follower of R' Chaikel Admurer (a *Rebbe* following Chagas ideas). They prayed in the same synagogue. In relation to prayer, we should preface that the Chagas Chassidim would pray with intense emotion, often raising their voices in song, shouting and using hand motions. A large part of Chabad Chassidism was contemplation before prayer. Rabbi Shneur Zalman wanted his Chassidim to contemplate concepts of Chassidism. Now, this follower wrote to Rabbi Shneur Zalman complaining: my friend prays with such feeling and emotion. He shouts and sings with passion and love of G-d. Meanwhile, I think and think; I try to contemplate in my mind, and if I am lucky, after some time I feel something. But my friend is burning with love of G-d!

Rabbi Shneur Zalman replied: *'He* is burning? *Chaikel* is burning in him! And we want that you alone should burn.' The follower of Reb Chaikel Admurer of Chagas was emotional because of the inspiration of his *Rebbe* 'burning in him'. The follower of R Shneur Zalman was expected to use his intellect and the intellectual ideas taught by his *Rebbe* to change himself.

This story encapsulates the difference between Chabad and Chagas. Rabbi Shneur Zalman did not say that the fire wasn't important. On the contrary, Rabbi Shneur Zalman's goal was also the fire, the emotion, the revelation of the essence of each Jew's soul to connect to G-d. While Chagas Chassidism goes straight to the emotion generated by the

Rebbe and the Chassidic court, Rabbi Shneur Zalman wanted to get to the emotion through intellectual communication – via the person's mind. Why? When a concept fits into a person's brain, when the person understands it completely, it is theirs– it has become a part of them. Rather than an external force, which affects them, it is a part of them, which they will use and live by. The emotion, the fire, is now generated from within – 'you alone should burn.' In Chasidic terminology, these different paths can fit under the titles of 'encompassing,' and 'internal.' The emotional communication of Chagas is an external, all-encompassing force, which inspires the follower. The internal communication of Chabad would bring an internal change in the follower himself.

In conclusion, a Chabad follower is expected to bring about an internal change to reveal the 'fire,' the emotional soul connection to G-d within himself, through the intellectual communication, teachings and example provided by his *Rebbe*.

Section Two

What is the approach of Chabad Chassidism to some contemporary issues? What is a Chabad follower's approach expected to be in relation to them?

Outreach

In the world today, everyone is exposed to all different types of people, with different beliefs. We will explore how Chabad followers are expected to take a role of outreach to the world around them.

As mentioned previously, Rabbi Yisrael Ba'al Shem Tov asked the Messiah "When are you coming?" He replied, "...When your wellsprings spread forth to the outside..." When he writes about this to his brother - in- law, he expresses distress that this would take so long.

We have already discussed above how Chabad and Chagas Chassidic groups understood this differently in the times of Rabbi Yisrael Ba'al Shem Tov. As the times and the situations changed, the result of their differing opinions on spreading Rabbi Yisrael Ba'al Shem Tov's teaching 'to the outside' also developed.

In 1929, the sixth Chabad *Rebbe*, Rabbi Yosef Yitzchak Schneersohn came on a visit to America. In a talk he gave on the festival of Simchat Torah, he introduced the idea that the Chabad Chassidim who had moved to America and now lived there were in a sense the 'outside.' In the free land of America, they lacked spiritual leaning and were not used to studying Chassidic teachings. He wanted them to start studying them. An example of this, is when some years later he instructed some of the advanced Chassidic students who had opened a Chabad school in Montreal, to spend time with the members of the Chassidic community there, encouraging them to learn Chassidic discourses and in that way to arouse their spiritual side.

Furthermore, Rabbi Yosef Yitzchak also addressed the 'outside' of non- religious Jews. When he came to America permanently and people said that 'America is different,' that religion need not be kept as it was in the old villages of Europe, he said 'AMERICA IS NOT DIFFERENT.' Judaism can and should be kept in America too. One of his actions towards this was the institution of the 'Religion Hour' program for Jewish children in public school. The Jewish, but non-observant children, would be taken out of school for one hour a week to be taught about Judaism by young Chabad followers. He also began to send '*Shluchim*'- emissaries (usually a husband and wife team) to live in countries around the world to teach Jewish practices and teachings, as well as Chassidic thought to Jews there. He saw this spreading to the 'outside' and rejuvenation of Jewish practise and spirit as a preparation for the Messiah, as he began to often say: 'Immediate repentance' – i.e., returning to Jewish life as G-d wants – 'brings immediate redemption' – the Messiah.

Finally, we come to the seventh and last *Rebbe* of Chabad, Rabbi Menachem Mendel Schneerson, who, although no longer alive, is still viewed by his followers as their current leader. His approach to the idea of spreading Rabbi Yisrael Ba'al Shem Tov's teachings to the 'outside' is clear to see. Under his direction, thousands of emissary couples have gone to far-flung cities across the globe to help and teach other Jews who may be totally estranged from their heritage and religion. Rabbi Menachem Mendel Schneerson, in his private audiences and later through distributing dollars, met with thousands of people from all Jewish backgrounds and beyond. Great Rabbinic leaders, members of Israeli government, simple Jews straight out of Communist Russia, American presidents and everyone in between, received his blessing and advice with the love characteristic of Rabbi Yisrael Ba'al Shem Tov's ideals: To love every single Jew, for they are each special and holy. In regards to the world at large, Rabbi Menachem Mendel encouraged that the Seven Noahide Laws for all mankind be promoted and taught to non-Jews, and wanted a 'Moment of Silence' to be introduced into public schools in order to implant an awareness of a Higher Being in every child. So, we can see that the Chabad approach today towards non-observant Jewry is to teach, educate and bring them close to G-d, especially through Chassidic teachings and ideals. This fulfils the idea of spreading Rabbi Yisrael Ba'al Shem Tov's teachings to the 'outside,' as Rabbi MM Schneerson would often say.

Meanwhile, when Jews began secularising and dropping traditional observance, especially due to the *Haskala* enlightenment and later the Reform movement, the general response of religious Jewry was to build metaphorical walls around themselves, so as not to be influenced negatively. Rabbi Moshe Sofer, the Chasam Sofer's 'motto' was 'new is forbidden from the Torah.' Meaning that no changes can be made in Torah law and even lifestyle. Chagas Chassidism took this approach. Today they mainly live in close, sheltered communities of Chassidic groups, such as Williamsburg in New York and Stamford Hill in London. They do not have the idea of going and spreading Jewish awareness to non–religious Jews, and will usually have little contact with them. Through this, they largely manage to keep out undesirable influences from the world around them. Satmar is an example of a Chagas Chassidic group that lives in a Chassidic enclave and doesn't usually engage in outreach. The first *Rebbe* of Satmar, R' Yoel Teitelbaum (1887-1979) said that 'The Torah of Rabbi Yisrael Ba'al Shem Tov has been forgotten.' Although Rabbi Yisrael Ba'al Shem Tov was able to reach out to all Jews, nowadays we cannot do this. Rabbi Yisrael Ba'al Shem Tov was reaching out to Jews who may have been unlearned, but they had a pure, simple faith in G-d and kept the commandments to the best of their ability. Nowadays, outreach would be to Jews who are completely estranged from Judaism and may not even believe in G-d, so the Satmar *Rebbe* does not agree to it.

The fact that Chabad Chassidism is geared towards spreading Torah knowledge and Chassidic teachings through outreach, in addition to being a result of their understanding of the Messiah's words, is also enabled by:

1) The intellectual communication of the system (rather than emotional).

2) The role of the *Rebbe* as teaching how to live (rather than enlivening, as discussed above).

If communication is based on emotion, the person is dependent. In a certain atmosphere, an emotional reaction is generated. So if one is in an atmosphere of excitement towards Judaism, one will be excited about Judaism. The advantage is that without working hard, the person is brought by the atmosphere to a place he couldn't have reached on his own. The disadvantage is that when the person leaves that atmosphere, the emotion leaves too. The *Rebbe* being the one enlivening you means that your vitality in Judaism is dependent on the *Rebbe*.

When communication is based on intellect, the person is more independent. Once a person understands a concept in Chassidic teachings that brings him emotion in his service of G-d, that concept has become a part of his brain and he can take it with him wherever he goes, no matter what environment he is in. When the *Rebbe* is teaching you how to live your life, then this way of living becomes your own independent way of living. The disadvantage is that it takes a long time and a lot of work to understand it and make it a part of you.

Therefore, a Chabad follower ideally is not dependant on the emotionalism of being close to their *Rebbe*'s court. The Chassidic teachings and lifestyle can become, independently, a part of them, and so they are able to travel to any location on the globe – and since it independently belongs to them, they can teach it to others in the role of emissaries. As a young man studying in Yeshiva, Rabbi Nachman Sudak asked the *Rebbe* if he could be sent as an emissary. The *Rebbe* replied that for now he should continue learning. The next time Rabbi Sudak asked, the *Rebbe* approved and he was assigned to be sent to England. He asked, "What should I do when I get there?" To this, the *Rebbe* said: "What should I tell you? You will get there, keep your eyes open, and you will find thousands of things to do." The first thing was to ensure that Rabbi Sudak had learned, understood and internalised Chassidic teachings. Once that was accomplished, The Lubavitcher *Rebbe* could send him across the sea to England and Rabbi Sudak would independently be able to know what needed to be done in the outreach work to Jews there, and by extension, the same would be demanded of any follower of Chabad Chassidism.

Technology

We will explore how Chabad followers are expected to respond to the recent explosion of technological development and use.

This brings us to the influence, which is probably largest and most significant today that did not exist in the times when Chabad and Chagas Chassidism first began: technology. The differing way in which Chabad and Chagas communities face technology is a direct continuation of how they understand

and carry out the directive of '*chutza* – spreading to the outside.' Chagas communities almost entirely shun TV, radio, and now the smartphone. A topic that *Rebbe*s of Chagas talk about frequently is the dangers and temptations that internet and the smartphone bring. It is extremely discouraged to own a smartphone and, having internet at home is looked down upon. The verse 'and your camp should be holy' is often reiterated to show that one must keep one's home and community holy, and not let the outside influences and threats to spirituality of technology enter.

The approach to technology in Chabad, is different. Rabbi Menachem Mendel Schneerson was strongly opposed to his followers having a TV in their homes. At the same time, Tanya lessons were broadcasted on radio and the *Rebbe's* talks shown on TV. Today, Chabad.org is a website that has huge amounts of Torah texts, teachings, contemporary Jewish writing, advice, multimedia etc. The majority of Chabad adults own a smartphone and will try to use it if not primarily, largely in order to help with their outreach work. We can get a clear understanding of the Chabad approach to technology from a talk of the Lubavitcher *Rebbe*. He quotes the Zohar, which predicts that in the sixth millennium there will be an outpouring of spiritual and worldly wisdoms. This time corresponds to when R' Shneur Zalman's '*Likkutei Torah*' was printed, an outpouring of deep Torah ideas. It also corresponds to the time of the Industrial Revolution. Both of these are to contribute to the coming of the Messiah, which (according to many opinions) will happen by the seventh millennium – if not earlier. There is a Midrash that states that the only reason gold was created, was to be used in the Holy Temple in Jerusalem, to glorify G-d. So too, the only reason for this outpouring of 'worldly' knowledge in the development of science and technology, is to bring awareness of G-d (which will also bring the Messiah). Science more and more shows how the world is really one. People used to think that there were millions of materials. Now we know that everything is made from the atom. Technology brings endless opportunity to reach and teach people all over the world. Therefore, if it can help them to fulfil the task of spreading Jewish teachings and specifically Chassidic teachings to the 'outside,' then a Chabad follower uses technology to do so.

Women

Nowadays, the significance of women's rights and women's activism is a very central topic. We will explore what the role of women is as followers of Chabad Chassidism, in contrast to that of women as followers of other Chassidic groups.

In Chagas, there is, of course, a range of approaches to the women's role. In previous generations in Europe, girls did not attend the Chassidic court of their *Rebbe* as their husbands, sons or brothers did. Generally, in Jewish society, girls learnt how to run a household and how to live according to Jewish law by example of their mother at home. Later when school became compulsory and the girls were going to non-Jewish government schools, now exposed to influences from all those around them, Sara Schneirer started the Beis Yaakov movement, educating girls in Judaism. Some Chassidic *Rebbe*'s gave her blessings of success – such as the Bobov *Rebbe* – but did not specifically tell their followers to send their daughters to her school. The Gerrer *Rebbe* fully endorsed and supported Beis Yaakov, and told his followers to send their daughters. The Satmar *Rebbe* in Hungary was against girls learning at all.

These approaches continue today. The Satmar Chassidic group is still mainly against women learning Jewish texts – they will learn Jewish law and stories, but usually not from inside the texts. A member of this Chassidic group told me that she thinks that the *Rebbe*'s goal may have been that "women are naturally more spiritual, more open to spirituality. A man has to do things from the external, from outside to make himself more open – he has to learn since he doesn't naturally have it. So it's about keeping women, women and men, men." In other Chassidic groups, girls will learn basic Jewish texts, but not so much Chassidic teachings. Gerrer Chassidism encourages girls to learn.

Now, let's look at Chabad in previous generations. In general, the women would not be learning Chassidic teachings, but there were some that did. Rabbi Shneur Zalman taught very deep Chassidic ideas to his daughter Fraida. The Beis Yaakov movement didn't really reach Chabad at first, since it was in Poland, while Chabad Chassidim were based in White Russia at the time. Rabbi Yosef Yitzchak Shneerson started 'Achos Hatemimim' – a group of teenage girls who learned Chassidic teachings together on a regular basis, and reported their progress to him. He once said: "In Chabad, there is no difference between a son and a daughter."

The Lubavitcher *Rebbe*, seventh of Chabad, would have personal meetings with many people, including women. He scheduled gatherings specifically to address women. He sought to empower women; in many talks, he stressed the unique power that women have. For example, he once said that since women are usually by nature more gentle than men are, they are more likely to influence non-religious Jews to come closer to Judaism. If a non- religious wife comes closer to Judaism, she is more likely to influence her family to join her than a husband would be. When newsletters were made for Jewish children, the *Rebbe* told the editors to make sure that both a boy and a girl are placed on the front page.

In Chabad girls' schools, the girls learn Jewish texts from inside the texts, as well as many Chassidic teachings including deep discourses.

In Chabad, the point is that the women - like the man - should learn and have intellectual communication of Chassidic ideas, and be empowered to use her unique traits as a woman. This outlook also enables the idea of emissaries, that we mentioned before. They are not a Rabbi who leads and teaches, whilst his wife remains at home. Emissaries are a team of man and woman who, together, make programs, lessons, activities etc. to bring Judaism and Chassidism to the 'outside.'

Conclusion

We have seen how the distinctive demands placed on a follower of Chabad Chassidism are to internalise the emotional connection to G-d through intellectual communication, since when one understands something, it becomes a part of their own beliefs, a part of themselves. We could say that Chagas followers are expected to be like a thermometer, whose temperature, fire, is based on its surroundings, while a Chabad follower is expected to be like a thermostat, which itself generates the heat for its surroundings. Their *Rebbe* provides the intellectual communication of the deep ideas of Chassidic teachings, and models how they themselves should live, and then both men and women who are Chabad followers, are expected to thus be able to communicate this to other Jews and the world at large.

ABOUT THE WRITER

Chaya Citron was born in Belfast but grew up in London, and is currently living in New York, where she is studying Chassidus and spending quality time with friends and family. She has always enjoyed learning and sharing what she has learned with others. Chaya hopes to always be able to pass on the passion she feels for Torah, Chassidus and a Jewish lifestyle.

CHAPTER THREE

WHAT IS THE JEWISH VIEW ON MUSIC?

Chayale Levy

This essay is about how music can affect both the mind and heart of the person listening to the tune. Music is a powerful creation and is not simple to use. Like everything in existence, it has one of the strongest effects on a person, as anything else can. I am going to explain the process in which music came into being and how it is used for different purposes, positive and negative according to the The Jewish/ Chassidic point of view and the psychological point of view.

I want to show how it can lead a person to change their entire point of view and being in existence for a better change.

The Jewish View

When G-d was creating the world, He wanted to gift the world with the present of music, but was not sure whether He should or not. He asked the angels on their opinion. They replied, "Don't bother, for humanity do not know how to appreciate music, they will abuse it and use it for the wrong purposes such as their business and to make money. Give us the power of melody and we will sing you praises, and we will sing you your songs, we will use the power of melody and bring it to its highest potential!" G-d thought about it and decided against the will of the angels and claimed, "The people might abuse music and its true reason for why it was created, but I will still give it to them, for it's something they can use to remember Me with, when they sing they will realize that there is more to life than just instant gratification. So yes, I shall give humans My unique language of music and song, so that they can use it to discover transcendence."

Everything that is created in this world has a specific purpose for its survival, a reason why it exists. The reason why G-d created music was so that we, His creations can use it to serve Him in the Temple and anywhere we may be. To praise Him, to thank Him and to honour Him with. For example, in the Temple, when the priests are offering sacrifices, the Levites would play music and sing praises to G-d, or when the people would pray, the Levites would lead with song. The first time that music is mentioned in the Torah is when it talks about the grandson of Adam, who's name was Yuvul. As it says, "…he was the forerunner of all those who play the harp and flute" Yuvul was known to have been a shepherd, and it is from here, that we see in all of Jewish history, shepherds are also ones to play the harp or flute.

Music is a whole world on its own. No one can fathom how strong and powerful music can be. The times that we see how music can change one's perspective in an instant, is scary, but reality. After a few generations people started to use music for the wrong purposes. Instead of using it to serve G-d, they used music to serve idolatry and to do business. Even if someone has a passion for music, but uses it for personal moneymaking reasons, which has an inappropriate meaning, it is completely wrong and not allowed.

When one uses music not for what it was created for, they are abusing the amazing gift that G-d gave to us. At the same time, creating an impure aura around them. Nowadays, the abusive behaviour to music is not even accountable, no matter how hard one can try to rectify the situation, it will never be enough. However, once the person has done a complete Teshuva and change their ways, the entire negative they had done in the past is forgiven.

There are two ways to split up a song:
1) The melody
2) The lyrics

Many people think that when creating a piece of music, it is another random tune, that some random person came up with, whilst doing a mundane matter, but it is not. When one creates a piece of music, it is coming from their inner self, they get inspired by something, then take it, and put it into a piece of music, so that others can appreciate their inspiration. Therefore, it is also when they write the piece of music that they are placing their whole being into their current work, so that they can get the best outcome. Their true essence creates the emotion of the melody. It is known somewhere in the

Jewish teachings of our elders, that when listening to music you are connecting yourself to the composer of the song.

How is that?

Because music is such a powerful thing, it has the power to connect two people from completely different sides of the world, who do not know one another, yet they are still connected through the music. Your soul connects itself to the soul of the composer.

The lyrics of a song is another expression of one's self, just not on such a high level as the melody. Sometimes, a song can be saying over a story that happened to someone, or a concept of society or a character trait or absolutely nothing of importance. The composer of the song and the composer of the lyrics can be two different people, but have the same intention, to express their current feelings, whether its gratitude, appreciation, anger, frustration, depression, sadness or loneliness. By listening to that song or piece of music, you are connecting yourself to the composer and their feelings. The power of music is so intense that it can change your emotions by listening to someone else's emotions placed into a tune/ melody/song.

We see from the beginning of creation how music can change a persons' being. Music started as being a time-passer for the shepherds in the field, waiting with their flock as the day went on. Then came another person, hearing the tune of the shepherd, and decided to create their own tune and expressing their emotions through it, just like the shepherd had. Although the shepherd had played the tune with the right intentions in mind, the person who heard, when he composed his tune, he may have not, and therefore, this led to something being created with a purpose to express their feelings, but with impure thoughts and emotions, which passes onto the person who listens to the melody.

As we see, not all songs have a pure intake and as history moves on, it becomes clearer to us on how music has changed. After all, there are so many different types of genres of music out there in today's modern society that anything is accessible. The Lubavitcher Rebbe said that even if the melody is that of the same of a rowdy song but the words have changed, the effect the song has on a person can change and instead of the person becoming a completely different person, it puts up boundaries. One should be careful on how they come to expressing and listening to the music around them.

The Psychological View

To get a better view on music overall, it is best to see it in the eyes of another, that being the psychological aspect, to how music can effect a person on a whole.

Music is a powerful concept that can change how the brain develops and plays a lot with one's emotions.

When listening to music, the brain concentrates on the melody and the lyrics, taking them in and sending messages through your body on how you should react to what you have just listened to.

The way the brain is, is that it has many sections and within each section, there is more parts within it. Each section is wired in a special way that sends messages throughout the body in a specific manner. It is very possible to change the way your brain is wired - nature versus nurture. One may have the nature to be exceedingly kind and considerate, but the way they were brought up, their surroundings etc. (nurture) changes them to be unfriendly and harsh. Therefore, when listening to music it can change the nature of the way your brain is wired, and you act according to the nurture of the effect the music had on yourself.

It is a known fact in the psychology world that one starts hearing sounds when they are just a fetes in the mothers' womb. Because of this, a lot of mother's are told to start communicating with their child when still expecting. There is no proof though that putting music on for the fetes to hear will improve their IQ at all.

It is also shown in that music can help with one's mental, emotional and physical health, helping one come out of depression or help in the process of it. Music can be used as a gateway to contentment and personal pleasure or seclusion from the world. Music can be your only true friend in times of pain and suffering, it's the only one who knows your true emotions and feelings. Music can encourage a person to change and help them through the process of becoming a different person all together.

Different genres of music have different types of effects on a person's behaviour. The simple classical music like '*Fur Elise*' or '*River Flows In You'* can bring a person to a calm, relaxed mood, placing them in a state of peace and tranquillity. A rock or pop song can cause a person excitement to rise and make them hyper and rowdy.

Besides for changing one's emotions and behaviours, music can also change a person's outlook / perspective on life and the situations surrounding them. Like someone who normally has a negative perspective on how they are treated by others, can listen to or express how they are feeling through a certain genre of music and they change to focusing on how they are treated is only to make them a better and stronger person.

Music being such a powerful thing, one may seem scared to enter the world of music whereas someone else may be desperate to enter the world of music.

Positive and Negative Effects

Someone can be a soft gentle person, but once they enter the fantasy world of music, they can drastically change to being a person with the personality that was very different to their previous self. It may seem impossible, but from my own experience, I know how suddenly a person can change by listening to music.

Music is not something that should be taken lightly. Yes, it can help someone, but it can also destroy someone without him or her realizing, it until it is too late.

Music can...

• By listening to music one can change for the better

• It can bring someone back onto the right path of life. It can change ones personality for the better on how they treat themselves and others

• By listening to music, one can develop an ear for music, a talent to play music or able to make note of changes in a piece of music

• One can come to appreciate their surroundings more

Alternatively, it can...

• Listening to certain types of music, can cause one to veer from the correct path. It can cause one to be more aggressive and rowdy

• It can change ones personality for the worse. I.e. how they treat themselves and others.

• Ones emotions can be mixed up and they can start to have inappropriate feelings.

• Listening to certain types of music can cause their evil inclinations to strengthen.

From what I went through in my high school years, I was trying to figure out what type of person I want to be and how to come about that path. Although I chose my path of who I want to be when I finished high school (and how I will come about that path is another matter) but as soon as I started paying attention to my surroundings, especially listening to the songs played in stores or exercise classes and connecting with them, it changed my outlook on life and made me doubt the path that I chose. I got involved in the wrong things because of listening to the wrong types of music and, even though I still know that what I have done in the past and currently doing is not what I should be doing, I had this addiction to music that changed me, and made me doubt all that I had decided for myself, all because of one song.

This addiction to music is not easy to overcome and I'm still in the process of overcoming it but still it is a factor that can change anyone.

Anything can change in a second and it can all start from one song that does or does not have the right intentions

Throughout the research that I have done for this essay I learnt a lot about music and came to a higher understanding on why I myself as person changed so much from listening to one song. I have tried my best to mention all the points, but there is so much more to add. Not all of it can be expressed into words, which is a reason we have something like music, for that which we cannot express through words can be expressed through something else instead.

ABOUT THE WRITER

Chayale Levy enjoys working with special needs kids and is a qualified hair stylist. She decided to write about music because she grew up playing guitar and piano and was inspired by her grandmother who was an incredible pianist who played by ear. When faced with struggles in terms of her personal music choices, she decided to research the effect of music according to Jewish thought, as well as the psychological effects music may have.

CHAPTER FOUR

INVESTIGATING THE INTERACTION BETWEEN GREEK PHILOSOPHY AND JEWISH THOUGHT, REJECTION OR ADAPTION?

Faigy Liberov

Philosophy, from the Greek word philosophia literally meaning "lover of wisdom," is the study of the fundamental nature of knowledge, reality and existence. Apart from the word, this branch of social science traces its origins back to Greece and more specifically to Pythagoras of Samos (c. 570 – 495 BCE) - the first to call himself a philosopher. His political and religious teachings quickly grew popular in Magna Graecia, influencing many diverse schools of thought, amongst them, the philosophies of Plato, Aristotle, and ultimately through them, Western philosophy as a whole.

Philosophy arose in Judaism due to Greek cultural influence. Prior to the rise of Greek philosophy, there is no evidence of disciplined philosophical Jewish thought. Up until that point, Jewish thought was purely based on Judaic themes found in various sections of the Bible and the Tanakh.

Origins of Jewish Religious Philosophy

Philo (15 BCE-45 CE) was a Jewish writer who lived in Alexandria, Egypt, which was then under the cultural influence of the Greeks. He had access to the philosophical works of the Greeks and was influenced by their writings, thus arguably the first to openly benefit from Greek philosophy by attempting to systematically explain the Hebrew Bible in Greek terminology. He showed that Greek philosophy and Jewish thought are compatible, by explaining that Greek philosophy is on some way an allegorical interpretation of the Bible. Philo may have influenced Christian thinkers. However, until recent years he was unknown even to the Jews.

The foundations of the articulation of Jewish philosophy was set in place by Rabbi Saadia Gaon (882/892-942). Who, as a pioneering medieval Jewish philosopher, plausibly one of the most elementary pillars of Jewish thought, contributed greatly to the scope of Jewish philosophy. Especially through his Magnum opus '*The Book of Beliefs and Opinions*,' which was written in response to Arabic and Greek philosophers. Rabbi Saadia was the founder of Jewish religious philosophy, combining Jewish theology with various aspects of

Greek philosophy. Up until that point, religion and philosophy were seen as irreconcilable, being that religion is based on faith and deeply rooted in sometimes super rational beliefs, whereas philosophy is all about conjecture and speculation. Being that it is a logical fallacy to have both faith and doubt, philosophers were unable to be religious and religious people were unable to be philosophers.

Whilst this argument has substantial reasoning, Rabbi Saadia was able to prove otherwise, by fusing the two together. Rabbi Saadia set up a Jewish philosophical system of thought, attempting to convey to his audience that by no means is philosophy and religion a contradiction.

Although Judaism is based off a rich historical background and can be traced back a long way. Rabbi Saadia insisted that Judaism is fully compatible with reason. In fact, religion and rational can be traced back to the same source, and if absorbed in the right manner, can be of use through harmonizing each other. Rabbi Saadia's works were focused towards annihilating the conclusions of the heretics, especially for those amongst the Jews. He was solely focused not on personal benefit or honour, but purely for the continuity of the practice of Judaism and the Jewish people. Throughout Saadia's works, he focused on bringing abstract concepts into rational terms, which was heavily influenced by the Kalam school of thought. Kalam differed in style to Greek philosophers, originating from Islamic thinkers and was used as a means to prove philosophical arguments through reason.

It took a man of such brilliance and skill to source every detail of his arguments in the Bible. Rabbi Saadia pointed out that although it is possible for man to reach the truth through logical reasoning, he is likely to go wrong along the way.

Thus, it is necessary to follow religion in which any person regardless of their intellectual capabilities is able to live a life of truth. Although he is guided by the rational, he strongly believes that faith is a moral necessity and can be practiced in a co-existing manner to logic.

In Rabbi Saadia's commentary on '*The Book of Creation*,' he discusses the origins of the universe, maintaining that the world is not eternal, but has been created by G-d through creation ex nihilo. He identifies the eternal aspect of the universe as G-d himself and His intellect rather than the world, which was, then a popular idea proposed by Aristotle. In a logical manner, he finds reasoning's for the existence of G-d, His absolute unity and Him not having a form.

Contrasting to Rabbi Saadia's philosophical works, Rabbi Judah Halevi (1075-1086) held an opposing view. As expressed in Judah Halevi's book, the *Kuzari*, these scholars believed that to bring the Torah, which expresses the infinite quality of Divine wisdom, into human understanding and the rational, is undermining the essential outlook on Judaism. Precisely due to the Divine origins of the Torah, it must be accepted as super-rational rather than irrational, hence totally transcending human intellect.

Opposition to Articulation of Jewish Philosophy

Judah Halevi greatly opposed philosophical and rational proofs for Judaism, for he felt that the Jewish religion is beyond rational and is not rooted in philosophy. Instead, he based the truth of the Hebrew Bible on the historical giving of the Bible. He bases his claims off the fact that all Jews were present at the giving of the Bible and thus witnessed the intense G-dly revelation. Therefore, it is just a matter of faith and trust. From Judah Halevi's perspective, revelation is far more convincing than philosophical proofs, for a hypothesis which is on the level of reason can be argued either way, however revelation being witnessed by many, has a higher level of authenticity, as its beyond human intellect and rational.

Judah Halevi was one of the only Jewish scholars at the time who greatly opposed the articulation of Jewish philosophy and response to Greek thought. However, many years later, various scholars stuck to his opinion and fought harshly against the works of Jewish philosophers such as Maimonides.

Maimonides As A Philosopher

Maimonides (1135-1204) was arguably one of the most fundamental Jewish philosophers of all time; expanding the scope of Jewish thought; articulating it in a clear and concise manner like never done before. His proficient philosophical treatise named '*Guide For the Perplexed*' set out to present man's perpetual questions on purpose, the nature and existence of G-d, origins of the universe, as well as many other philosophical ideas.

Aimed at the many Jewish intellectuals captured by the wisdom and theories of the Greek philosophers under Islamic cultural influence, this book was written to clarify the conflict between Aristotelian philosophies and Jewish thought. Popular Muslim translators such as Al Kindi (873) and his disciples made this very accessible in its Arabic formulation, which was then the language spoken by the Jews. Greek philosophy seeped its way into the minds of the Jews, interfering   with   fundamental   Torah principles. Philosophically oriented Jews, although firmly committed to life values and practice set by the Torah, were left perplexed and unguided between the conflict of faith and reason.

Maimonides, deeply concerned for the spiritual welfare of the Jews, felt impelled to organize a systematic and clear articulation of the core philosophical Jewish beliefs. With his wisdom and vast knowledge both in Jewish and secular studies, he was able to compose this masterpiece. It took a man of such high calibre and depth to answer complex questions such as paradoxical role of anthropomorphisms when the Torah stresses the monotheistic and absolute unity of the Divine. Much heed was given to this philosophical piece and its popularity grew tremendously amongst the Jewish people, as well as Islamic and European philosophers who benefited greatly from the Latin edition.

Although Maimonides work was a highly respected piece and greeted with much enthusiasm, it stimulated a powerful opposition in the Jewish world. A long and bitter controversy arose, and his ideas were fiercely attacked by those who thought that Judaism would be endangered if it were to be put in rational terms and should be looked at from a purely traditionalist view.

Talmudic scholars such as Rabbi Shlomo ben Avraham of Montpellier and his disciples fought fervently against the works of Maimonides. They went as far as reporting his works to the Inquisition and the Church as being a threat to religion. The Church, being deep-rooted, bitter enemies of the Jews, used this opportunity to their own advantage and ordered a public burning of Maimonides books in Paris (1234).

Although there was an opposing, harsh response to Greek thought within Jewish circles, many great Jewish scholars such as Maimonides, Solomon ibn Gabirol, Rav Bachya ibn Pakuda and Gersonides benefited greatly from Greek philosophy and used it to bring people closer to Jewish belief and understanding of the Bible.

Ibn Rushd, (1126-1198) an Islamic philosopher and contemporary of Maimonides once said, "Better not to tell the simple people that they are wrong, they're not going to get it right anyway." For Ibn Rushd, truth is found in philosophy - the speculation of the mind. He therefore claims that religion is for the masses, as they cannot comprehend the abstract. Judaism and more specifically, Maimonides disagreed with this and composed the fundamental thirteen principles of faith, which is directed at the masses.

The Tanakh, which was originally the only source of Jewish text and learning, and continues to be the base of Jewish practice, was not written for the intellectual elite but for the masses. Therefore, there is lots of anthropomorphisms and imagery to make it more understandable to the average reader.

Throughout Jewish thought, philosophy is often seen as a step to enhancing religion, promoting ones understanding of the Bible. However, it is never found as a replacement to the practice of Judaism. Philosophy is a means in which to understand Judaism in a deeper intellectual manner.

Aristotelian Thought within Judaism

Maimonides is an example of one who stood out for his interaction with Greek thought and the great benefits he derived from Greek philosophers' writings. Maimonides was arguably an Aristotelian, in most instances agreeing with the ideas of Aristotle.

Aristotle (384-322 BC) begins his quest for the origins of humanity and the cosmos as a whole, by starting with himself - humanity and then finding a cause and another etc. until he reaches the point of the concept of G-d, in his phraseology known as the 'Prime Mover.' As according to logic, causes cannot be infinite and there must be an underlying cause, different to all those that follow. He then goes on to theorize and elaborate on the idea that the greatest achievement of mankind is the fusion of oneself with the Divine, which is achieved through involving oneself in deep abstractions and contemplations that allows one to conceptualize external and abstract concepts, creating a unique unity of divinity with oneself. Aristotle clarifies the meaning of abstract as being anything beyond sensory perception, and stresses that man can attain such heights through the power of intellect. At this point, man can become Divine and blend with the ultimate, creating an eternal and everlasting effect.

The concept of the fusion of man and divinity is not only found within Greek thought, but also greatly expanded upon in various Judaic philosophies and especially Chabad Chasidic philosophy. Rabbi Schneur Zalman of Liadi (1745-1813) founder of the Chabad Chasidic movement and author of the book of Tanya elaborates on the idea of the bond between man and G-d via learning His wisdom and intellectually absorbing abstract concepts of G-dliness.

However, it is important to note that according to Chabad Chasidic philosophy, unlike Aristotle's idea, this is not the greatest of man's achievements. For man can reach higher through taking action in this physical world, hence making the world fit for the Divine.

Therefore, it is fair to say that Maimonides as a Jewish philosopher heavily agreed to Aristotle's ideal goal of man and purpose in creation. Just like Aristotle, Maimonides believes that through intense contemplations and abstractions, man can unite with the Divine and achieve the most one can in this world. He stresses on the idea that this is what man leaves after his departure in this world and it is our abstractions and contemplations that are eternal. Therefore, it is through the tool of the mind that one can unite with the Divine and achieve true ecstasy.

The Bible, being the base of Judaism begins with the story of creation and how the world came into being in seven days, each day another aspect of creation coming in to place. It is therefore not surprising to say that from the many diverse aspects within Judaism, creation is a basic and simple belief. One could therefore conclude that Judaism does not agree to all of Aristotle's teachings. As Aristotle believed that the universe is eternal, based on his logical reasoning that if G-d were perfect and unchanging, at what point, could a change occur that He would need creation. According to logic, want implies a lack, however, G-d by definition is not lacking and so how could he desire creation? As with all other Aristotle's ideas, we can find it within the realms of Jewish thought. Gersonides, (1288-1344) a famous Jewish scholar and commentator, interprets the story of creation in the Bible as being stages of revelation and believes that the universe is eternal coexisting with G-d. Although this is not the basic widespread Jewish belief, it can be found amongst religious Jewish scholars. It is therefore quite evident that Aristotelian thought was able to penetrate, contrasting and even conflicting Jewish thinkers.

For Aristotle, G-d is just there in His simplicity, knowing G-d's self, which in turn, sets off secondary reactions, the world on the other hand, is inspired to participate and grasp it. Aristotle reasons that whatever is ultimate, is necessary and permanent, implying no change whatsoever. Therefore, from this perspective, G-d does not need the world in any way and does not care about the cosmos and life. This conclusion has been made numerous times and the Rabbi Menachem Mendel Schneerson (1902-1994) seventh and final leader of the Chabad Chasidic movement also talks of the aspect of G-d as being perfect and complete having no need for us. However, this idea negates the fundamental Jewish idea that G-d truly cares and about life, creation, and it precisely His will that everything occur as it does.

The reasons the Greeks felt that change is imperfection is because they started with looking at themselves, concluding that there must be a necessary existence as it's a logical fallacy to say that there is no end. Therefore, there must be something in of itself, identified as the Prime Mover.

Maimonides says that the underlying truth of all axioms and sciences is to know that there is a first, primary Being. Both Maimonides and Aristotle convey the idea that a constant spinning universe must have an infinite power beyond, in Aristotle's terms, an unmoved mover in a total state of simplicity and purity. In order for us humans to relate to the

Divine we draw inspiration for the finite to reach the infinite, almost like climbing up the ladder to divinity.

In Aristotle's book, '*The Anima*,' he discusses the idea that intellect comprise two parts, the part that becomes and the part that activates, in Chassidic terminology the "Sechel Hapoel." There is an ongoing debate between the interpreters of Aristotle on the exact meaning of this generating intellect. It is generally agreed that it is the power to go from sense perception to abstraction. There is some conflict about this concept, as some believe it is a Divine power outside of the person, whereas others believe it is an internal Divine power.

Particularly, the concept of intellect is the one thing we attain from beyond ourselves, a level much higher than humans, and according to Maimonides is the one thing a person leaves after they die. Aristotle claims that one starts with a *tabula rasa,* Latin for a clean state. Through abstractions and contemplations, one can unite with the Divine. One should not just live their life off sense perception, but also abstractions within the conscience, this is due to the possibility of man having an activated intellect. Man can even achieve the ultimate intelligible and become the Divine through this. Maimonides also mentions this idea of becoming Divine. This idea of fusing with G-d is developed and later discussed by diverse Greek, Islamic and Jewish philosophers. From Maimonides to Rabbi Shneur Zalman of Liadi this idea repeatedly comes up.

We can experience the ultimate divinity within ourselves through learning and comprehending G-d's wisdom. As doing is superficial, whereas knowing is far greater, we can become our conscience as we fuse with divinity, hence the advantage of the Torah over the commandments. Therefore, we see how within Judaism the ultimate expression of Aristotle's idea in his book, *Anima,* is expressed; in short, whatever ineligibles we create, we become.

Other than the idea of the mystical union, Aristotle's ideas are generally compatible with Judaic philosophy. However, Chabad philosophy is a lot closer to Neo-Platonic ideas, which disagrees with Aristotle and claim that divinity is present within every aspect of physicality, as later on elaborated by Rabbi Shneur of Liadi.

Neo-Platonic Thought within Judaism

Shifting from Aristotle to Plato and more specifically Neo-Platonism. Plotinus (204-270 AD), founder of Neo-Platonic thought, speculated that due to G-d's absolute perfection, there is an abundance and an intense overflow of divinity, which causes a Divine flow towards the cosmos and life. Hence, we come into being due to G-d's absolute overflow and goodness. This differs to the way of Pre-Socratic thinkers, who started with the limitations of their own existence, then concluded that there must be an infinite power beyond us.

However, according to Kabbalistic and Chabad Chasidic teachings, the Bible starts off with an entirely opposite view, firstly and primarily there is G-d and then within Him there is an innermost desire and will that we come into being, therefore He contracts Himself to a level in which creation can come about, essentially humanity. Thus, the result of our actions is rooted within G-d's quintessential point, for all of creation is precisely so that the will of G-d be fulfilled. Therefore, all that the Creator has undergone in order to bring our world into being is so that divinity can dwell amongst corporeality, fusing both physicality and spirituality.

According to Jewish teachings, the will of G-d is found through studying the Bible and carrying out the commandments of G-d, elevating the physical world making, it a dwelling for the Divine.

G-d is not spiritual, nor physical, and unlike what is generally believed, spirituality is no closer to G-d than the physical. Aristotle views life from a linear perspective and very much focuses on the hierarchy needed to reach a level of ultimate purity. Chabad Chassidus views life from a circular perspective, where the essence of the initial thought is found in the end and it is down here in the most physical elements of the world, that G-d's quintessential point is found. Thus, it is the role of humankind to reveal G-d in mundane actions, elevating and uplifting the physical. Rabbi Schneur Zalman of Liadi explains that despite the purifications one must undergo and the abstractions one works towards, in actuality it is in the bottom, or lower world that has most meaning and significance. As expressed in the saying "all beginnings are wedged into the end."

This concept comes up in 'Sefer Yetzira'- the Book of Creation, which is the heart of Kabbalistic thought. Every beginning makes its way down to the end, which then starts the next level, leading an infinite chain bridging the gap between humanity and the Creator.

Plotinus describes seeing great revelations when going up, elevating himself to high levels. However, upon coming down, he becomes depressed, which hints to that idea that he believes that the ultimate is not found within this world. Many Jewish thinkers agree to an idea that the ultimate is not found amongst the physicality, as does Maimonides. He holds that the ultimate is found in the World to Come, not in this mundane world. This heavily contradicts Chabad Chassidic philosophy, which is much focused on the ultimate levels, and greatest pleasure man can give to G-d is found in this world by elevating and transforming the physical, making the world fit for the Divine.

In the *Guide For the Perplexed*, Maimonides speaks of the greatest people, such as Abraham, as being physically in this world in bodies, however their heart and mind were elsewhere, "here but not here." Maimonides sees more potential and meaning in the World to Come.

One might then say that one's sense of self is the biggest contradiction to the Oneness and absolute unity of G-d. In fact, it may be the most similar to G-dliness, for just as G-d is in a state of Self, so can we. The greatest point of Divinity can be found within oneself!

There are many similarities between Plato's teachings and Chassidism. This may be due to the influence the Jewish sages had on Plato. Jeremiah the prophet is believed to have taught Plato. Plato (428 BC) originally made a mockery of Jeremiah, however later came to greatly respect and acknowledge his teachings. In the words of Plato "his words are words from the living G-d, and he is a wise man and a prophet."

Neo-Platonism seeped its way into the minds of various Judaic philosophers, particularly into the works of Ibn Gabirol. Solomon Ibn Gabirol (1021-1070) was a medieval Jewish thinker, famous as a poet and especially for his poem named "*Keser Malchus*." His philosophical magnum opus was "*Mekor Chaim*," meaning "fountain of life," Gabirol wrote a lot about philosophical ideas such as form and matter. Usually the form and concept are regarded higher than the vessel/matter shaping it; however, Ibn Gabirol believed they arc of equal importance. This differs to the opinion of both Aristotle and Maimonides, whom disagree and claim that form is more important, and matter is a mere vessel.

On the idea of Divine will, Gabirol explains that will is a part of and excluded from the Divine essence. He explains that in essence, Divine will is unlimited however; in action, Divine will is finite. Will as described in many Jewish sources, serves as the link between creation and G-d's essence. Ibn Gabirol's work achieved much fame and adherence throughout the Christian, Islamic and the Jewish world. He explained key philosophical ideas from the perspective of Jewish belief in Greek terminology.

There is much conflict between Aristotelians and Platonists, Plato speaks of lofty ideas and concepts, physicality just being a manifestation of the concept. However, Aristotle goes to say there is no Divine paradigm for things and there must be a distinct separation between the physical and spiritual.

Long Term Effects of Greek Philosophy on Jewish Thought

Besides for this fundamental idea of the mystical union, many concepts and phraseology of Aristotle seeped its way into Jewish philosophies, not only to that of medieval minds, but also to the thinkers of much later centuries. The book of Tanya uses many terms that come straight from Aristotle, such as the different aspects of the soul, intellectual, animalistic and common terms, such as the power of potential actuality. It is essential to understand the depth and significance of the ideas of the Greek philosophers, for they were able to both consciously and subconsciously permeate the scope of western thought effecting a very diverse audience.

In Judaic philosophy, there is a world of ideas that would not be fully articulated if not for Greek philosophy. The popularity of the Greek philosophical works prompted the Jewish sages to develop their own system of philosophy. However, it is important to note that the works of the Greek philosophers were not new to the Jews, for tradition has it that Aristotle had in fact borrowed many teachings and wisdom from King Solomon of the Jews, however he altered and adjusted some points.

Rabbi Menachem Mendel Schneerson, the seventh and final rabbi of the Chabad Chassidic movement, expands on the roots of Greek and Jewish philosophy. He explains how essentially Greek philosophy stems from the same source as Jewish philosophy. Although not all aspects of Greek philosophy be adapted to Jewish thought, there are definitely certain aspects that the Jews adapted and benefitted from, such as the ideas of Greek astronomy.

He explains that since every wisdom is sourced in the Bible, whatever the learning may be, self-nullification is needed to excel in the subject. For one must put themselves aside in order to fully absorb and internalize a concept, especially if one is to reveal new aspects. Self-nullification is the vessel to reach great intellectual heights.

Jewish thought recognizes absolute Divine unity within everything, even the most physical elements, this is absolute unity. The Jewish perspective is that essentially there is no concept of plurality, everything to mankind seems as different components, however, in essence, we are all one. Greek thought recognizes Divine unity however still acknowledges differentiated components and then concludes that it is sourced in the absolute unity of the Divine. Therefore, although on the surface they are both stating the same idea, the way they both reach that conclusion is rather different.

This may explain the difference in perspective on the four elements making up our physical world. Maimonides elaborates on the four elements, explaining that everything physical on our planet is made of a combination of the four elements. Essentially, there is no pure element only containing that aspect, for even each distinct element is a combination of the other ones and we only see the dominant one. However, Greek philosophy differs in this idea, as they believe that each of the four elements can exist within their pure state, and do not agree to that idea that each element contains the other three. This apparent contradiction explains both views on Divine unity, as Jews view everything as essentially unified; they do not see the elements as being pure in itself and therefore must contain the other three elements. Whereas Greek philosophy recognizes distinctions.

Much of modern-day Jewish philosophy such as Chassidism, benefited greatly from the articulation of Greek philosophy and uses terminology directly from Greek sources. Arguably, the articulation of Jewish thought only came about due to the rise in popularity of Greek thought. Jewish sages felt like they had to provide a clear articulation of the Bible perspective to ensure the continuity of Judaism. This is not to say that Judaism changed or adapted to Greek thought, as all of Judaism is sourced in the Bible. However, it was the articulation of Greek thought that brought about lofty Jewish concepts to be brought in to writing, by virtue strengthening the commitment of the Jews.

Divine Will and Care, the Point of Conflict between Greek and Jewish Philosophy

One thing all Jewish thinker's share in contradiction to all other philosophers, is the idea of Divine will, termed in Hebrew as '*rotzon*.' Despite the most diverse range within Jewish thought, all agree on the idea that G-d is not mechanical and thus there is some sort of care and relationship between man and G-d.

For most other philosophers' creation is in some way just a result of divinity, just as the sun's rays are a result of the sun, but by no means integral as having an effect on the sun and in essence just nullified to its source. In Kabbalistic thought in terms of the *sefirot*, there is the idea of *Kesser,* which links the *sefirot* to G-d. Rabbi Sholom Dov Ber Schneerson (1869-1920) also agrees with this unchanging G-d, who paradoxically has a care and desire for us.

It is an obvious logical fallacy to say that perfection can have a desire, as by definition want implies a lack however in the case of G-d, His desire is an integral component of Him, being in a total state of unity to G-d and therefore does not imply imperfection.

Some Greek philosophers answer this by saying that there no change in G-d brought about His desire, but rather an overflow from His abundance of goodness.

The idea of Divine care and desire is fundamental within Judaism and is expressed in the Tanakh, as it is not only a philosophical belief. Rabbi Shneur Zalman Of Liadi explains that when one operates on a certain manner, they don't matter to G-d, however, as we are rooted in the most quintessential part of G-d, through Divine service, we discover the permanence and absolute unity of G-d, as well as the unchanging essence within ourselves which unites us to G-d's core. Chabad Chassidic philosophy is all about discovering the ultimate Oneness in the finitude.

According to Jewish philosophies instead of there being one and intellect as expanded on by Greek philosophers, there is one, will and intellect, the Divine will being the crucial link between man and G-d, directing man's purpose in this world.

Therefore, throughout the scope of Jewish philosophy, and particularly medieval Jewish philosophy. Divine will stand out as being the one aspect that is not found entirely in Greek philosophy. For all other aspects of Jewish philosophy can be found in Greek philosophy and vice versa. Although it is particularly only one aspect that stands out, in actuality its effects are enormous for it heavily effects the behaviour and actions of mankind and the relationship between man and His Creator.

ABOUT THE WRITER

Faigy Liberov is a passionate individual with a deep love for philosophy, learning, teaching and traveling. Her journey in life has been fuel by a profound curiosity and a thirst for knowledge, constantly seeking to understand the complexities of the world and human experience.

She is passionate about mental health and is a certified Emotion Code practitioner, helping people heal and find peace. But it doesn't end there! Faigy loves breaking down complex ideas into relatable nuggets of knowledge and hopes to author numerous books one day.

Currently teaching and studying psychology, she is excited to further her passions and help people be more connected to their true selves.

CHAPTER FIVE

WHY WE DO WHAT WE DO, WHEN WE KNOW WHAT WE KNOW

Rivky Osdaba

How we can practically alter our thought process and do what we know is best for us, gaining self-control? The methodology used in this essay is using ideas from Psychology, Chassidic teachings and practical 'tools' on each topic, applying the science to back up these tools.

Thesis: both Psychological techniques and Chassidic ideas can help a person gain self-control.

Through my research, I gained a deeper insight and understanding into this field and I understood that it's not automatic for one's knowledge and action to be connected. A person must actively connect what he knows to his behaviour.

There is a Chassidic parable of a farmer who was illiterate. One day, the farmer received a letter and asked the teacher on the farm to read the letter to him. The teacher read the letter to the farmer, which informed the farmer of his father's passing. The farmer then fainted. Later, people asked the teacher why he didn't faint as well, he was closer to the information so why did the famer get so deeply affected? The farmer answered that it was not _my_ father; it was the farmer's father. This demonstrates that information needs to be relevant to a person and close to his heart to have a profound impact; just knowledge itself is not sufficient.

The research helped me discover certain techniques that help a person connect his knowledge and action and do what he knows is best for him. This answers the second part of my question, "**How** to align our knowledge and action?"

- Observe – Mindfulness
- SMART – Plan to achieve
- Positive Thoughts – Table with coping thoughts
- Smiling – Pencil in mouth
- Breathing – Colour Breathing

Haim Ginnot, (1922-1973) a teacher, psychotherapist, parent educator and child psychologist once said, "You cannot teach a child how to swim when he is drowning."All these tools need to be practised when the sea is calm, before stress and panic set in, to ensure that we know what to do when the sea is rough. What all these tools have in common is that it gives a person time to pause, reflect and align a person's knowledge and action, what one knows is best to what he then does.

I became aware that these tools need to be practised throughout our lifetime, because as we experience new and varied challenges, our thoughts need to adapt and be realigncd.

Psychology and Chassidic Teachings

It is not clear when psychology became a self-help system. Psychology's origins was used solely for people who were dealing with mental illness. 'Self-help' books based on psychological principles are becoming increasingly popular. The U.S self-help industry as of 2016 was worth $9.9 billion. This started in 1859 with Samuel Smiles book, "Self-Help," and it became more popular in recent years.

In the 1960's Aaron T Beck and Albert Ellis founded something called Cognitive Therapy, which later developed into Cognitive Behavioural Therapy (CBT) as we know it today.[4] This area of psychology has become a focus in this project.

What is CBT?

To understand what the exponents of CBT think, we can look at what it stands for. Cognitive is what we think and Behavioural is what we do. Therapy is the way in which this is brought into practice. According to its practitioners, CBT helps us deal with the issue at hand through understanding our behaviour and tracing it back to our thought process. They claim that by deconstructing our thinking patterns, beliefs, assumptions and attitudes, we can decide what works to create a more productive way of thinking. CBT teaches how to utilise the skills that we already have, which enables us to independently practise these skills, coming from the person himself. What sets us apart from animals is the ability to think consciously, using our brain to make choices that are best for our environment and us, even though these choices may make one feel uncomfortable.

The theory of CBT takes this saying seriously, "what we think decides how we feel." In this therapy, it is crucial to address the client's thoughts to change his behaviour, seeing the thought process as the root cause of the problem and therefore, treating it first and focusing on the client's thinking process. This could be the reason why CBT is often called the, "psychology of common sense."

When I began looking into CBT, what really fascinated me was that CBT is described as being psycho-educational, meaning that it aims to teach the clients to be their own therapist. This is Haim Ginnot's view when it comes to parenting, giving the child his autonomy to learn, grow, and even experience pain, in his own terms.

Moving to the Chassidic teachings, the founder of the Chabad Chassidic movement was R' Shneur Zalman of Liadi. The name 'Chabad' is an acronym for Chochmah, Binah and Daat - Wisdom, Understanding and Knowledge, and uses these three faculties to affect one's emotions and actions.

Chabad Chassidism focuses on spiritual service of G-d through intellect, which means spiritual transformation using one's wisdom, understanding and knowledge.

Mindfulness – Being in the Moment

In the hectic world that we live in, it's very easy to get caught up living in the past and future, but what about living in the present moment? We all know too well how it feels to be rehashing conversations of the past and planning and calculating what will happen tomorrow.

Linehan (1993) introduced a mindfulness skill called "observe." Noticing the present and observing. This is claimed to help us check in with our feelings therefore enabling us to make better decisions about what is right for us at the moment.

This technique involves observing the breath and physical sensations, e.g. Heart beating, legs pressing into the seat. Then observing sounds, smells and the physical space around you.

Lets look at the Chabad Chassidic approach to what each moment means, fully living in it and being immersed in the moment:

In January 1970, thousands of followers gathered in New York to mark 20 years of leadership of the Lubavitcher Rebbe, Rabbi Menachem Mendel Schneerson. The Rebbe conducted a public gathering and amongst his followers, a group of visitors from Israel began to worry. Time was ticking and they needed to pack, say goodbye and catch a plane back to Israel. But they didn't want to leave when the Rebbe was talking.

Noticing their worries, the Rebbe told the following story of his father in law, Rabbi Yosef Yitzchak Schneersohn the sixth Lubavitcher Rebbe. In Communist Russia, in 1927, Rabbi Yosef Yitzchak singlehandedly ran an underground network of Torah schools, which was illegal at the time and punishable by death. He fearlessly spread Judaism in Communist Russia.

One night, he had to undertake a journey to Moscow to meet a foreign businessman, all whilst travelling under the heavy shadow of the secret police. Before making the trip, Rabbi Yosef Yitzchak spent hours in private audiences with individuals. After doing this, he had half an hour to himself before embarking on this trip.

The Rebbe, his son-in-law, then went into his office and found him sitting totally relaxed concentrating on his work as if he had just begun his day. In shock, the Rebbe exclaimed, "to such an extent?"

This was Rabbi Yosef Yitzchak's reply: "Although you cannot add hours to the day, the time with which you already have you should maximise to its fullest. When you are doing something, what you have done before or will do afterward doesn't distract you at that moment. It is as if they don't exist!"

Rabbi Yosef Yitzchak called this in Hebrew "*Hatzlacha Bizman*" – literally translated, "to be successful with time," in other words, time management. The fourth Chabad Rebbe, Reb Shmuel, quoted this. Rabbi Yosef Yitzchak continued, bringing an example of a 13th Century Sage called Rabbi Shlomo ben Aderet of Barcelona (the Rash'ba.) He delivered three Torah classes each day to intelligent men, he composed responsa of Torah law answering the many questions that he received, he was also a medical doctor and despite such a schedule, he took a walk every day.

How did the Rash"ba fit all of this into his schedule on a regular basis?

When he went on the walk, when he was with his patients, when he delivered a Torah class and when he was composing responsa <u>nothing else existed</u>! Each segment of time he regarded as a world of its own.

Back to the Chassidic gathering, the Rebbe concluded the story and turned to address the visitors from Israel. The Rebbe said that the El-Al plane has not yet been created, Kennedy airport doesn't exist. Right now, being in the gathering; that is all that should be their focus. This illustrates that every moment has a purpose of its own and that we should use it to its fullest.

Mindfulness is the space where our knowledge turns into the outcomes that we want by being focused and giving ourselves that space to align our intentions and needs with our actions.

This helps us understand the question on **why** we do what we do, when we know what we know, explaining **how** we can practically align our knowledge and actions through the lens of being mindful.

Delayed Gratification

When the Apple watch came out, a close relative of mine, who was 10 years old at the time, desired this watch. His mother told him that he would have to save up money to purchase it. He calculated and realized that it would take him 6 months to get the money needed.

Lately, I discussed this with his mother, and she told me, "It was a big challenge for him to wait for the watch and when he was nearing his goal, he begged me and his father to pay the shortfall and he would pay us back in time. I was tempted to give in, but the point of this exercise was to teach him to wait, so that he should learn delayed gratification.

Delayed gratification is understood in an experimental setting. In the 1960's Mischel Walter created something called the 'Marshmallow Test' in Stanford University's Bing Nursery School. He and his team took children, of all ages, into a room and gave them the option to ring the bell and eat the plate with one marshmallow. The other option is to wait until the researcher comes back into the room, 15-20 minutes later, and get the plate with two marshmallows.

They followed the children to adulthood and discovered that those children able to wait for the second marshmallow succeeded disproportionality in all areas in life. Financially, emotionally, in relationships and education. This research opened up the discussion for the impact of self-discipline and its consequences in life.

Children who succeeded in the first 10 seconds were most likely to succeed waiting until the researcher came back. This illustrates that the time helped the child align and connect his knowledge and action. We need time to process what we know is best in order to apply it to our actions.

Mischel Walter once asked a child "What would an intelligent child do?"

The child responded, "He would wait for another marshmallow."

Mischel Walter then asked the child, "What are you going to do?"

The child responded, "I'll eat it now."

This shows just how disconnected one's knowledge and action can be.

In my experience with children, becoming an EYP (Early Years Practitioner) I've noticed how the children deal with impulse control. Either by distracting or talking aloud to themselves, saying "NO!" I have also tried to implement different ways to help the children and give advice on how they can make it easier to control themselves.

For example, in the case of the Marshmallow Test, discussing with the child whether keeping the marshmallow in sight, on the plate, or out of sight, under the plate, will help the child succeed. Or, distracting oneself e.g. Count until 100.

Haim Ginnot once said, "The intellect can only absorb what the emotions allow." From this quote, we infer that when the child eats the marshmallow right away, his emotions are in play and the intellect cannot influence that decision, therefore disabling the child to practice self-control.

This helps us understand the question on **why** we do what we do, when we know what we know, as our emotions can limit what see and think.

Responding vs. Reacting

The brain is made up of two parts. One of which is the Mammal brain, that is shared with the animal kingdom and is the part of the brain that is fully formed in utero, before being born. The human brain, otherwise known as the prefrontal cortex, is the logical part of us, enabling self-control. This part creates goals and makes decisions.

Similar to animals, the mammal brain is concerned about the here and now and mainly concerned about survival. In order to survive, it creates fear.

In the 1920's, Walter Cannon defined this process as the 'fight or flight' response, whilst he was observing the digestive reactions of animals under stress. The Mammal brain of the human has an innate 'fight or flight' response as soon as it detects fear.

The Amygdala is responsible for the fight or flight response that causes you to react to threat. When the amygdala is activated, it prevents the prefrontal cortex from being engaged in logical decision-making and impulse control.

Does the fight or flight response have any benefit?

When there is a threat to life, the fight and flight response is there to protect us and enables us to do things that we would normally never do. This is a lifesaving mechanism.

The downside to this is that the amygdala cannot differentiate between what is threatening e.g. A soldier in war, or what is not life threatening e.g. Getting stuck in traffic on the way to work.

When a baby is born, his mammal brain is fully formed, and his human brain has all the neurons he will need, but they are not yet connected. Throughout his childhood, specifically in first two years of life, he is creating neural pathways, connecting the neurons.

Bringing back the example of the child who is sitting in front of the marshmallow, in his logical brain he knows that he will get more if he waits. If his mammal brain is sensitive to frustration, then logic cannot win. The mammal brain is more powerful in children, because the neurons aren't yet connected in the human brain.

As humans, our ability to respond by thinking logically needs to be practiced.

However, the mammal brain is an inborn instinct that can overpower the human brain when it's not exercised.

The child who ate the marshmallow reacted to the situation. However, the child who waited and thought about the benefits of getting another marshmallow *responded* to the situation.

What the difference between reacting and responding? When one reacts, it is with one's emotion and impulse. However, a response is with one's intellect and application of one's knowledge.

Here is a table that I put together to summarise:

HOT SYSTEM/REACT	COOL SYSTEM/RESPOND
FAST	Slow
AMYGDALA/MAMMAL BRAIN	Prefrontal Cortex /Human brain
REFLEXIVE	Reflective
EAT THE MARSHMALLOW NOW!	Wait for another Marshmallow

Going back to the "Fight or Flight Response," what happens to the brain when one is in a situation in which they feel fear, anxiety, and anger?

Physiologically, the heart beats faster, which elevates blood pressure and the breath gets shallow. This lights up the Amygdala and shuts off the blood flow to the prefrontal cortex which robs one from making rational decisions.

Chabad Chassidic teachings claim that every person is capable of using their minds' innate ability to rule over the heart. As illustrated by the following story.

The sixth Chabad Rebbe, Rabbi Yosef Yitzchak, once wrote in a letter about a man called Reb Moshe Maizlish and his capability to utilize the mind's ability to rule over the heart.

When Napoleon invaded Russia in 1812, the Chabad Rebbe at the time, R.Shneur Zalman of Liadi, sided with the Czar. This was because he saw the consequences of Napoleon's victory, being that the Jews will prosper materially, but falter spiritually. However, if the Czar will win the Jews will falter materially, but prosper spiritually.

Reb Moshe, who was a Chassidic follower, was a spy for the Czar, posing as translator for the French and communicating their military secrets to the Russians. Once, when the French strategists laid out their maps to plan their next attack, Napoleon became suspicious of Reb Moshe's presence.

Napoleon suddenly questioned Reb Moshe, sharply accusing him of being a spy, whilst he placed his hand on Reb Moshe's heart to determine what his instinctive reaction would be. Reb Moshe's heartbeat remained calm, contrary to how one would naturally react. He answered with such confidence that Napoleon was convinced of his innocence.

In Chassidic teachings, it is brought down that humans are in an upright position, naturally putting our mind above our heart. We see in the anatomy of most animals that their heart and brain are on the same level. This explains the idea that as humans, we have the ability to control instinct and impulse.

Cognitive Behavioral Therapy

Arron Beck, the founder of Cognitive Behavioural Therapy, considered consciousness as a state of awareness in which decisions can be made on a rational and realistic basis, using our prefrontal cortex.

Aron Beck gave three things that this state of conscious attention allows us to do:

1) Assess our interactions with people and the environment.
2) Link our past memories with present experiences.

3) Control and plan future actions.

When one is in the reactive response of 'Barge in, Give in or Shut down' or what is known commonly as the 'Fight, Flight or Freeze response,' CBT gives the patient the tools to stop and take a breath. After which, his heart rate is lowered, sending calming signals to the Amygdala, which brings the blood flow back to the prefrontal cortex, which gives him access to rational thinking.

The next step in this process is for the client to observe his own reactions, thoughts and feelings from a bird's eye view. He then evaluates what is the best course of action to determine what works. After this, he is ready to practice what is most effective and helpful in this situation.

Ellis and Beck created an **ABC** model that describes the interaction between thoughts, feelings and behaviour.

Activating triggers/event.

What was I doing? Who with? Where? When? How was I feeling before?

Beliefs.

What was going through my mind at the time? Thoughts/ images. (Worst case scenario.)

Consequences.

Physical sensations. What did I do? What did I feel like doing?(Actions and urges.)

This helps us understand why we may do something contrary to what we know. Although our human brain has the information about what we *should* be doing, when the fight and flight response is activated, the mammal brain is engaged, disregarding any knowledge that the human brain has accumulated, making it impossible to make logical decisions and have self-control.

Plan to Achieve

Joseph Luciania, a clinical psychologist in the US, led a study by the University of Scranton, which said, "Just 8% of people achieve their New Year's goals, while around 80% failed to keep their New Year's resolutions." Many people make a resolution to go to the gym, when around 80% of Americans who have gym membership don't use the gym.

What is happening? We all know that exercise is good for us, how come so many of us can't get ourselves to do it?

Joseph Luciania wanted to emphasize that just wanting to do something, is not enough to actually follow it through. As humans, we need motivation and most importantly, a plan of action.

In the book, *'Managing Anxiety with CBT for Dummies,'* it highlights the importance of having a goal in mind in order to grow,a motivation as to why you want to overcome that specific challenge and situation. Research proves that the results of creating a motivation is that we are more likely to achieve what is important to us.

The advantage of having a goal in mind is that you become specific.

Take a look at these two to-do lists.

To – Do list	To – Do list
-Homework	-p29 in History book
-Supper	-Review last section for Maths quiz tomorrow
-Exercise	-Cook Pasta
	-Cut a salad
	-10 min of favourite Yoga video.

Which one are you most likely to complete?

According to the practices of CBT, when the tasks are more specific, they are easier to accomplish and make you more motivated. Specific is breaking it down into small steps making the process gradual and more easily digestible, implementing bit by bit into one's daily schedule and routine.

I followed this advice and I personally found it to be helpful when working on this EPQ. It is called, "being **SMART**."

Specific

Measurable

Achievable

Realistic

Time oriented

The details, purpose and benefit of achieving this goal. How will you know when it is accomplished? What will you feel and think? Is it feasible? Do I have the skills and motivation to achieve it? When is this goal going to be achieved?

From discussions with friends, I have found that a factor as to why people don't do what they know is best for them is because the goal is seen as one big chunk, as opposed to being broken down into pieces, therefore they feel overwhelmed and fail to achieve it.

Thinking Habits

As humans, we tend to predict, judge, mind- read, compare, despair and put ourselves down through self-criticism. These are all examples of unhelpful thinking habits that we accumulate. Being aware of the way we think and what we tell ourselves is critical.

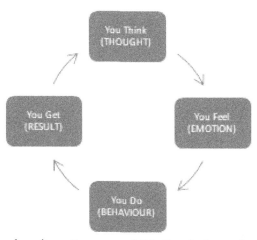

Why does it matter so much? Is it only in my head?

It matters because what you think affects what you feel, and what you feel affects what you do, and what you do affects what you get, and what you get affects what you think! Therefore, we will go around circles.

Hellen Keller (1880 – 1968) said, "Happiness cannot come from without. It must come from within. It is not what we see and touch, but that which <u>we think and feel and do…</u>"[35]

In this quote, we see the order of events. First, we think, then we feel; emotion, and then we do; behaviour.

The first Chabad Rebbe, Rabbi Shneur Zalman of Liadi addresses this in his book of Tanya (1800). "The mind controls over the heart." This is a natural ability that every human being was created with, being able to be in control over our desires in our heart. This is done through changing the subject in our brain from that desire to something else.

King Solomon says in the Book of Ecclesiastes 2:13, "And I saw that there is an advantage to wisdom over stupidity, like the advantage of light over darkness." Isn't this obvious, we all know that wisdom is preferable to stupidity, and light is preferable to darkness? What is King Solomon coming to teach us with comparing light and darkness to wisdom and stupidity?

Light has an automatic upper hand over darkness. When light is introduced into a dark room, it automatically and effortlessly pushes the darkness away. The same is true with wisdom and stupidity. When you bring wisdom, holy thoughts, into your head it automatically pushes away a huge amount of dark thoughts. So even though we cannot stop the flow of our thoughts, we can steer them in the right direction.

A man once came to the third Chabad Rebbe and asked for a blessing, as he was severely ill. The Rebbe replied in Yiddish, "Think good and it will be good." This combats sadness, which is severely detrimental to making good and informative decisions.

Implying from this quote, that positive thoughts will actually bring about positive results, giving tremendous power to our thoughts.

Carol Vivyan, a Cognitive Behavioural Psychotherapist from Guernsey, suggests trying to use a table, so when you're in a difficult situation you know what to tell yourself.

Difficult or distressing situation	Coping thought/Positive statement
E.g. Having to speak in front of a crowd	Stop, and breathe, I can do this

Here are examples of coping thoughts I found helpful:
- This feels bad, it is a normal body reaction – it will pass.

- I have survived before, I will survive now
- I feel this way because of my past experiences, but I am safe right now.
- It's okay to feel this way, it's a normal reaction
- This is difficult and uncomfortable but it's only temporary

Reflecting on the question of **why** people do what they do, even when they know better, training our brain to think positively so that our emotions and actions that follow, will be more aligned to what we know is best for us. This also gives us an insight into **how** we can align our knowledge to our actions.

Tricks We Can Play On Ourselves

In 1988, psychologists did an experiment where they instructed participants to rate how funny a cartoon was in two scenarios. Once with their teeth biting a pen causing a 'smile,' and another with a pen in their lips, causing a 'pout.' They rated the cartoon funnier when having the pen in their teeth, 'smiling.'

The conclusion of this experiment was to show how much just smiling, not even truly being happy, makes us receptive to positivity, which enables us to get in touch with the conscious part of our brain.

When we smile, it lowers the heart rate, which sends the blood flow back to the prefrontal cortex. The prefrontal cortex enables us to respond, rather than react, using the rational part of the brain.

The fifth Chabad Rebbe says that joy brings one's brain to the heart, intellect into feeling, which connects what we know to what we do.

According to Carol Vivyan (2010), we can use colour to help influence our emotions and ability to cope by the following four ways.

1) Wearing colour
2) Drinking or eating colour
3) Visualising or mediating with colour
4) Surrounding ourselves with colour (e.g. Green garden)

Colour Breathing is a technique that people use to help with insomnia, stress, anxiety, depression and to improve overall health and wellness.

One way in which to calm ourselves down when we are stressed and panicked is to visualise breathing in calm blue and breathing out red tension. Practitioners in colour breathing suggest that if you find it difficult to visualise the colour, imagine something that is that colour – for instance blue sky, orange sunset, red fire.

Colour	Promotes	Good for
Red	Energy, strength, confidence, courage, motivation	Depression, shyness, negativity
Orange	Self-esteem, optimism, self-expression, happiness	Depression, negativity, trauma, stress
Yellow	Uplifting, cleansing, self-respect and confidence	Depression, despair, negativity, lack of confidence

Green	Balance, self-acceptance, compassion	Stress, anxiety, self – pity, confusion
Turquoise	Calm, cleansing, healing, sharing	Stress, anxiety, anger.
Blue	Calm, peace, relaxation, honesty, creativity	Insomnia, stress, anxiety, over-excitement, anger

The Hebrew word for breathing is נשימה – *Neshimah*, which comes from the same root as נשמה – *Neshamah*, the Soul. When one breathes, they connect with their soul and all external triggers and events lose their importance. This shifts one's perception of pressure and urgency.

The science behind why breathing has such a big impact is similar to that which we discussed previously about happiness. When we breathe, our heart rate lowers which sends the blood flow back to the prefrontal cortex, informing the body that it is safe.

Conclusion

Why we do what we do, when we know what we know?
How we can practically alter our thought process and do what we know is best for us, gaining self-control.

Through my research, I have gained a deeper understanding that we must actively connect what we know to what we do. Through certain techniques of mindfulness, SMART planning, positive/coping thoughts, smiling and breathing, we can gain control and connect our vast knowledge into action. Doing what we know is best for us in that particular situation.

The methodology I used are ideas from Psychology and Chassidic teachings. I learned that these two school of thoughts at first glance seemed similar but the more I researched in depth, the clearer it became on how different they are.

Many aspects of Psychology give room for the person to be 'excused' for their behaviour due to circumstance and nurture. In contrast, Chassidic teachings reinforce time and again that the only person that can dictate your future and actions is you, emphasizing that we are in full control of ourselves despite our circumstances and experiences.

This may seem demanding but I find this very empowering.

ABOUT THE WRITER

Rivky Osdaba enjoys delving into subjects that are based on Chassidus and highlighting the psychological insights that are woven in the fabric of Torah. She also enjoys playing the violin and sharing her knowledge and experiences with others. In the future Rivky aspires to helping women and girls to live fuller and healthier lives physically, emotionally and spiritually, taking a wholesome and integrative approach to health and wellness.

CHAPTER SIX

HOW AND WHY SHOULD I LEAVE MY CULT?

Brocha Overlander

Should cults be allowed to exist under the right of freedom of religion?

Is the abuse simply religious practice?

How does human sacrifice become culture?

Where is the line between freedom of religion, and actual abuse of power?

In this essay, I will explore the different aspects of a cult:

- The leaders and how their childhood may have affected who they became later on in life
- How exactly the cults do such a great job of recruitment

- How cult leaders use manipulation tactics to control their congregation
- The benefit of a cult, although incomparable with the harm they cause, to the general society
- The terrible abuse that goes on in many cults, and why the number of cults should not be allowed to grow
- The different ways to get out of a cult

Finally, I will discuss if deprogramming as a method to get out of a cult should be banned, due to allegations of cruelty.

My claim in this essay, is that a cult is a form of abuse and therefore it is reasonable to use drastic measures to deprogram a person in order to reintroduce them into the regular society, as long as no lasting damage may occur.

The Leaders

Many cult leaders are narcissists; people with a mental condition where they have an inflated sense of their own importance, and a deep need for excessive attention and admiration. They also have a lack of empathy for others and show a pattern of self-centred and arrogant thinking and behaviour.

Cult leaders, like many narcissists, don't care about the damage they're causing. They have a goal, and they're willing to go to extreme lengths to accomplish what they see as their "Divine mission."

They're usually great speakers and creative strategists with a great ability to attract and inspire followers. Narcissists make great leaders, but can often lead to a dark side, where the narcissist thinks that he deserves everything, whenever and however.

One of the differences which distinguish a cult from a religion, is that a cult leader stands apart from and above the cult's rules and disciplines, often covertly, sometimes brazenly. On the other hand, a leader of a true religion is held even more accountable for his actions than his followers. In short: religious leaders are men of G-d, cult leaders are gods.

Very often, a cult leader may be transgressing the very laws he set for his congregation; in a cult where members are told to stay celibate, the cult leader may be having sexual relations even though he claimed it was immoral. If he is caught doing the things he denounced and forbade; he may change the rules on the spot, or claim that the rules only apply at certain times and/ or to certain people. This shows an inconsistency in the cult's philosophy.

In the event that a cult member is questioned on any contradictions that might be apparent to someone who is not trapped in the cult, he will either refuse to rationalize, or give the lame excuses that the victim has been brainwashed to respond to anyone who may try to turn him away from the cult.

However, sometimes, in the event that the lies are exposed in broad daylight, it may cause people to leave, as will be explained later in the essay.

Many studies have shown how childhood trauma can affect the way a person leads his life in the future. Trauma during childhood chips away at a child's stability and sense of self, undermining self-worth and often staying with the child into adulthood. In addition to this, trauma can impact a person into adulthood; they may feel disconnected and unable to relate to others.

Many cult leaders prove these studies to be true, as many cult leaders went through significant trauma as a child and as an adult, show signs of narcissism, where their self-worth is over-inflated to compensate for feelings of low self-worth.

One cult, known as The Gatekeeper, was run by a man named Chris Turgeon. His father was a drunk who beat his mother. When Chris was still young, she married his stepfather, named Edward, after his biological father left them. This obviously left a profound imprint on Chris as he later went on to turn a group of his friends into a cult that followed his every command, even when he ordered them to commit murder.

Chris claimed that G-d told him he was a prophet and was meant to prepare Christians for judgement. Simon McCarthy Jones and Elanor Longden of the British Psychological Society, note that hearing G-d's voice is often a symptom of brain disease, synonymous with schizophrenia.

According to NY Times journalist Fred Bratman, in his article *Cult of Personality*, he explains how leaders who wish to appear infallible often create images of themselves designed to invoke adoration from their subjects. So they might paint as if even in their childhood, they were close to G-d, and would wander the fields, deep in meditation, when truthfully they may have just been slacking off chores. They may portray themselves to be diligent and hardworking when in reality this could not be further from the truth.

One such man was Victor Paul Wierwille, leader of The Way International, a cult focused on preaching the gospel. As a young child, Victor Paul would practice preaching to the trees on his family farm. It is worthwhile to note, had Victor Paul actually been inspired by G-d, he might have shared his revelations with his family and friends. But instead, he "practised" a performance in front of a silent and willing audience.

Additionally, he claimed that when he prayed, he got a direct response out loud from G-d, a voice which told him that if he would teach it to others, G-d would share with him explanations of the Bible such as had never been learnt before.

Evangelists believe that Divine revelation and miracles are a thing of the past, so by making this announcement, Wierwille was making a clear break from his past beliefs, and, in addition to this, was also deeming himself a prophet to whom G-d spoke to directly.

It is also worth noting that some leaders do start off enthusiastic for G-d, and only soon does it come out that their true desires are for sex, money and control. Either deep down these were always their desires, or as their power and control grew, they saw that they could now fulfil any desires they wished to.

One cult leader by the name of George Feigley, ran a cult called The Light of the World. He opened a school in his home where he taught the children, unbeknownst to the parents, that sexual exploration was but a way to get closer to G-d, and was a sign of maturity. In addition to this, he groomed the young victims by giving them rings that signified his bond to them.

Abusers work to gain the trust of their intended victims by giving them small gifts, attention, or sharing secrets. This makes the child feel special and makes them believe that they have a caring relationship with the abuser.

Psychiatrist Michael Garret explains that some individuals use grandiose illusions to maintain their self-esteem. In the event that one is unable to achieve ordinary successes in work and love, they may resort to delusional narratives rather than looking for actual respectable markers of self-esteem. Delusions, if unchallenged, may last a lifetime.

The Trap

The new-wave cult religions seek out people who are at a low point in their stability. Cult victims are not intellectually weak. They are usually far above average intelligence. However, they tend to be emotionally unstable at the time that they are proselytized.

The most common targets the cults aim at are young men or women between the ages of 18 and 24 who cannot cope with the current state of their personal lives. He or she lacks the courage to face problems, make decisions and deal with responsibility. In the event that a person like this is dealt a rough blow in life or meets with a series of minor setbacks, the cults will find them an easy catch.

This is why cults hit college campuses so hard. They work mostly on the sophomores and juniors, since the freshmen are too spirited and idealistic, and the seniors are aware of where they are heading in the world. But in the two intermediate years, at ages 19 and 20, students are often confused and disappointed, without direction, so they become susceptible to a cult's religious activities.

Similarly, the cults concentrate their recruiting work at bus stations, airports, parks and other places where they can find young people in transit or without direction. If it's a girl, they send a boy to go after him and vice versa. This is because there is a connection that forms instantly with a member of the other gender even when just passing on the street, especially in the case where the person they are trying to attract is single.

Often, cult members are drawn in using deceptive ploys. A common tactic is sending out young members of the cult to go chat with a person of the opposite gender. So if it's a male they're after, they'll send a pretty female to go talk to him. She'll invite him to one meeting where they'll discuss their problems. There they'll give out snacks, talk, and cultivate a warm family atmosphere.

A cult known by the name the Divine Light Mission, would send out young men and women to distribute brochures for their housecleaning service. The advantage of this was that besides for it being lucrative, bringing in lots of money for their leader, it also provided excellent opportunities for proselytising and bringing in new members. The cult member gains access to an individual's home and spends hours there. They'll strike up a friendly conversation and before long, the homeowner becomes enthralled by the religious and philosophical ideas that are expressed. If the homeowner is among the middle-class Americans who are frustrated, lost and confused about their own value system, he or she can very easily become involved with the cult.

This is also one of the differences between a cult and a true religion; a cult is seductive and ensnaring. Cults use deceptive ploys to draw new converts. It's goal is to build an ever-expanding power base for the cult leader and its activities. A true religion, however, even in the circumstances where it does seek converts, is guileless. It presents its views openly, in a straightforward and understandable manner. This is because they would like the potential convert to accept and believe in what is being presented, rather than just complying without really understanding.

The Control

There are many tactics cult leaders use to keep their followers in check. Cults will often hold sessions where they chant, either incoherent syllables or simple mantras. These sessions work to stop any deviant thoughts from popping up and distracting them.

Using loaded language (phrases without any real definite meaning behind the words) helps to isolate, indoctrinate and control the thoughts of their cult members. Creating a new dictionary of words that help the doctrine, but have no actual definition, also creates an elitist mentality. Those who question, are regarded as inferior or not as smart as the rest of the group, who "understand" exactly what is meant by all these made-up terms.

The cult doctrine is a black and white mentality; either you're with us or against us. Anyone not in the cult is completely wrong in regard to everything and should not be trusted.

Cults program their victims to expect persecution-people telling them they're in a cult and are therefore indoctrinated to be unable to hold a rational conversation. Anyone critical of the cult's movement would be deemed sacrilegious and to be excommunicated.

In the Emin cult, membership created, in both the individual and the group, a feeling of superiority with regard to non-members. Additionally they used loaded language such as the term "electrical barnacles," which has a clear paranoid flavour. Such beliefs created a special way of looking at non-members and of interacting with them, the feeling of superiority and the supercilious attitude towards non-members, justified by the special, secret knowledge open only to insiders, created an obvious resentment among outsiders.

In 1985, Monte Kim Miller was an anti-cult activist, speaking at churches to warn against brainwashing and manipulation—until he began using the same tactics he preached against to extort, coerce, and compel his followers into radical behaviour. No one suspected him of indoctrination; because that was the very thing he was so against.

Many cults claim that the destruction of the world is imminent, and the only way to be saved is through their leader. This results in the followers relying on the cult leader, rather than G-d.

Cult leaders will implement strict rules to control their cult members. These laws might dictate whether they are allowed to engage in intimate acts; watch television; read newspapers, etc.

The members usually trust the leader, and fear the repercussions of misdemeanours, so they are obedient. Penalties for questioning the leaders can range from the threat of eternal damnation, to much harsher measures. In one cult, parents were made to beat their own children with paddles, in the event that the leader thought that the children were misbehaving.

Another difference between a cult and a real religion is that a cult destroys the individual's ability to think independently and make reasoned decisions. Religion does the opposite. Religion teaches philosophical principles that enable us to make choices based on intellect rather than emotion. Religion increases free will, cults seek to destroy it.

One cult which perfectly characterizes the practice of destroying an individual's ability to think is the Divine Light Mission. This group, led by a guru named Maharaj Ji, teaches that rational though is an obstacle to enlightenment and the human mind is the devil. It stresses meditation and its own form of yoga discipline, promising to liberate its members from the bondage of worldly existence. The results are entirely the opposite; DLM enslaves its victims mind, body and soul.

DLM primarily serves as a financial power base for its leader, who lives lavishly through the unthinking self-sacrifice of its members. The members (called Premies) are required to tithe their incomes to the cult, after first giving up all they own as part of the initiation process.

Premies meditate at least two hours a day in a cross-legged pose; many of them do it for up to six hours. This, together with the constant repetition of a supposed magic formula, or mantra, which blocks natural thought processes, brings the victim to the mindless state that the cult wants them in.

In the Tvevnoc cult, only one hour of "free time" was allowed each day, but even then, members were forbidden from being alone, even in an unsupervised group. Rather, they were required to remain together whilst being monitored by cult leaders.

A very common way of keeping the followers in the cult is by cutting them off from the outside world, so that even in the event in which they were to escape they'd have nowhere to go and no-one to help them. Cult leaders will often force the cult members to cut off any relationships outside of the cult, claiming that they will be a bad influence, or are somehow on the bad side. This includes close family members, friends, teachers and anyone else who might try to help get the person out of the cult. Cult leaders will pit their followers against the world, even their own family members, to ensure their complete dependence on the group.

On one occasion, one man claimed to have "discovered" through hypnosis that he had been sexually abused by both his sister and his mother. The shocked family categorically denied that any such thing took place; and in spite of the fact that their counter claims were likely to have been the truth, their son refused to listen, and cut off all communication with them, saying he could not have anything to do with such disgusting people. The young man with his therapist/ cult leader travelled around, telling his story of childhood sexual abuse. What was concerning at the time, was that all of this therapist's patients seemed to be recovering memories of childhood abuse and were then being encouraged by this therapist to cut off all ties with their family and accept her as their new parental figure. Normal therapeutic boundaries seemed to be broken as every aspect of this man's life seemed to be controlled by his therapist. The total devotion he had towards her was similar to the relationship between cult leaders and followers. This is an example of the extent to which cult leaders may go to discredit the parents of the cult members.

The Good Side

To push their narrative, cult leaders will often take their members to food drives and other charitable events to push their narrative of being a caring, helpful group of people seeking to fulfil G-d's command in the best way possible.

Often a group's "good works" and "charitable activities" are publicized through elaborate brochures illustrated with beautiful photographs, but these descriptions frequently turn out to be either mostly exaggerated, or entirely false.

Therefore, it is hard to separate whether the good reports that do come out are even to be believed or are just fabricated in order to hide the abuse that's really going on behind closed doors.

However, some cult ideology encourages the member to be a good person. The Emin cult emphasizes hard work and respect for the law. It is opposed to the use of drugs, other than nicotine and alcohol. Additionally there is an emphasis on punctuality, good manners, and formal dress.

The Abuse

It's widely known that cult leaders use their followers to grow their power and money. One of the ways they do this is by forcing their members to sell items on the streets, with all revenue going straight to the pockets of the cult leader.

In many cults, members are forced, or pressured to donate a percentage, if not all of the income they may be making, to the cult.

One cult leader organized theft and fraud, claiming G-d would never let them be put in jail. He made his followers believe they were doing G-d's will, but really, they were just building their leader an arsenal of weapons to arm the group and stuffing his pockets with cash. The cult leader knew eventually they would be caught, but since he wasn't the one to break into the stores, he would not be prosecuted. He was not concerned of any repercussions that may occur and rather sent hundreds of followers to their doom to grow his wealth and power.

Another example of the mistreatment of cult members is in the case of the leader of the Divine Light Mission, who became known for erratic behaviour, including physical cruelty, like kicking initiates for the sheer sport of it. He did so to exercise his power over the initiate, making them think that if they protested, they wouldn't be accepted into this elite group of people who one day would save the world.

One of the most well known instances where the harm a cult can cause was revealed to the world was in the case of the Jonestown cult, which was led by a man by the name of Jim Jones, who established a settlement in Guyana. He created a community, which preached that anyone could come and feel comfortable in, no matter your background, race, ethnic identity etc.

He had gotten into trouble with the IRS and slowly started insinuating the idea of revolutionary suicide into his followers' heads. Jim jones used this term as a device to achieve a specific goal. In one recorded tape, he said that the people of Jonestown would commit suicide unless they were "given freedom from harassment and given asylum." In essence, he defined it as "protesting the conditions of an inhumane world."

On November 18, 1978, 909 people were found dead from apparent cyanide poisoning. As reported afterwards, the followers drank - willingly or unwillingly - fruit punch which was laced with cyanide. Over 300 children were made to drink it and syringes full of the mixture were emptied into infants' mouths. Those who didn't want to join in were injected with poison. Those who tried to run for the surrounding jungle were shot by one of Jones' armed guards.

Later, the recovery workers who had to load up and transport the bodies of the masses of victims detailed that the staggering number of children they saw there was the most disturbing thing they had ever seen in their lives. "Can't sleep," one worker reported, "cannot get the small children out of my mind."

The immediate emotional impact on seeing "three or four babies per [body] bag" kept workers up at night. They were so traumatized at these shocking images, it haunted them long after they delivered the bodies to their final destinations.

When this event occurred, people around the world were outraged at how such a thing could happen. The few survivors came forth and told their stories and people were finally shocked into the reality of what cults really can do.

The Exit

One of the ways to extract someone from a cult is through deprogramming, where the basic objective is to shock the cult member into thinking. Once his resistance is worn down by making him think that he might be locked up forever, he gets scared, and the protective bubble of cult-faith bursts. As soon as he can once again function with his intellect and is willing to argue, debate, or discuss his beliefs rationally, the job of the deprogrammers is essentially complete. After this "cracking," the cult member is easily shown that he has swallowed a complex and cleverly contrived lie. Once the protective bubble has popped, almost all cult members see the truth, rarely do they go back to the cult. They realize quite clearly that they have made a terrible error.

One way to deprogram is to emotionally assault the individual and deprive him of sleep, in order to get them to listen, but on the other hand, some deprogrammers have made it their practice to give the person lots of sleep and healthy, protein filled foods. They are then able to function better. This can turn out positively and negatively. On the one hand, the person is finally being given adequate food and sleep (contrary to what he would have experienced during his time in the cult) and is therefore able to function better, and think rationally. On the other hand, it may make their resistance stronger, and harder to crack. In each case, the situation must be weighed out to see if it is worth it.

In short, the cult member is held against their will and emotionally assaulted until they are ready to reason. This has been thought to be controversial, since the cult group can claim that the victim was kidnapped and held against his will. Obviously, this is all done for his benefit, but there still is a legal problem with that approach, as will be explained in the following section.

In some cases, bringing in an ex-cult member to speak to the person who is being deprogrammed may help shock them into thinking rationally. When he sees that there is someone in front of him, using the same language and lingo as used in the cult, yet disproving all he thought to be true, can get him to finally start realizing that everything he was taught is a lie.

However deprogramming does nothing except safeguard the victim against returning to the cult. The former cult member is still searching, facing an enormous void, which often makes him/her feel different from the crowd.

In some cases, the cult member may realize on his own, with no outside input, that what is going on in their cult is actual abuse.

In one cult, called the Kingston clan, one member came to that realization when his mother got ill and the cult leader barred them from going to a doctor, claiming that G-d would save her, and instead of getting her proper treatment, attempted to pray the sickness away. Understandably, his mother died shortly afterwards. This shocked the son into realizing what kind of community he was part of and he managed to escape on his own.

Another time where this happened, was where a cultish missionary group called Bnai Yeshua (a branch of the Hineni organization), sent someone into Jewish community in Crown Heights to take a photograph of an elderly Chasid as he was returning home from synagogue in the morning. The photograph appeared a couple weeks later in a Bnai Yeshua periodical in an article titled: "*Orthodox Jews Turning to Pork for Sabbath Meals.*" The Chasid was outraged when he learned that they had used his picture to ensnare other Jews. He got an attorney and sued, and he was awarded a judgement of $125,000. The missionary group, thinking to turn a failure into victory, sent out a mailing that publicized its loss of money as the basis of a plea for more funds. When people read and saw that, by its own admission, the group was perpetrating lies to achieve its goals, there was a wholesale desertion of membership. A few months later, the group was dismantled due to lack of funds.

For many ex-cult members, reintegrating back into normal society can be incredibly difficult. It often takes years for them to admit that they were ever in a cult.

Once they are truly out of the cult, ex- cult members are very special people who have gone through a difficult learning experience and are better people for it.

Is Deprogramming Cruel?

There has been debate around the topic of deprogramming. Despite it being ultimately for the person's own good, they are being held against their will, which is seen by some as immoral. Sometimes they are deprived from sleep or adequate food, all to shock them into thinking rationally to enable them to have a functional discussion.

Cult members have tried to obtain legal protection against deprogrammers but it has yielded mixed results.

The defendants' (the deprogrammers') claim is that they break a law in order to prevent a greater evil than the law against abduction was created to prevent. In other words, the reason why abduction is illegal is to prevent bad people from abducting innocent people, whereas in this case, the abductors are good people trying to help victims who have been, or will end up in the future, in a terrible situation.

For example, one who stole a car under the premise of delivering someone to the hospital and thereby saving his life may be acquitted under the charge that he did so to prevent a greater harm from occurring, which would be letting the person die without taking the necessary steps to save the man.

Lawmakers have debated over whether punishing the person who stole the car will discourage other people in similar situations from taking the necessary steps to enact the socially and morally right thing to do.

I personally believe that a cult is a form of abuse and therefore it is necessary to take drastic measures in order to save the person from future emotional, physical and spiritual damage. However, I do not believe that any course of action in which to convince the victim to rationalize is permissible. The necessary steps may be taken in order to help this person, but anything that will cause long-lasting damage on the victim, who has already been through enough, should be considered abuse and therefore not be allowed under the premise of saving the person.

In conclusion, many factors influence how a cult leader behaves. The many tactics cults use to attract followers show how deceptive cults are. The abuse that happens in many cults is enough of a reason why deprogramming should be permissible, even if the victim does feel short-term discomfort, it is ultimately to prevent an even greater, long-term damage from occurring and messing up the person's entire life.

ABOUT THE WRITER

Brocha Overlander was born in London, England. Growing up in a household filled with an abundance of books, she developed passion for reading at an early age. At seventeen, she left to continue her religious studies in New York, where learned about Judaism and gainied valuable insights into the meaning of life. Brocha has an interest in music, paticularly the guitar and ukulele, in addition to her talent on the piano. Brochas's also has a passion for traveling. Her journeys to different countries allowed her to gain a deeper appreciation for the beauty and complexity of different cultures.

CHAPTER SEVEN

WHAT MAKES LIFE MEANINGFUL?

Mika Vogel

For thousands of years, many have been plagued with trying to find an answer to the question that lies at the root of all existentialism. What is the meaning of life? However, despite the emergence of many philosophies and ideas, there has been a failure to reconsider and even reconstruct the question. Rather than contemplate the meaning of life, consider why meaning is important at all. The most suited to help explain this question is perhaps Viktor E. Frankl, (1905-1997) author of the international bestseller '*Man's Search for Meaning.*'

Why is Meaning Important?

Frankl, after spending three years in the Nazi concentration camps refined and coined his theory, "logotherapy," a school of thought entirely dedicated to the search for meaning in life. He believed that meaning was the primary motivational force in a person's life and so this search for meaning would create a struggle between man's desire for instant gratification, and his desire to reach upward, for meaning. This tension also meant that there would be a gap, a gap between what man is, and what he can and ought to be. To relieve the tension, the gap must be imbued.

Frankl proposed that every man had what he called a "will to meaning" which equates to every man's desire to find meaning in life. Each man's will to meaning is particular and specific to him. Only when fulfilled by him, and him alone, will it achieve significance and satisfy his own will to meaning.

One of the characteristics introduced in the formation of logotherapy was what Frankl termed as "the self-transcendence of human existence," where meaning is created when a person begins to point to something other than himself, towards something, or someone else. This involvement with things other than himself allows him to actualise himself and create meaning in his life. However, the term self-actualisation would be deemed unattainable, as self-actualisation would come only as a by-product of self-transcendence.

Going further, Frankl's logotherapy suggests that meaning in life can be found in three distinct ways: (1) by creating a work or doing a deed; (2) by experiencing something or encountering someone; and (3) by the attitude we take towards unavoidable suffering. As Nietzsche says "he who has a 'why' to live for can bear almost any 'how.'" The first way is self-explanatory. Meaning can be found through accomplishments and achievements, the act of completing a project or working towards an end goal.

Number two involves creating meaning through dedication to a person or experiencing nature and culture. Frankl called this "the meaning of love" coined alongside "the meaning of life" and "the meaning of suffering." Frankl himself said, "If we take man as he is, we make him worse, but if we take him as he should be, we make him capable of becoming what he can be." He implied that through love, and the potential that is discovered through loving a person, man would enable his loved one to self-actualise and thus create meaning.

The third and final way concerns "the meaning of suffering." When a man is faced with a tragedy and cannot change the aspects of his circumstances, he is then forced to change himself. This links to Frankl's idea of "the self-transcendence of human nature." Not that suffering is necessary to find meaning, but rather, meaning can be found despite suffering. In fact, suffering ceases to be suffering at the moment it finds meaning.

This element can be further explained after considering the 'logotherapy triangle,' the three main ideas as to which logotherapy was founded upon. Firstly, "the meaning of life," that can be found in any situation, often associated with a stimulus, something happening. Secondly, "the will to meaning," the conscious, yet innate motivation to find meaning. And lastly, the "freedom of will," whose definition is termed as "the freedom to choose attitudes towards conditions." Conclusively, this attitude is what shapes man's perspective and approach to finding meaning in life, and whether or not he ends up doing so.

Ultimately, man cannot grasp the meaning of life, due to his limited intellectual capacity. Frankl calls this the "Super-Meaning" where rather than endure the meaninglessness of life, as practiced by past philosophers, he offers that man learn to endure his inability to completely understand the full meaning of life in logical terms. For meaning is beyond logic.

It is also important to consider what makes life meaningful from a spiritual perspective, how there is usually an aimlessness that stems from a lack of spiritual connection. Over time, man has tried and failed to compensate for it, filling the emptiness with superficial achievements, such as chasing careers or making money. Rather than pursuing that which is temporary, pursue that which is meaningful.

The Torah teaches us that every man has a soul, an endless reservoir of the most powerful force in a person's life. For every challenge a man is faced with, he has all the resources to deal with it. He has all the answers inside of himself.

Discovering a meaningful life begins when man realizes that he is significant, that he is indispensable. That his value is based solely on the fact that he exists, that he is himself and no one else. Not on his performance, or production or looks, youth or power. Birth, in itself, is G-d saying you matter.

There is a Jewish prayer, said every morning as soon as one wakes up, that acknowledges - in man's first conscious moments - G-d and the fact that He has decided to return his soul to him. "*Modeh Ani*"- "I give thanks to You, for returning my soul to me." This isn't just thanks for life however, it is thanks for being significant, being indispensable, and meaningful.

Meaningfulness is created when one aims to discover his indispensable contribution to the world. The lack of meaning usually arises when one forgets or questions their significance. Even then, our soul speaks to us. Anxiety is a voice of the soul speaking to us when we're in pain, telling us that something is not right, something is misaligned. This is precisely what makes life meaningful, the challenges. The challenge of a life of meaning is to achieve spirituality and spiritual serenity in a world of difficulties.

Meaning vs. Purpose

Many times, it is believed that meaning and purpose are the same, or at least that they are synonymous with each other. However, upon further inspection, these two terms can be both defined and explained separately from each other. Meaning can be defined as an "intention," or "reason for doing something." On the other hand, purpose can be characterised as "the fulfilment" or "the consummation" of the said meaning. Whilst one intends, the other accomplishes.

According to Aristotle (384-322 BC), purpose, or rather "*telos*" in Greek, refers to the full potential or inherent purpose or objective of a person or thing. Likewise, the word "meaning" originates from the Greek word "*logos*" and can also be translated as "reason" or "discourse." In Greek philosophy, *Logos* was thought to be the Divine reason implicit in the cosmos, ordering it and giving it form and meaning, an eternal truth present to whoever sought it.

The "Meaning vs Purpose" discussion can additionally be explained from an alternate perspective, specifically the Chabad perspective. In his magnum opus, the Tanya (1796), Rabbi Shneur Zalman of Liadi (1745-1812) founder and first

Rebbe of Chabad, introduces what he terms as "Chabad," an acronym for a man's three intellectual faculties. These are Chochmah, Binah, and Daat (abbreviated as ChaBaD).

Chochmah ("wisdom") is the first flash of intellect, the beginning of an intellectual revelation. The details and implications of the idea are present, yet they are still concentrated and obscured. Following this, comes the faculty of Binah ("understanding"). Through the contemplation of Binah, all the obscurities present in Chochmah are revealed and understood. Lastly, the third and final faculty is Daat ("knowledge"). After a person fully understands an idea, with all its nuances and ramifications, he must then immerse himself wholly in it, so much, so that he not only understands the idea, but now also can feel it. Only in this way can he be affected by it. If a man's understanding turns or points to the appeal of a particular thing, his understanding of that appeal will give birth to love for it. So too, if his understanding indicates the harm of a particular thing, the birth will be that of fear.

The second and third faculties can be used to explain meaning and purpose. Binah provides us with the steps and complete idea, which then leads to Daat, where this final idea can be implemented and acted upon. The faculty of Daat brings the abstract concept into actuality, as in the verse "And Adam *knew* Eve" (*yada* – from the word Daat) denoting attachment and union. Binah and Daat - the intention and the accomplishment.

Now that the difference between meaning and purpose has been explained, as well as what meaning is and why it is important (as mentioned in the first unit), it is now necessary to address the purpose and the Chassidic approach to explaining what it is.

To answer this query, one must look into the very book of life itself - the Torah. Even the word "Torah" in itself means "instruction," or "lesson," acting as a guide to understand and attain our life's goal and purpose. In the very beginning of the Torah, G-d creates Adam - the first man - and tells him that his purpose in life would be to, "Fill the earth and master it; and rule the fish of the sea, the birds of the sky, and all the living things that creep on earth."

Adam, and consequently man, was commanded and given the power to conquer the world, for when G-d created him, his soul – his Divine image – infused his entire being thereupon making him ruler of all creation. After, the creatures of nature came to crown him as their creator, Adam indicated their mistake and exclaimed, "Let us come and worship our Creator."

This "world conquest" given to man as his mission and purpose in life, was to elevate and purify the world, including all the creatures and animals, as well as ensuring that the world and all of humanity would be permeated and infused with the light of the Divine Image until all of creation would recognise G-d as their Maker.

However, before man could conquer the world, he would first have to conquer himself and his ego, through the domination of the "animal" within his own nature. This is done when one follows the directions of the Torah, so that his actions become imbued with the light of G-d.

As mentioned above, G-d created Adam, the first man, as a single entity, unlike the rest of the creatures on earth, who were created in large numbers. This signifies that one single individual – each and every person- has the power to influence and thereby bring the entire world to fulfilment. If a person fails to utilize his invaluable Divine powers in his task of conquering the world, it is not only a personal loss but also one that could affect the fate of the entire world.

Adam serves as an example for each and every person to follow, as the Rabbis teach us that "one person is equivalent to an entire world." This means that every man has the ability, as well as the inherent duty, to attain the highest degree of fulfilment, in addition to doing so for the entire world.

This degree of fulfilment is accomplished through subjugation, as Adam cried to all animals to "prostrate themselves before G-d their Maker," for it is only through prostration – self-abnegation – that a creation can be fully united with its Creator and achieve this highest degree of completion.

This idea can also be further explained through the exploration of a specific event in Jewish history. After the Jewish people were liberated from their exile in Egypt, passed through the desert, and received the Torah at Mount Sinai, G-d commanded them to build the Tabernacle: "Make for Me a sanctuary, so that I may dwell among *them*." Upon first glance, this sentence seems to be grammatically incorrect, being that it should have said: "it" and not "them." However, the Sages come to explain that the choice of words acts as a hint for each man to create a dwelling place for G-d within himself, a place where the Divine Presence can rest.

The Role of the Soul

In order to better understand how to achieve one's purpose, and create meaning in one's life, one must first begin to understand the role of the soul, and better yet, what the soul is. The soul is usually undefinable, an infinite part of ourselves that comes directly from G-d. On many occasions, the soul has been likened to an energy, a spirit of some sort, usually defined as an immortal material that can never be tarnished. Where the soul is infinite, the body is finite, weak, mortal, and short-lived. However, the body acts as a vessel that caters to the spiritual needs of the soul, and so, it is integral to understand the relationship between the two.

The body acts as a device for the soul, a container, just as music is contained or packaged within the notes, or a ship is manoeuvred through the visions and desires of its captain. A popular analogy used to describe the relation between them is that of a flame, where the soul is constantly rising upward and is transcendent, yet is grounded by the wick, the physical body, which also demands fulfilment of its own wants, desires, and needs. This creates tension within their relationship, where the body seeks animal bliss, tempted to procrastinate and remain in its comfort zone, and the soul, which continually wishes to improve, learn and transform. Feeling restless or angsty is a healthy element, as too much calm is not consistent with the human spirit, but at the same time, there is also an anxiety that stems from the frustration due to not reaching certain heights. However, one would find a balance, as life is about waves and cycles, peaks and valleys, finding a balance between the tensions and resolutions present in one's life.

Despite this tension, one can strive to live a soul-centric life, a life that is lived when one begins looking inside out, towards purpose, a calling deeper than its own bodily inclinations. Soul-centric thinking starts when the focus is turned to one's "inner," the part of a person that yearns for something bigger than himself. This then allows a person to recognise this part in others and that everything in life has a soul, an inner narrative that is not defined by superficial limitations such as race, or gender, but by its Divine mission. By nourishing, nurturing, and responding to it, one can unlock their voice, the song that is uniquely theirs, which then, combined with the songs of others, creates a symphony that can transform the world.

However, in order to live a soul-centric life, one must delve even further into understanding the soul, even before comprehending its relationship with the body. In his magnum opus, the Tanya (1796), Rabbi Shneur Zalman of Liadi (1745-1812) explains how every Jew has two souls. An animal soul, present from birth, and a Divine soul that is introduced at the time of spiritual maturation, at the age of twelve for a girl, and age thirteen for a boy.

There are many differences between the two souls, one being that the Divine soul is likened to the reflective mind, in comparison to the animalistic soul, which is likened to an impulsive heart. Essentially, the main difference is that the animalistic soul is the primal voice, whereas the Divine soul is the voice of transcendence. This can be seen in the way an animal differs from a human being. Because an animal looks down, its head is then level with its body, in contrast to man, whose head rests above the rest of his body. This hints to man's ever-aspiring spirit, as man looks up, towards G-d.

The two souls are often compared to two kings, both of whom wish to rule the same city, the body. Contrary to popular belief, the goal is not to vanquish the opposing soul but to dominate it and later transform it. This is done by dominating the metaphorical "garments" with which the soul uses to express itself: thought, speech, and action. These elements are used to manifest the intentions of the governing soul and so, the objective of the battle between the souls is to rule them.

As stated previously, the souls are compared to mind and heart, control and impulse. Now, one can argue that the impulse of the animalistic soul is unavoidable, as deep down, man is a selfish creature. It is only through the development that comes with maturing, that man does not revert to his inherently selfish ways. However, Chassidic teachings assure us that every person possesses the quality of "*Moach Shalit al halev*"- the mind rules the heart. This idea is explored in Tanya and proposes that self-control is innate, which links to the Jewish law that states that accountability of our actions is an obligation.

Just like there is no battle between light and dark, so too, the mind has natural dominance over the heart. This can be seen in the way that a smart man rules over the fool, or the way light has natural dominance over the dark. The reason why most temptations are fed despite this explanation is that the mind is not given enough time to express itself before our impulses kick in. Impulse has the power to seduce us before we can reflect when the blood of our heart rushes and 'takes over' the brain. By giving the mind and heart equal time, one can ensure that there is now a choice. Given the understanding of this concept, one can appreciate how choice is inherent and how, regardless of the many battles present every day, one still has the power to choose. To be selfish, or to allow the Divine soul to express itself.

Both souls are necessary. One deals with the world, while the other elevates it. One cannot exist in this world without the other, much like the body and the soul, dependant on each other to fulfil the purpose they were both put into this world for. However, the G-dly soul must remain in control, the ruling king of the city and all of its expressions.

Ultimately, this is the purpose of man. Because the Divine soul manifests itself within a physical body, it is man's job to train, educate and harness the animal soul that lives alongside the Divine one. The very function of the Divine soul is to understand, not what it needs, but what it is needed for, something greater than itself. However, this is not abstinence, for its entire role consists of ensuring the elevation of the physical components of the world, accomplished through interactions, by cause of the animal soul.

An example of this is the transcendent experience behind feeding the body. On the surface, it would seem that the animalistic soul is in control, feeding the body to indulge it's selfish desires. Nonetheless, the Divine soul is elevating the body, by causing it to participate in spiritual affairs, such as eating foods associated with spiritual events, as well as elevating the food itself. Unleavened bread on Passover, or indulging in delicious foods on Sabbath, so that the body is elevated for spiritual purposes, but by using means that the body can appreciate.

Meaning between Man and Woman

Now that creating meaning has been considered in relation to the role as an individual, it is now relevant to examine meaning regarding connections and relationships between two people, namely husband and wife. What is the inner meaning of marriage? Why get married at all? Before this question can be answered, it is necessary to acknowledge what a "standard" relationship might look like.

When looking at a relationship between a man and a woman, there are usually three components taken into account that pertain to the compatibility between two people. Physical compatibility, where both parties feel a physical attraction to one another, a sexual appeal. Emotional compatibility, where an emotional connection prompts an intense understanding of each other, and lastly, intellectual compatibility, that includes stimulation and respect for each other's particular way of thinking. All of these constituent parts, however wonderful, are subject to change. Youth and beauty fade, there are disagreements and misunderstandings and time shifts these factors, in all relationships.

Here, enters the fourth element. Spiritual compatibility. While the first three are considered selfish, regarding the needs of only oneself and his/her spouse, spiritual compatibility is selfless in the way that it concerns a shared appreciation of values, an appreciation of something greater than the both of them, allowing them to consider how they will make their unique mark on the world. Unlike the others, spiritual compatibility is unchangeable in the way that its impact is felt even after the couple is old or lifeless. The spiritual connection between man and wife is not subject to mortality because it is larger than they are. Therein lies the true meaning of marriage. Celebrating transcendence and allowing eternity to enter through the spiritual connection built.

Not to say that meaning cannot be found in non-marital relationships, but what makes a marriage truly meaningful, is the fact that a marriage union fuses the souls of man and woman, making them one, for until then, both had been separate halves of a whole. After the wedding ceremony, the couple emerges as one soul, both embarking on their mission to refine and purify the world as one unit. For without one's other half, it would prove impossible for one to reach his/her Divine potential. This is because without one's soulmate, eternally bonded through marriage, one would not be able to go beyond the individuality into which they were born.

Love has, according to the Darwinian perspective, been defined as a means to the perpetuation of a species. Likewise, from a Freudian viewpoint, love acts on the pleasure principle, suggesting that people engage in relationships because it is mutually beneficial. Consequently, according to both of these theories, marriage would prove rather pointless, being that relationships would still achieve what the theories would assume need be achieved. However, the Torah states how man and woman are two parts of one, created in the Divine image and split, to seek each other out and together seek transcendence. As it says "and G-d created man in His image, in the image of G-d He created him; male and female He created them."

Being that man and woman were created in His Divine image, a meaningful marriage requires that both remember their third partner, G-d, who joins the relationship upon its sanctification – the marriage ceremony. This commitment to G-d as a part of their marriage allows for an eternal foundation upon which the couple would build their life, which then instils a commitment toward their future children, their home, and the world around them. Inviting G-d into the relationship includes the fulfilment of the commandment that man was given upon his creation, to "be fruitful and multiply," for having children is G-d blessing the couple in their union and is the most rewarding goal that a man and woman can hope to achieve together.

Man and woman represent two energies, the masculine, and the feminine, from which the whole world was created and is kept alive. When balanced, these energies can complement each other to the point where the entire environment is affected, for within the man, exists the feminine, just as within the woman, exists the masculine. Although one is usually dominant within a person, both coexist within him. The masculine energy represents one's interactions with others, whilst the feminine symbolises one's interactions with oneself. The introvert versus the extrovert.

To better understand, one can use the analogy of a garden. In this case, the feminine energy would be symbolised in the nurturing of the garden, the watering, and the growing, just as one may recognise such qualities in a mother. Soft, tender, subtle. On the other hand, the masculine would appear through the weeding of the garden. This is the role of man and woman. Whilst the man actively seeks G-d, tasked with refining the world, the woman absorbs G-d, tasked with revealing G-d within the world. By claiming the energies of both genders, by recognising the masculine in the feminine and vice versa, man and woman cultivate the forces with which they can change the world.

This creates a synergy between the genders, between man and woman, strengthened and intensified when they are joined in marriage and so become husband and wife, after which true meaningfulness is found.

Family

Once a man and woman become parents, they are now entrusted with the most important task granted. Ensuring that their children grow to become healthy, good-hearted people. This starts with the building of their home, establishing an environment where children feel loved and cared for, heard and understood, so that they may grow up to create the same sort of home. The atmosphere of a home contributes greatly to the upbringing of a child. It shapes their attitude and perceptions of the world and builds their self-esteem and confidence in their abilities. A home where the family has a shared appreciation of values, yet allows room for self-expression, is a home where the children can learn to walk in the ways of G-d.

A healthy home not only consists of emotional warmth, providing and nurturing the children's physical and emotional needs, but also introduces spiritual warmth, where G-d is welcomed into the home until it is infused with life, a source of energy and hope. Allowing G-d to enter the home through the fulfilment of His commandments creates peace between family members, which then translates outwardly, towards other families and communities. For, in order to create meaningfulness within the world, one must start with one's own world, one's family, and home.

Society

Finally, society. Creating meaning within communities, within the world. Rabbi Menachem Mendel Schneerson (1902-1994), also known as the Lubavitcher Rebbe, advocated for such a world, believed in it whole-heartedly.

One of his most relevant ideas has been loosely termed as "The Principle of Reciprocity," in which he believed that society and all of its members would only achieve personal success and happiness "through a reciprocal dynamic of giving and receiving."

The Rebbe's definition of 'reciprocity,' however, differs from the conventional one, in the way that he understood it to mean that reciprocity lies in satisfying the needs of another, and not just as a by-product of self-benefit. He then went on to further explain this concept. Once a person comes into the presence of another, they must understand that this indeed is by Divine Providence, and not by chance. Then, the person may become aware of two things. That he was placed in this position so that he may benefit from the person, and so that the person may benefit from him.

The Lubavitcher Rebbe teaches that, as seen in the natural order of creation, no one thing was created to be solely recipient or giver, as "Everyone is obligated by the commandment to give charity, even a pauper." However, he emphasizes that this charity also refers to spiritual charity, that whilst one man may be able to give physical charity, another person's role is to help another spiritually. This is because just as every person has the need and ability to give, they also have the need and ability to receive.

Denying either of these needs is to deny a part of an individual that makes one human. Rather than seeing these needs as a flaw, the Rebbe reconstructs it as a form of giving, by which each person has the opportunity to become complete, for both parties to become whole, through the act of reciprocity. Moreover, "a reciprocal relationship transcends the sum of its parts," meaning that when two people get together, they must expand to include a third individual who isn't present, to do something for him. By doing so, it not only empowers the participants but also finds them in a wider pattern of relationships, integrating into community.

This idea was encouraged to be applied on a wider social scale, where instead of defining humanity through materialistic standards, such as money and power, one would envision a "reciprocal society where each individual is empowered to achieve meaning and happiness through his incomparable contribution to the welfare of others." Through this contribution, to something outside of ourselves, to others, and to G-d, that is where one can find true meaningfulness.

ABOUT THE WRITER

Mika Vogel is a former student at Lubavitch Senior Girls School. She has completed her EPQ, which targeted the question, "What makes life meaningful?" She has also completed A-levels in Psychology and English Language. Mika has always been particularly inspired by understanding the "why" of things, and joined with her great love of books and writing, she chose this topic, hoping to shed a little light on one of the greatest questions ever asked. She is currently working towards her Bachelor's in Psychology.

CHAPTER EIGHT

HOW DOES JEWISH LAW VIEW DEBATES CONCERNING LIFE, DEATH AND RELATED MEDICAL ISSUES?

Baila Golomb

Judaism believes in the sanctity of the body, "for in the image of G-d, man was created," the preservation of life, "Do not stand idly by the blood of your brother," and that no man can weigh the value of one life against another, "one life is not preferable to another."

In a pluralistic society, where one's life is dictated by either religion, a personal belief system or secular values, how can we set universal criteria with which to tackle medical dilemma? Thus was born the need to define life and death.

It is simple enough to say that a fundamental dichotomy, such as life and death should have clear boundaries. Alas,

Western civilisation, as early as the Romans, has played around with different definitions as to when we determine death.

In this paper, I will be exploring secular Western ideas pertaining to the boundaries of life and death, and the value that a life holds. I will be juxtaposing this with Jewish Scripture and contemporary responses from the last few decades. My desired outcome is to be able to display many opinions and unify them into what I believe to be the purest and kindest display of humanity.

After conducting my investigations, I found that Jewish Law does not have set rules that I can unify because it looks at each medical situation individually.

Respect for the Physical Body

How does one measure the value and significance of the human body?

Judaism believes in appreciating the sanctity of the body, "for, in the image of G-d, man was created." This provides insight into Judaism's perspective on the treatment of the human body and cadaver dissections.

The popular opinion was against dissections until the Church legalised the practice, circa 12th-century. However, dissections were not available to all medical professionals. Up until then, dissections were performed on animals, and the information learned was applied.

"*Human Cadaveric Dissection: A Historical Account From Ancient Greece to the Modern Era,*" written by Sanjib Kumar Ghosh, discusses how the Church did not specifically forbid dissection, but their opposition was regarded and adhered to. Pope Alexander III made his statement, "The church abhors blood." This led to physicians not studying human anatomy until it was sanctioned by Frederick II, the Roman emperor during this time. He stated, "a human body should be dissected at least once every five years for anatomical studies." He regarded this as necessary for the progression of medicine, but still held the values of the church.

Cadaver dissections were performed with strict instructions, such as having the cadavers supplied by authorities, and said cadavers only belonging to male or female executed criminals. They were performed as "anatomy teaching sessions, comprising of four day exhibitions, held once or twice a year."

This respect for the human body was widely accepted until these methods were deemed insufficient. The universities that were granted cadavers were limited and therefore the knowledge was regarded as such. This led to students stealing bodies from graves to dissect them.

Popularity for dissection arose outside of the medical field as well. Artists such as Leonardo DaVinci saw the human body as a manifestation of beauty and consequently wanted to learn all they could so that their work could be a replica. They not only attended dissections, which had now become a public affair, but performed some themselves. We can see this depicted in Michelangelo's fresco where one of the figures is seen holding his skin.

But despite all of this, the human body was still seen as beautiful and holy, a manifestation of G-d.

In most situations, both modern and those from the previous century, Judaism rules against dissections and autopsies. ''In the image of G-d, man was created'' and therefore Jews do not defile the body, as an act of science, or in the interest of finding the cause of death.

There is a story recorded by Rabbi Ezekiel Landau of Prague (1713-1793) about rabbinic leaders discussing the need for an autopsy, their reasoning, to save another's life.

The scenario: London, the 18th-century, a child is operated on to treat his gallstone but succumbs to his injuries. A discussion took place asking if it is appropriate for a post-mortem to be performed on the cadaver in the hope of gaining insight into the disease and how to treat it. The conclusion, for this scenario, was to not perform the autopsy seeing as there was no immediate need for information, only the acknowledgement that this information may be needed to treat this illness in the future.

Organ Donation

After consulting a Rabbi to gain information about organ donation within Judaism, I learnt: Organ donation is permissible under Jewish law. This includes live and post-mortem donations. Live donations consist of liver, kidney, blood, bone marrow and plasma.

End-of-life donations are trickier; will the removal of this organ hasten or subsequently cause the person to die?

This question is posed for heart donations. A patient can survive on a life support machine with a failing liver, kidneys and multi-organ failure. During this decline of functioning organs, the patient will be asked if they would like to be an organ donor and will be informed, of which organs they can donate.

Once the heart has been removed from the body, that body will no longer have flowing oxygen and will die. This will be discussed further, when brain stem versus whole brain death is analysed.

Donating to Science

There is a recorded letter written by the Lubavitcher Rebbe, Rabbi M.M Schneerson (1902-1994) responding to a letter he received, regarding donating one's organs to science.

This letter was written April 14th 1969. The question posed asked the Rebbe his opinion of donating one's eye to an eye bank after death.

The Rebbe starts his answer by addressing if there is a need for the question and how relevant it was seeing as the person was to live a long and healthy life, but continues to answer him as follows:

The Rebbe talks about how it is not only the soul that tethers man to G-d, but also the body, "the body of the Jew is sacred and is the property of G-d, while the Jew is no more than a guardian of it."

He continues to explain that many rulings in the Torah are a derivative of this concept, for example, there are many mitzvot around hygiene and keeping our bodies clean.

Therefore, the rabbinical opinion regarding these matters, is regular prohibitions against the mutilation of the body. The Rebbe explains, in fewer words than this, that the donation of organs for science is completely prohibited within Judaism, and that our body holds more value to G-d than we realise. The quote taken from the Rebbe can be seen in modern-day literature as, "your body is not your own, get your hands off of it," which highlights the same point; that we are not the sole owner of our body, but just its guardian.

Redefining the Boundaries of Death

"*The Redefinition of Death Debate*," written by Susan F. Jones and Anthony S. Kessel, outlines how the definition of death evolved throughout the 20th century, and how it always will, due to medical advances.

The definition of death morphed throughout the century as follows:

In the 1960's, the definition of death was the cessation of heartbeat, with the gradual decrease in body temperature.

In the 1980's, the definition of death was whole brain/brain stem death.

Now, the current widely accepted definition of death is the cessation of heartbeat and breathing and/or whole brain/brain stem death.

This timeline is taken from Western countries.

The 60's posed an influential time when many medical advances took place, globally, such as the first human heart transplant performed by Dr Christiaan Barnard in South Africa, 1967. The Embolectomy Catheter was developed by Dr Thomas J Fogarty, 1961. And the legalisation of abortion, in the UK, 1967.

These advances changed the face of medicine, but also created ambiguity because some forms of irreversible death have become reversible. Cessation of cardio-pulmonary function can now be reversed with CPR, and cessation of breathing can be reversed through artificial ventilation. Whole and brain stem death remains irreversible, but all these advances, have contributed to medical ambiguity.

A consequence of mentioned ambiguity has left the criteria for brain death to be not universal.

In the UK, brain death is confirmation of a non-functioning brain stem, whereas, in the USA, brain death also includes the cerebrum, also known as, whole-brain death. This shows how two advanced Western cultures cannot agree on a definition of death that is synonymous. Most Western cultures view whole/stem death or cardiopulmonary failure as an ethical and legal definition of death.

Despite this, debates still rage around procedures performed on the dying patient. England and Wales state that EV, 'elective ventilation,' to increase the supply of viable organs constitutes an 'unlawful battery' because the procedure is not done in the interest of the patient, but rather for someone else.

The AMA, American Medical Association, states, "no specific duration of time predicts unsuccessful resuscitation." There are numerous records of procedures being performed that are classified, as autopsies in one country, but these same procedures will be called an 'end of life procedure' in another, due to the lack of unity on what constitutes a dead versus a dying patient.

Therefore, the concept of 'personhood' arises. Personhood dictates the quality or condition of a person, meaning the person's link with their brain, and their cognitive function. Following this logic, a comatose state is synonymous with death, because there is a broken link between the body and the brain.

Personhood has evolved from the Cartesian concept that the body is a machine. This means that if the engine in the machine is faulty and disconnected from the body of the machine, the machine no longer functions and is rendered useless.

The first official human heart transplant, 1967, mentioned above, borrowed this logic when classifying the heart-donor as dead. The transplant team used the victim's irreversible coma as the necessary criterion when diagnosing him as dead. As a result of this, in 1968, Harvard Medical School agreed and verified that irreversible coma is synonymous with cessation of vital functions, such as those located in the cerebrum, not the brain stem.

This verification led to several malpractice suits against American physicians. Therefore, this definition was no longer adhered to after the 1970's.

A decade later, in 1981, the Uniform Determination of Death Act stated that whole-brain death constitutes a lack of neurological integration. Thus, all that remains is, "no longer a functional or organic unit, but merely a mechanical complex."

This allows the 'person' to no longer exist, aligning with the idea of personhood. An example of this logic being applied comes up when diagnosing anencephalic babies, babies born without parts of their skull or brain, as non-persons because of their obvious lack of neurological integration. This ignores the fact that anencephalic babies breathe spontaneously without intervention.

Descartes writes that the body is a machine and represents mortality, while the mind is the soul that makes us, our conscience, immortal. This dichotomy seems to align with the above stated Act, that once consciousness has left the body, what remains is merely a body, a piece of flesh.

The Jewish opinion would be in favour of viewing the body as much a part of what makes up man, as the conscience. The Jewish belief in being 'created in the Divine image' sustains the belief that the human body is man, not just it's vessel. The artistry that is the body, proves this.

What is conscience, if the body is not there to wield it?

Intrinsic Value vs. Instrumental Value

Judaism believes that man holds intrinsic value, rather than instrumental value. As stated by the Lubavitcher Rebbe, the physical body does hold meaning and sentience. The body is holy and has G-dliness within it, all of this circles back to humans being created in the Divine image.

Therefore, does your intrinsic value depend on you being designed in the image of G-d and does this logic apply to all forms of life?

Judaism prohibits unnecessary animal harm. There are specifications put in place on how to feed and care for one's livestock. These *halachot* (specifications) still apply today.

For example, the fourth of the seven Noahide laws states, "You must not eat flesh with its life-blood in it." The Talmud explains this to mean not eating the flesh of an animal while it is still alive.

And the Sabbath law to feed your animals before you feed yourself derives from, "I will give grass in your fields for your animal, and you shall eat and be satisfied," prioritising the feeding of the animal before man, this leans in the opinion that animal life also holds intrinsic value.

What happens when one intrinsically valuable life is measured against another, whom do you choose?

Dennis Prager, a Jewish American political voice, debated this and came up with an experiment to see who the wider public would view as more intrinsically valuable.

This experiment posed the following question: who would one choose to save from drowning, their dog or a stranger?

The results Prager gathered from his audience are quite diverse: One third chose to save their dog, one third chose to save the stranger and one third was undecided. Prager understood from these results that two-thirds of his audience chose to not save the stranger.

Members of the experiment wrote to Prager saying, "I would never sacrifice my dog for someone I don't know, my dog is my family... I would throw a stranger in front of a bus to save my dog."

Another response Prager received said, "I think you're a monster if you don't pick your dog over a stranger."

These two responses seem to show that one's intrinsic value, and how it is measured by someone else, is dependent on your affiliation to them. In other words, human beings do not have intrinsic value, but rather instrumental or situational value; the value of your life is dependent on someone else's emotional feelings towards you.

It is written in the Talmud that the value of one life is at equilibrium with the value of the world. The Talmud explains that Adam, the first man, was created alone, lacking a companion. This teaches us the significance of the individual's life, that to kill one life is synonymous with killing all of life.

Abortion

Abortion is another scenario where the intrinsic value of a life is being measured by society. But as concluded above, some believe that humans don't have intrinsic value, so what are these people's opinions when regarding that of an unborn child?

Joshua Lederberg, Nobel Prize winner in Physiology, states: "the foetus is by no measure criterion (sic) nearer to being a human being than the unborn ape or chick," he continues this point with, "the new-born infant must undergo further development to achieve the full measure of humanity." Lederberg is saying that a foetus only becomes human once it has grown, once man has matured, both physically and neurologically.

Michael Tooley, American philosopher, takes an almost identical approach to Ledeberg when referring to human infants as "potential persons." He not only believes that the "destruction of potential persons" is a neutral action, but uses this logic to determine infanticide as "morally acceptable." Tooley delves more into the abortion aspect of the potential life, whereas Lederberg analyses the journey it will take for these potential lives to evolve into human adults.

Following the logic that value is reliant on affiliation, as shown when discussing if humans have intrinsic value, a foetus is biologically and emotionally affiliated with the mother, whether the child is wanted or not.

On the other hand, if the foetus is no more than a cluster of cells, it does not matter that it is affiliated with the mother, because it holds no instrumental value.

The Value of a Foetus

Ben Shapiro, Jewish American political debater has spoken about abortions many times. He spoke at the University of California, Berkeley on September 15, 2017, and was asked why he believed that a first-trimester foetus has moral value.

Shapiro first stated that the 'cluster of cells' being formed during pregnancy will inevitably grow into a baby, meaning it will always be a potential human life. If we say that the heartbeat is the first sign of human life, we have created a null line by end-of-life care, because there are patients whose faulty hearts are only beating due to a pacemaker; an external device.

If we say that brain activity is the first sign of human life, the same logic applies. There are patients who are in potentially permanent comas or vegetative states who have little to no brain function.

"Any time you draw any line other than the inception of the child, you end up drawing a false line that can also be applied to people who are adults."

He continues to say that we should acknowledge adult human life as having intrinsic value.

The debate continues by classing sentience as having value. Again, the argument leans in the direction of those in end-of-life care who are not sentient, patients in a comatose state.

Shapiro questions if it is ethical to stab a patient who is in a comatose state because they no longer have sentience and therefore lack intrinsic value. The answer given was that a comatose patient has potential sentience.

Shapiro answers, "You know what else is potential sentience? Being a foetus."

Therefore, if the concern is how we ascribe moral value, Shapiro eloquently extinguishes this line of questioning by proving that the gestation period of the foetus hosts intrinsic value and that this should not be dismissed. If the question is about which life has more intrinsic value, we can look at scenarios when the health of the mother is being threatened by the foetus.

The Jewish Opinion

In Judaism, there is a concept '*rodef*' translated as 'the pursuer.' This term is applied when the foetus poses a threat to the mother's life or overall wellbeing. When tackling these situations, rabbinical leaders will always value the life of the mother over the life of the foetus and permit abortion.

Rabbi Shlomo Zalman Auerbach, Orthodox Israeli Rabbi, writes about specific situations and when he believes abortion is permissible. For example, he prohibits abortions for a foetus with Tay Sachs, but allows for the abortion of an Anencephalic baby.

When a Rabbinical leader publicises these types of prohibitions, they do not pose as a definitive ruling for all similar cases. Within every medical situation, there are several variables to entertain. According to Orthodox Judaism, if a woman, G-d forbid, finds herself in this situation, she should get a personal recommendation from her Rabbi and medical liaison, and these three parties will come up with the next appropriate step.

Rabbi Auerbach also writes about contraception; a woman who suffers from postpartum depression is allowed, in his opinion, to use contraception to prevent depression. Once more, we see how Rabbi Auerbach rules in favour of the mother's physical and mental wellbeing over the foetus, even before conception.

According to Jewish Law, society's opinion on a foetus is irrelevant. The value of your foetus is not reliant on your affiliation to it or what society ascribes, but rather, the fact that it is a foetus who has sentience. If the life of the mother is being threatened by carrying a child, it does not matter the value that it has, the life of the mother takes precedence. Therefore, although society may ascribe a value to your foetus that you do not agree with, society does not have the right to dictate when or if you should carry a child.

Euthanasia

Euthanasia is a derivative of two Latin words, *eu-thanatos,* meaning "easy-death," but it is colloquially translated to be mercy killing.

There are five different types of euthanasia:
1) Active
2) Passive
3) Non/voluntary
4) Involuntary
5) Assisted suicide

Active euthanasia is described as actively administering a lethal drug that will kill the patient. Active euthanasia can be referred to as aggressive euthanasia.

Passive euthanasia is described as intentionally withholding external life support. For example, turning off the ventilator or removing the feeding tube.

Voluntary/non-voluntary euthanasia is based on consent. If the patient is unconscious and their wants are unknown, we classify this as non-voluntary euthanasia.

Involuntary euthanasia is when doctors intentionally ignore the wants of the patient and/or their surrogate decision-maker and euthanise the patient against their wishes.

Assisted suicide is described as knowingly helping a patient to commit suicide. Assisted suicide can be as simple as a family member getting hold of the lethal sedative that the patient intends on using to end his life.

Physician-Assisted Suicide

The AMA on Euthanasia and Assisted Suicide written by Steven Luper talks about the different types of harm inflicted on a patient and how we can classify different procedures.

The Hippocratic Oath says, "First, do no harm." Every doctor takes on this oath when entering the medical field and becoming a doctor.

Harm, refers to the effect this medical intervention will have on the patient's overall wellbeing. There is a difference between something being 'intrinsically good' for the patient and 'overall good' for the patient. To expand, 'intrinsically good' would be something that is positive in and of itself, while 'overall good' means the effect it will have on the patients even if the method it uses might be seen as 'bad.' An 'overall bad' procedure may have such a negative overall effect that it is now classed as harmful. Therefore it is possible to say that the overall 'welfare level is a sum of the intrinsic goods and evils she accrues over the course of her life.'

If a doctor were to prick someone with a needle, they would use the terminology that the doctor harmed them, because, even though the pain was temporary, the person still suffered. From this, we see that harm is classified as any action that inflicts pain. This definition is so broad, that we see it in medicine the whole time. Medicine is full of 'pro tanto' harms, the Latin word 'existing,' for example breaking a bone to reset it. Pro tanto harm can fit into the category 'overall good' because breaking the bone, causing temporary pain, was done to heal the existing injury, and the result was positive.

Is it appropriate to start banning procedures because of the assumed harm it may cause to a patient, *pro tanto* and otherwise?

The blatant answer is no, there are little to no medical procedures that are entirely risk-free, this would eliminate hundreds of procedures that cause minimal damage. It is illogical that we should ban basic procedures because it might cause overall bad welfare for a discrete number of people.

This would include the administration of anaesthesia, which would ironically cause more harm to the patient.

Luper rewrites that we should incorporate all of these considerations and writes the statement: "physicians should treat no patient in a way that is likely to be overall bad for them."

Euthanasia is not covered as being harmful, if you subscribe to the definitions of harm as stated above, because the harm inflicted on the patient is not overall bad. After all, this is the desired outcome for the patient. There are requirements that need to be met by a person who wants to terminate their life:

The participant must be over eighteen years old, must be informed about alternative treatment plans such as palliative care and be suffering from an illness likely to terminate within six months.

The last requirement is the most relaxed because of the unreliability of the timeframe, as well as the fact that there are patients who have a larger time frame that might be suffering more whilst partaking in palliative care.

Ergo the question poses itself, is it the euthanasia or the continued suffering that is considered a harmful event?

Involuntary Passive Euthanasia

Medical Futility and Involuntary Passive Euthanasia written by Michael Nair-Collins talks about new versions of medical terminology and how misleading they may be by referencing four medical cases.

Medical futility is defined as medical intervention that is unlikely to yield results. Distributive justice is the event of deciding whom to give the medical attention or resources to. A new concept that has been published, calls conflicts of end of life care, "potentially inappropriate treatment." Nair-Collins explains that this simply means, 'physicians and hospitals should have the authority to forgo life-sustaining treatments over objection.'

Nair-Collins brings up four medical cases "allegedly involving medical futility:"

Case 1: An 85-year-old woman suffered anoxic encephalopathy after cardiac arrest and has been on ventilation in ICU for three months with no improvement. Her son wants her treatment continued. Meanwhile, patients are on ventilators in the emergency department, because there are no beds in the ICU. The hospital wishes to remove ventilation to allow space for patients with better prognoses, and believes this is justified because further treatment is futile.

Case 1 discusses distributive justice, masking as futility. The mechanical ventilation is preventing hypoxemia and the cardiac arrest that would follow. Therefore, the interventions are doing their job at keeping the patient alive, even if she is unlikely to regain consciousness.

The concern here is that other patients would be able to benefit from the resources in the ICU and therefore keeping this patient in the ICU may be seen as 'an unjust distribution of limited resources.'

Case 1 shows us that we must be able to distinguish between cases of futility and distribution. Futility never applies to cases of clearly beneficial treatment, for Case 1 the beneficial treatment is the ventilation that is preventing cardiac arrest.

Case 2: An elderly man is in the ICU with a poor prognosis and several new ailments. He has said that he wanted one, but never signed a formal DNR. His surrogate nephew insists that he would never have wanted a DNR. Physicians say that further treatment is futile. It is discovered that the nephew has been using his uncle's medical compensation.

Case 2 is a situation where the surrogate has obvious ulterior motives and his wishes are not in the best interest of the patient. For Case 2, fiduciary responsibility overrides surrogate decision making, 'On grounds of respect for patient's precedent autonomy.'

Case 3: An infant is born with multiple abnormalities. His survival was slim when gangrene developed, his parents demanded amputations of several limbs to "do everything they can to save his life."

Case 3 shares similarities with Case 2 as the concern lies in surrogate decision making. The balance between the harm and its benefits is not obvious here and the 'clinicians are appropriately concerned.' Therefore, the logic applied in Case 2 applies here as well, fiduciary response eclipses surrogate decision-making.

Case 4: A 56-year-old male has cardiomyopathy and other ailments. He has a brainstem stroke and is ventilated and transferred to the ICU. He is unresponsive and apneic and will not recover to awareness. Earlier, he discussed with his wife and physician that he wants every chance at life, no matter how others perceive his quality of life. His wife, his surrogate, wants his treatment continued. The ICU is empty, insurance is paying for all treatments; however, the physicians believe that further treatment is futile and want to dismiss life-sustaining treatment.

Case 4 is purely concerned with medical futility. Continuing the treatment will allegedly cause no benefits. The patient is apnoeic and unconscious, and "cannot appreciate the benefits of treatment as a benefit." Conclusively, "Effects must be distinguished from benefits." The treatments given should benefit, not just affect the patient's anatomy and physiological health. The treatments for the patient in Case 4 will indeed have a physiological effect, but won't help the patient in his entirety.

"Medicine requires providing the patient with the capacity to participate in the human community." Therefore continuing this patient's treatment is futile.

The Jewish Case against Euthanasia

Life As An Intrinsic Rather Than Instrumental Good: the 'Spiritual' Case Against Euthanasia, written by David J. Bleich discusses the Jewish perspective on euthanasia.

Bleich recounts an event the Talmud discusses concerning the adulterous woman and how she was punished. The adulterous woman was to drink from the "bitter waters," if she had committed adultery, she would die. Within this set of circumstances, there were women, proven guilty of infidelity, that did not die instantly. These women had done something of merit that deserved a reward, therefore the effect of the water did not take place immediately.

The lengthening of her sentence may have afflicted more pain due to the nature of how the water works, nevertheless this was seen as a privilege.

'Life accompanied by pain is thus viewed as preferable to death.' Bleich quotes Psalm 118, "The Lord had indeed punished me, but He had not left me to die," which illustrates the same idea, that pain or punishment is preferable to death.

Bleich switches gears to discuss if our life affects G-d's grandeur:

There was a legal case in the sixteenth century concerning suicide prevention. The thoughts explained were, that if a king is measured by the number of his subjects, then suicide is a lack of respect for the king. They even go as far as to say that suicide should become a punishable offence because it 'interferes with his rights as a monarch.'

This case juxtaposes with the mourning prayer that is recited in memory of lost ones. The prayer starts with the words, "exalted and hallowed be G-d's great name," Rabbi Meir Shapiro explains that the loss of even one life 'diminishes Divine glory.'

Bleich questions if mankind actually contributes to G-d's glory and strengthens this by bringing up those who are not able-bodied. He answers by quoting a metaphor of an orchestra.

Due to the several types of instruments and the sheer amount that play in an orchestral piece, there will be moments throughout the performance when a string or a wind instrument will stay silent. This does not diminish the beauty of the instrument or the music, by just being on stage the musician adds to the ambience of the performance.

Not every member of society is given the ability to do his assigned role at any given moment; this could be due to a physical setback. In spite of this, "his very existence constitutes an act of Divine service."

We see here that the very existence of man, whether he is actively praising G-d or doing His bidding, fulfils his moral obligation to be a subject of G-d.

Plato writes that man serves as the "chattel of the gods" reinforcing this boundary. Man was made to be subservient to G-d. When it comes to decisions made using personal autonomy, man must remember that his autonomy is accompanied by G–d.

We can assume that most people desire to live long and healthy lives. In situations such as a terminally ill patient or one in a comatose state, end of life care will be discussed with next of kin. In this event, the family is less likely to have the same zest for the preservation of life that they have for themselves. Therefore, one must remember to be cognizant that G-d is the sole 'proprietor of human life.' And taking the opinion that this person does not want to live anymore, is not the job of man.

The Task of the Soul

Rabbi Shneur Zalman explains that the task of the soul is to make a dwelling place for G-d. He also explains how man has both G-d and physicality within him, presenting as his body and his soul. Therefore, man is the perfect life form to fulfil this mission, but how?

Simply by being alive, being a reflection of G-dliness in the physical world. Hence, every moment in time is significant.

If someone is suffering and feels alone in this world, Psalm 23 says, "Even though I walk through the valley of the shadow of death, I will fear no evil, for you are with me," signifying the belief that even though you may feel alone, G-d is always with you. Rabbi MM Schneerson explains that the soul comes down just to do one thing, this moment of belief in G-d may be this person's task.

Conclusion

After critically analysing many medical scenarios, it is now apparent that when it comes to Jewish Law and medicine, there is no simple answer.

Medicine, as displayed earlier, exploded, and as proven in the above essays, will continue to do so. Therefore, it is impossible to set a standard for how to deal with significantly specific, delicate and intricate medical issues.

If you look at the surface level answer that Jewish Law gives for dissections and autopsies, you will find the simplistic and unadulterated answer; no.

But if you conduct exploration and delve deeper you will find that it's not all cut and dry, the prohibition for autopsies, for example, is not universal but historically appropriate.

The same applies to Organ Donation. My original understanding before undertaking this project was that Organ Donation is forbidden. Yet after just one conversation with a Rabbi, I learnt that Organ Donation is not forbidden and statistically apparent within Orthodox Charedi communities.

Therefore, when looking at delicate matters such as those laid out within the essay, you will find sources in the Torah that say one thing, and a source from the Mishna that might say different.

However, no rabbinical publication or Biblical source will ever disregard the three fundamental beliefs: a) to believe that man is created in the Divine image, b) that no man's life is of less value than another and c) no life is preferable to another.

ABOUT THE WRITER

Baila Golomb is a LSGS graduate who was always academically inclined and enjoyed independent learning outside the constraints of school. In sixth form, she studied Psychology, Mathematics and completed an EPQ, due to her interest in what dictates human behaviour and how we value life according to Judaism and Western views. This drove her to write an EPQ surrounding topics of organ donation, the euthanasia debate and the sanctity of the body. Due to her religious upbringing, she delved into this topic through the lens of Judaism and how Judaism juxtaposed Western and archaic opinions on the value of a life. Her father, who was a blood donor, also influenced her and this was the foundation on which her EPQ was born.

CHAPTER NINE

HOW DOES RELIGION AFFECT YOUR HAPPINESS?

Yehudis Gruber

"...Religiosity is, on almost every conceivable account, opposed to the normal goals of mental health."

That is what the high profile psychotherapist, Albert Ellis, had to say about religions role in happiness.

Though from a differing psychological school of thought, Sigmund Freud agreed with this sentiment. "It is religions which delude us with the promise of happiness; they" – and here Freud referred primarily to Judaism – "also have traditions which internalise aggression and nourish a sense of guilt."

It may be true. From the outside, the religious worshipper appears frighteningly similar to an obsessional neurotic, the latter being quintessentially anxious and unhappy. They both spend hours performing certain rituals, and when omitted, they both feel a sense of guilt and fear.

So does religion, especially Judaism hinder the pursuit of happiness? Or does religion play a profound role in engendering happiness for an individual?

In my essay, I will investigate the effectiveness of religion's role in happiness, in terms of both personal satisfaction and wellbeing and how the religion is constructed in a way that ensures the happiness of its members.

But first: What is happiness?

Happiness

Dictionaries seem to struggle to define happiness. The Oxford dictionary defines happiness as, "The quality or condition of being happy," which tells us nothing of its nature or experience.

Jeremy Bentham (d. 1832) sees happiness as the "balance of pleasure over pain." Some modern dictionaries concur by defining happiness as, "the state of feeling or showing pleasure."

So if happiness is defined as pleasure, what is pleasure?

Pleasure is the gratitude of the extra. Rabbi Manis Freidman defines it as, "the feeling you get when you have more than you need." Pleasure implies that happiness is acquired from the outside, be it from an object (a new car) or from another person (being in love).

The sense of pleasure is experienced on both an emotional and cognitive level, making it easier for a person experiencing the pleasure to define. Perhaps this is why happiness and pleasure are often used interchangeably. They are not, by any means, the same thing.

Aristotle warned against confusing the definition of happiness as pleasure. A pleasurable sensation merely comes and goes without much impact on one's inner self. It does not make one a happier *person*. True happiness, Aristotle argued, is found in leading a virtuous life. He dubbed this kind of happiness '*Eudemonia.*' It is associated with fulfilling responsibilities, investing in long-term goals, concern for the welfare of other people, and living up to personal ideals. In Greek, '*daimon*' means G-d, which suggests that people thought that happiness came by the will of G-d.

Indeed, this is the view that endures for the better part of early modern history.

As the Enlightenment unfolded, something changed. Religion was no longer sought to answer questions of happiness. The American Declaration of Independence posits the view that all men should be free in their 'pursuit of happiness.' This was a watershed moment. For the first time, people were being encouraged to seek their own private happiness. It also introduced the idea that happiness must be actively pursued instead of simply relying on G-d to provide it for you.

Nowadays, the definitions of happiness are largely determined by psychologists, mostly in terms of wellbeing.

Martin Seligman suggests happiness is found in working for and achieving long-term goals. For example, participating in charity work has a much more lasting effect on wellbeing than watching a TV show.

Seligman believes that exercising one's 'signature strengths' strengthens one's sense of self and therefore brings him happiness. These qualities include curiosity, leadership, integrity, enthusiasm. He advises to "use your signature strengths every day in the main realms of your life to bring abundant gratification and authentic joy." This can be regarded as higher than pleasure, because it takes into account long-term goals and adds meaning to life.

Humanistic psychology adopts a similar approach. Abraham Maslow, deemed self-actualisation as the ultimate goal in human happiness, the topmost in the "Hierarchy of Needs." 'Self-actualisation' can be defined as fulfilment of one's potential. Humanists argue one needs to 'self-actualise' to find happiness and achieve the healthiest well-being.

However, 'self-actualising' is very subjective. A murderer may feel he is actualising every time he kills people. There is no moral threshold; no sense of connecting to anything higher than ambition.

Another criticism of Maslow's' theory is that he posits that self-actualisation can only happen after all the lower rungs of the hierarchy are fulfilled, meaning that self-actualisation (and consequently happiness) cannot be fulfilled until more basic needs are met, like shelter and food. This is simply untrue. There are many instances of people who are in the most depraved of circumstances and still manage to achieve happiness.

Coupled together, these points show how self-actualisation cannot be taken as a complete explanation for happiness. Something deeper, more universal must be at the root of all happiness.

Meaning

Rabbi Mendel Futerfas, (d. 1995) was a famous Chabad Chassid, who was deported to Siberia during the oppressive Soviet reign. There, the inmates would try to amuse themselves by playing cards and telling jokes. One night, when everyone was huddled around some cards, one prisoner suddenly burst into sobs.

"Why are you crying?" the prisoners asked him.

"How can I not cry?" he replied, "Look at me! I was a respected doctor in a large hospital just six months ago! How I have fallen!"

The others too, began to sob.

"I was a lawyer," said another prisoner, "I had a whole office of diplomas. What use are they to me now? I feel like nothing!"

"I was so wealthy!" wailed another.

"Everyone in Moscow came to watch me sing!"

Soon, the inmates turned to Reb Mendel.

"What were you?" they demanded, "What titles and importance did you lose?"

Reb Mendel replied, "Before I was arrested I was a Chassid, trying my best to devote myself to G-d. Now," he smiled, "I am a Chassid too!"

Later, when retelling this story, Reb Mendel would describe his fellow inmates who, despite being healthy and robust, would simply not wake up in the morning. They had lost their meaning, lost the will to live. So they perished.

What was so powerful about Reb Mendel's meaning in life, that it compelled him to live with joy despite his grim surrounding?

Victor Frankl had a similar question. Whilst imprisoned in Auschwitz he would ask himself, "Has all this suffering, this dying around us, a meaning? For if not, then ultimately there is no meaning in survival; for a life whose meaning depends on a happenstance - whether one escapes or not - ultimately would not be worth living at all."

Even if one were to be living a liberated, suffering-less life, the meaning they ascribe to their life must be one that could be applied to suffering. Meaning must be transportable. It must be something that one can carry inside themself, through anything that could happen.

Pleasure is tied to happenstance. Happiness is not, because its very essence is the meaning it engenders and meaning is unbound from circumstance.

Reb Mendel had this kind of meaning. His happiness wasn't based on his success, his talents or his intelligence. His happiness stemmed from his connection to G-d, the Divinity inside him. In this way, Reb Mendel was able to endure his sufferings.

Just like in Reb Mendel's case, religion is found to be "particularly helpful in moments of great stress." A study by Pargament and Brant found that "Attributions of negative events to the will of G-d or to a loving G-d are generally tied with better outcomes." When widows and widowers were asked an open-ended question about their sources of comfort, 59% stated that their religious beliefs were a major source of comfort.

This is the gift of religion. It provides meaning to life, in a way that can transcend anything.

Indeed, in one study, religious belief was found to be the primary factor contributing to meaning in life, which in turn contributed to well-being. A study done in Northwestern University, amongst two thousand people, found the most common answer to 'Why are you religious?' was 'religion gives meaning to life.'

After his experiences in the death camps during the war, Frankl developed his own school of psychological thought. He called it 'logotherapy' after the Greek word for meaning - *logos*. He argued that an individual's search for meaning is the "primary motivation in his life."

According to Frankl, depression is caused by a *noogenic neurosis,* which is a feeling of "existential frustration," an absence of meaning. Conversely, it would seem that meaning is the *cause* of happiness.

So is it that easy? Being religious means being happy?

Not quite. Gordon W. Allport outlines the differences between immature and mature religiosity. The immature religious sentiment is marked by conformity and self-gratification. Allport calls this 'extrinsic religiosity.' The extrinsically religious person uses religion as a means of obtaining security or status, and has not progressed further than the childish acceptance of his religion. A person like this finds no joy and meaning in his religions. For him, religion is merely a tool for social or personal survival.

Real meaning is only found in the mature religious sentiment. Central to the mature religious sentiment is the concept of 'functional autonomy.' It is the term used to describe the idea that the forces that motivated us early in life become independent of its childish origins and become reaffirmed in an adult consciousness. It is when a person decides to 'own' his beliefs. The intrinsically religious person internalises his religious beliefs and lives by them regardless of social pressure. The main symptom that a person has graduated into the 'mature religious sentiment' is one's lack of self-interest.

A parallel to Allport's ideas can be found in Chassidic teachings. A person could be described as a *'penimi'* or a *'chitzon.'* The best translation for these terms is 'innerness' and 'superficiality.' A *penimi* is not necessarily perfect, but is sincere, honest and consistent in the journey towards the Divine. A *penimi* is uncaring of any social accolades religiosity might win for them. Such service can be called 'intrinsic' religiosity. Research has shown that only intrinsic rather than extrinsic religiosity is significantly related to the meaning of life.

Perhaps this is why research done by Kravetz and Vilchinsky found that "religious belief, not religious behaviour is related positively to meaning in life and psychological wellbeing." Rituals are meaningless if they are not motivated by the individual's inner conviction, like a soul without a body.

Happiness According to Judaism

Jews have a **moral obligation to be joyful**. There is commandment to "עִבְדוּ אֶת־ה' בְּשִׂמְחָה Serve the Lord with joy," because without it, there is something in ones Divine service that is lacking.

Furthermore, happiness itself is an expression of the Divine, as it says, "There is only pleasantness and strength in G-d's space" meaning that happiness and G-d co-exist together. Wherever He is found, joy can be found too. If one finds themselves sad for seemingly no reason, it is their soul begging for G-dliness.

In the following section, I will examine two branches of Orthodox Judaism's perspectives of happiness: The Mussar movement and the Chassidic approach.

The **Mussar** movement is an approach to Judaism that was developed in 19th century Lithuania, particularly among Orthodox Lithuanian (*Litvish*) Jews. It is based on a the pursuit of ethical and spiritual acomplishments, especially in the field of studying Torah and character refinement.

Rabbi Eliyahu Dessler, one of the most illustrious figures of the Mussar movement, said, "The world, as G-d made it is a happy one. It's we who have removed ourselves from the world of happiness." All that is needed to prove this statement is a glance at an infant. Though infants are far from being fulfilled, are usually found gurgling and smiling. The Western notion of the 'pursuit of happiness' denies the value of the joy that is innately within us. It means one is chasing something outside when happiness already exists within.

Mussar teachings explains how the main avenue to happiness is the study of Torah, following the idiom that, "the pursuit of wisdom leads to happiness." They see rejoicing with the study of Torah, as rejoicing with the G-dly component within them. "To achieve inner happiness," Rabbi Chaim Eisenstien says, "Each individual with his unique capabilities should revel in their toil and accomplishments in Torah." The study of Torah is often grueling, but the triumph of intellect creates a deep, spiritual happiness.

Mussar's adherents also find happiness in achieving their goal of character refinement, even when, ironically, this brings them to uncomfortable situations. Early students of Novardok (a branch of the Mussar movement) would purposely perform embarrassing acts such as wearing ties made out of hay and asking for nails in a bakery. This brought them great joy as they saw their embarrassment as part of the process of self-refinement.

By refraining from pleasure in this world, followers of Mussar understand that they were securing pleasure in the World to Come. Rabbi Eliyahu Dessler said, "The one who enjoys a rich spiritual life is happy. There is no other kind of happiness in existence." The abstention of wordly *pleasure* is a source of *happiness* for them.

Chassidism is a movement that was founded by Rabbi Yisrael Baal Shem Tov, who taught love, joy and humility—both in our service of G-d and in our treatment of fellow human beings. In fact, the early Chassidim were dubbed '*der freilichers,*' the cheerful ones, because of the emphasis they placed on serving G-d with joy.

Why? Because happiness is essential for Divine service. In Chassidic teachings, happiness is never seen as the goal, rather, it's the *means* to the goal. It is the fuel that propels a person on their journey towards the Divine.

In a parable given by Rabbi Schneur Zalman of Liadi (d. 1812), he describes a pair of wrestlers. One of them is stronger, but depressed. The other is perhaps weak, but his energy is focused, determined and cheerful. Who of the two is more likely to win?

In the battle that takes place every moment between the good and evil inclination inside us, the good inclination (Yetzer Tov) must be fortified with happiness. If a person is sad, the evil inclination (Yetzer Hara) is more likely to win.

Chassidic teachings argue that it's not enough to be happy whilst studying Torah learning or doing good deeds, but that one should bring joy to every single aspect of life, be it mundane, be it dirty. In Hebrew, the word for happiness 'בשמחה' has the same letters as thought, 'מַחֲשָׁבָה,' the Hebrew word for 'thought' implying that happiness is not based on our circumstances, but how we choose to view them. Every moment can bring one joy, even that which seems so far from spirituality and G-d.

A story is told of the two Chassidic brothers, Reb Zusya of Anipoli and Reb Elimelech of Lizhensk who found themselves thrown into a prison by an anti-Semitic policeman. In their cell there was a bucket of excrement, and the smell was so putrid that the brothers found themselves unable (according to Jewish law) to learn and pray. Reb Elimelech began to sob, "How lowly is our position that we cannot even pray to G-d or learn His holy Torah? Woe is us!"

Reb Zusya shook his head, "No! On the contrary. The fact that we cannot pray or learn is due to the circumstance that G-d Himself put us in, so it must be good!"

Face shining, he grabbed his brother, "Come let us dance to the G-d who decreed we cannot pray or learn."

Reb Elimelech stood up and together, the brothers began to dance. They danced and danced and danced and created such a furor that the anti-Semitic policeman returned.

"Crazies!" he roared, "Why are you dancing in this prison-cell?"

Another prisoner who had observed the brothers' exchange replied, "They are dancing because of that bucket of excrement."

"Fools!" the policeman yelled, "If it makes you so happy, I'm taking it away!"

He grabbed the bucket and stalked off. Now, the brothers could pray and learn.

This story teaches a profound lesson. Every single occurrence in life, even one that feels spiritually damaging can be an opportunity for growth and joy. It all depends on one's perception.

That is why Judaism prescribes the manner of ordinary activities, such as the order of donning clothes and the manner of eating. By performing ordinary actions in the manner prescribed by G-d, every moment becomes an opportunity for cosmic happiness.

But how can such happiness be achieved? How can we find it in ourselves to rise above the corporeal and infuse it with joy and meaning?

Bitul

"Happiness cannot be pursued," Victor Frankl wrote in his bestselling book, *Mans Search for Meaning*, "It must ensue and it only does so as the unintended side-effect of one's personal dedication to a cause greater then himself."
A man once wrote to the Lubavitcher Rebbe complaining he was depressed and that everything seemed meaningless. In reply, the Rebbe simply circled the word that began every sentence in the man's letter. The word was 'I'.

The road to happiness? Abandon the 'I' and focus on the 'you.'

In Chassidic philosophy this is called '*Bitul*'- self-nullification. It's forgetting the 'I' for the sake of the larger picture. Shloma Majeski, the author of The Chassidic Approach to Joy, gives an example. A doctor can perform a surgery in order to advance his career or, he can go in with the intention of saving a life. The first approach focuses on the doctor's self. Failure of the surgery will erode his confidence and diminish his sense of self. In contrast, in the second approach, the doctor was never dependent on any external factors such as self-advancement, so although he will be saddened on behalf of his ill patient, his happiness remains intact. Because it was never about him to begin with.

One must internalise that G-d has placed them in this world for a purpose. Life is not about indulging the 'self.' It's taking that 'self' and turning it to the world. With Bitul, we see things through G-d's lens. True joy can only be experienced when one leaves himself behind and connects to G-d.

Majeski urges people to ask themselves, 'How can the G-dliness inside me achieve something for G-ds plan?' Or, in Victor Frankl's words, "Ask not what you can expect of life rather what life is expecting of you."

Someone who has Bitul doesn't act as if the world owes him everything. Someone like that is more giving, more responsible, more grateful. The more one rises above himself in ecstasy of the Divine or in service of others, the happier he will be.

Psychotherapy and religion are both similar in that they aim to rectify conflicts within a person, be it spiritual or emotional. Sometimes, psychotherapy even mimics religious sentiments. One psychiatrist instructed his patients to visit patients within the same ward with worse symptoms than themselves, exercising the virtue of charity, but in an irreligious manner.

There is something about the ritualistic acts of Judaism, even when divorced from their meaning, which enables better wellbeing.

Indeed, Professor Kate Loewenthal found that "the more strongly committed [to religion] - are more hopeful and optimistic ... the more liberal groups tend to be more depressive."

Why is this? What can be found in organised religion that faith alone cannot provide?

In the following sections, I will explain how religion, Judaism in particular, is constructed in a way that is most conducive for mental and emotional well-being.

The Community

"Judaism is an insistently communal faith," Rabbi Sacks said. Every milestone, be it a birth or a death, brings the community together.

Even if one were to be a recluse, religious obligations would require him to meet with people. Men are obligated to pray with another nine men thrice a day. Study is usually done in a *shiur* (groups) or with a *chavrusa* (partner). The *Mikveh*, (ritual baths) which men go to daily or weekly, is often a place of socialising.

In addition, Chassidic sects often hold gatherings called '*farbrengens.*' During a *farbrengen*, people are encouraged to express their raw emotions and be honest. It is almost like a therapy circle, but for spiritual matters.

All this constant social is helpful in preventing loneliness and providing a scaffold of support around a person. Studies have shown it to be related to greater satisfaction with life and perceived health.

The Jewish community generates untold support. They have their own volunteer emergency response service called Hatzalah, who are equipped with their own ambulances and medical paraphernalia. There is also Chaverim who provide assistance to those stranded on the road, locked in or out of their house among many other situations. 'Gemachs' (free-lending societies) provide anything from interest-free loans to oxygen tanks to wedding gowns. Through giving, a community is woven together. Religion sustains these bonds.

The sense of responsibility is ingrained within every individual of the community, contributing to one's sense of importance and self-worth. It makes one a happier person to know that they are needed.

In Judaism, people often define themselves by their community and corresponding ideology. This creates a stong sense of identity in religious Jews, which known to be significantly linked to wellbeing.

Community is a blessing, but not all aspects of it are positive. Conformity can be common in these tight-knit communities. One of the reasons for this is that Orthodox Jewish marriages are mostly arranged. This means that each side will investigate the other side before agreeing to the match. Therefore, a person has to be on guard to 'behave' and live up to community standards or risk losing marriage prospects. (Or, more often the case, one's children's marriage prospects.) This could create a sense of fear because one thinks they are constantly being judged and can lead to 'extrinsic religiosity' mentioned above.

Some groups of religious people snub each other due to ideological differences. One group of Jews might be made to feel inferior to another, when in line with basic Jewish law, they have done nothing wrong. Sometimes, the leaders of different sects have disagreements, causing their followers to shun each other. Even within a sect, there can be tension. Illustrious lineage is highly regarded in Orthodox Jewish circles which could increase snobbery towards those of a 'lesser' pedigree.

However, despite any superficial tension, Jews of any sect and origin pray together, dance together, and mourn together. Jews feel as though the pain of their brother - religious or not- is their pain. There is invisible brotherhood that binds Jews together, even if in reality they are strangers.

This not only contributes to one's self-worth, but also encourages a feeling of security. As one girl from the religious Jewish community said, "I feel safer when a Jewish person is on the bus with me. I know I can rely on them."

Another aspect of the community is its community leader. Research by Lazar and Bjorck found that, "support from spiritual leaders remained associated with less emotional distress and more satisfaction with life." Orthodox Jewish youths are encouraged to find a personal spiritual mentor (*mashpia*) or a Rabbi they connect with. The *mashpia* or Rabbi offers spiritual and emotional support and the relationship becomes lifelong. Gordon Allport asserts that, "the therapist's techniques are in the main so similar to the pastors." This implies that a rabbi's relationship with his congregants has the same psychological effect that a therapist has.

Gordon W. Allport (d. 1967) even argues that philosophy of religion may even be superior to psychological methods. A therapist, though his techniques are sound intellectually, is encouraged to remain at a professional distance from his patient. A pastor or rabbi's affiliation to their congregation is born out of love. That is the essential ingredient; it is what makes religion most effective.

Prayer

The early psychologist, Knight Dunlap (d. 1949) was wrong when he said, "Prayer certainly is an expression of desire." Desire is certainly part of prayer. But prayer is not a sum of demands.

"Prayer, like love, is mostly about losing yourself," Tzvi Freeman said. In Judaism, it is called the 'service of the heart' because it is an act suffused with love. Prayer is the cement in our relationship to G-d.

Through prayer, one can weave together the strands that tie us to the Creator, G-d. This relationship has not an insignificant impact on our mental hygiene.

Pollner found people "who reported a close relationship with G-d also indicated more happiness and life-satisfaction." Pargament and Brant propose that when a person feels supported by G-d, they are better able to cope with tragedy. Lazar and Bjorck also found that "G-d support was associated with better psychological functioning." In a survey of Black Americans, who were asked which method helped them cope with a personal problem, 44% answered prayer helped them most.

Why is this? What about prayer makes it so potent?

In the Morning Blessings, Orthodox Jews thank G-d for their clothes, shoes, sight and even posture. There are prayer for eating, for sleeping, even for visiting the facilities, highlighting what is otherwise taken for granted. "Prayers of thanksgiving bring to the foreground what is usually in the background." Rabbi Sacks said, "I learn to cherish what I have, not be diminished by what I do not have."

It's called gratitude. It is one of religions' most profound gifts.

Music

The mark of a happy man is the tune he dribbles from his lips. For Jews, the mark of a successful prayer or learning session is how much song was infused in it. "Sing every day," says Rashi, a medieval commentator on the Talmud, "Even if one has reviewed his learning, he should sing it every day, and this will cause your life in the World to Come to be with happiness and songs."

When King Saul was struck by depression, his remedy was the song of the harp. Maimonides (d. 1204) encourages one suffering from 'melancholia' to listen to music, so that their sadness will subside. Sefer HaMiddot also highlights the virtues of music; "Music will make you happy and bring you enthusiasm."

Music is central to the Jewish sentiment. Song, like most things in Judaism, has a distinct purpose in Jewish life. Farbrengens (mentioned above) are built around songs. Most Chassidic songs are wordless, because sometimes, confining emotion into words shatters the untouchable mystic of a song.

Music has the unique power to sweep the soul from its humdrums and spirit her towards the Divine.

Parallel to the emphasis on music is dancing. Chassidim especially are known for expressing their spiritual joy with somersaults and '*kazatzke*' dances.

Most of all, music brings everyone together. It binds us the way no philosophy ever will. That's why it's so joyful; music melts the barriers between us all.

Shabbos

"I can't imagine people who live without Shabbos," David* told The American Journal for Occupational Therapy, "Jews who really understand and appreciate Shabbos can't wait for it. It's really our day of rest. It's our day to gain a little spirituality, to get closer to the things that we are and we do. It's a way to regroup and look at ourselves and look at our surroundings and relax and enjoy it."

All week we chase achievement, hounded by the pressure to perform well. Is one ever able to appreciate an achievement before chasing after the next?

Shabbos is one day of the week to be instead of do. Shabbos in Rabbi Sack's words is "an antidote to stress, the most effective I know."

Shabbos allows one to spend time with family and friends. Families shares Torah insights and enjoys philosophical and Talmudic discussions. They sing *zemiros*. Most of all, we switch off from the week; living, instead of making a living.

One's entire week is centered around Shabbos. It gives one's week the tug of a goal. "Pleasures taste better when you have time to let them linger on your tongue," Rabbi Sacks said. That is what Shabbos achieves. Shabbos magnifies all the things that make one happy, allowing one to enjoy and appreciate them.

Family

The first commandment in the Torah is to procreate. Marriage in Judaism is all about creating a family; in this way, Orthodox Jews are extremely pronatalist.

This seems counter to the Western idea of marriage. Are marriages happier this way?

American Orthodox Jews have a 10% divorce rate. Considering the large marriage rate within the community (between 80 and 85 percent of Orthodox American Jews are married) this indicates of the stability of Orthodox Jewish marriages. This is especially poignant when considering that nearly half of American marriages are doomed to fail, with a 48% divorce rate.

This centres back to bitul. One has come into marriage as a partner, not a taker. One's focus is centered on the future that he and his spouse will create together.

Research has shown that childless people do less housework, exercise more, travel more, and spend more money on restaurants and entertainment. How can raising children – often a dirty, time-consuming, and challenging task – make people happier?

The Durkheimian theory explains how parenthood structures people's lives and integrates them into social networks, thus providing a meaning and purpose in life.

Giving and receiving affection, feeling love, and feeling valued are known to correlate to well-being.

In Judaism there is a special happiness called '*nachas*,' the term used to describe the joy of successfully rearing children. The Lubavitcher Rebbe (d. 1994) spoke fervently about not allowing the deliberations above – like resturants and entertainment - from dissuading you from the eternal joy of parenthood. The Rebbe directs people to look at their grandfathers and grandmothers, satisfied and fulfilled with generations of offspring surrounding them. That is authentic '*nachas*.'

Women

Films like 'Unorthodox' and 'My Orthodox Life,' paint the role of Jewish women in dark colours. They are seen as micromanaged by their husbands, coerced into childbearing and are too downtrodden to realise it. Twenty percent of former religious women left their Jewish communities because of the role of women.

But how do women who are currently in the religious community feel? Are they happy?

It is true that religious Jewish society is largely dominated by males. Leadership and most religious jobs (*kli kodesh*) are roles that are almost exclusive to men. Men and women are also often segregated in Orthodox circles, which could lead to feelings of inferiority.

In addition, most religious Jewish women don't have professional careers, and bear large families and the brunt of household work. In general, these factors are associated with lower wellbeing in women.

A study done in the Anglo-Jewish community revealed that this is not the case. The study found that the very factors that are the cause of depression in the latter group, like child rearing and housework, are actually sources of happiness for Orthodox Jewish women. Ironically, in general society, where women supposedly have more autonomy, women are three times more likely to suffer from depression than men are.

A high profile feminist, Jeanette Kupferman, describes her encounter with Chassidic women: "...they laughed often and easily and for women who by modern standards were severely restricted in everything they did ...showed a remarkable energy, spontaneity and ease of manner."

Contrary to popular belief, the role of women is often highlighted in Jewish teachings. She is called the akeres habayis - the mainstay of the home. Every Friday night her husband sings to her an ancient poem, 'Aishes Chayil' extolling her virtues and thanking her for her service to the family.

But it is not only her family that the Jewish woman influences. The Lubavitcher Rebbe (d. 1994) especially emphasised the role of Jewish women, saying that they possess a great deal of "empathy, good-heartedness and loving-kindness," which enables them to influence others in their journey toward the Divine.

The high-esteem that a Jewish woman is held in, coupled with her fulfilling role as mother and wife is conducive to her happiness. Loewenthal discovered that "wellbeing is higher among those whose 'foundation of the home is intact." In other words, a woman who doesn't chase after a man's job is happier. She is secure in the pull and tug of loving and being loved. By using her innate sensitivity and warmth, she has a unique role; different, but not inferior to the role of man.

Conclusion

All my research, both pyschological studies and theory, has shown that, in fact, religious people are happier than the rest of the population. Religion is associated with positive moods and religious people are less likely to suffer from psychopathological problems. Religious people live longer, have greater perceived health and are less lonely.

A study among Israeli students, found that both religious behaviour and belief were associated with healthy well-being. Aryeh Lazar and Jeffery P. Bjorck applied the *Fiala Multidimensional Model of Religious Support* to religious Jews. They found that all three supports (religious community support, religious leader support, and G-d support) are linked with positive psychological functioning and better satisfaction with life. This supports the idea that religion, specifically Judaism, is a symbiotic interplay between the intrinsic aspects of religion, like meaning and *bitul,* and the extrinsic factors religion offers, like community.

In essence, Jewish teachings on happiness are intertwined with the pursuit of a meaningful and purposeful life, both within oneself and within the larger community.

ABOUT THE WRITER

Yehudis Gruber is eighteen years old. As of the writing of this bio, she hasn't quite graduated yet, so she can still identify as a student of LSGS where she is working towards her A-Levels in English Language, Graphics, Psychology and of course, EPQ. She feels extremely privileged to be a part of the Chabad-Chassidic movement, because she feels it gives her a HUGE sense of personal meaning and purpose (read her EPQ for more ;)). In her spare time, you will find her quoting her favorite podcasts, vibing to a TYH song and hiking in the horse-farm up her road.

CHAPTER TEN

HOW DID THE HOLOCAUST AFFECT JEWISH CHILDREN?

Sorale Labkowski

The Holocaust took place during the years 1939 and 1945.
The Holocaust was the effort of the Nazis to make the world
'Judenrein' – 'clean of Jews,' through systematic murder, by
death of starvation, disease, exhaustion and other forms of
brutal killing, implementing the 'Final Solution.'

The Nazis knew that the children are the hope for the
continuity of the Jewish People and therefore, their main
focus was to annihilate every Jewish child. In addition, the
Nazis tried to prevent the continuity of the Jewish People
through forced abortion, castration and other means, in
various forms.

After the war as well, many children were scarred physically, spiritually and psychologically. Many issues arose when it came to reuniting surviving relatives and for many, the scars of the Holocaust continued into decades and generations later.

More than 1.5 million Jewish children perished in the Holocaust, which is estimated around 90% of Europe's Jewish children.

Pre-War
Kindertransport

Between 1938 and 1939, almost 10,000 Jewish children left Nazi Germany, Austria, Czechoslovakia and Poland on the lifesaving mission that would later become known as the 'Kindertransport.' Many of these children never saw their parents again; orphaned due to the subsequent six years of systematic murder by the Nazis. From one group that came over, who were cared for by the Sainsburys, only two children had surviving parents!

The older children were responsible for the younger children. Generally, children under seven years old were sent to Holland, Belgium or France, whereas older children were sent to England. Unfortunately, many of those children who were sent to Holland ended up being killed by the Nazis, when Holland was invaded. Many of the younger children did not understand what was happening; why were they leaving their parents? Some were told they were going on holiday, but then why were Mother and Papa crying?

Despite the seriousness of the situation that had caused them to leave their families and homes, the children were able to joke. "The realisation that we could say what we liked with impunity engendered an atmosphere of enormous gaiety." They would tell each other political jokes that they had picked up at home from the adults and created new friendships, in their state of being overexcited and enjoying their first moments of freedom.

Upon arrival in England, there were several reactions. Some children were bitter that they could not live with their parents, while others viewed this trip "not the story of a sad refugee, but is sort of adventure."

Dr Solomon Schonfeld was distressed about the situation of the Jews in German controlled Europe, but he was also very concerned about the assimilation of the Jewish children arriving in Britain. Dr Schonfeld, organised the 'Schonfeld Kindertransport.' He tried very hard to ensure that the Jewish children would, if possible, stay with Jewish hosts, or at least get a religious education, so they would not be lost to the Jewish People.

War
Algeria

The Nazi forces entered France in May 1940. France was divided into unoccupied, Vichy France and occupied France, under German control. The French colonies of North Africa came under the rule of Vichy France.

Anti-Semitic laws in Algeria were set out by the Vichy government and were extremely harsh. Some of their laws were stricter than what was imposed in Vichy France itself!

In Algeria, a 'numerus clausus' was imposed, limiting the number of Jewish schoolchildren to 14% and was later reduced to only 7%. Therefore, private education was set up for the elementary and secondary students who had been

expelled, with 20,000 Jewish children attending the 70 elementary and 5 secondary newly established schools. Majority of Algerian Jewry were assimilated, and therefore, the schools set up focused on French nationality and not on religion. It's ironic that though they had been stripped of their French citizenship and were being persecuted by the French, they still held on to their French nationality with pride and were trying to raise the next generation on that. "We are French and we state loudly that... there is no power in this world that can affect the deep feeling that unites us to our country, to its culture, to its dead."

Due to this strong feeling of patriotism, many young Jews joined the resistance, formed in 1940, contacting other resistance groups. They were contacted in May 1942, by the American army, for help in invading Casablanca, Algiers and Oran. The capture of Algiers was the only battle that succeeded, on 7-8 November 1942. However, the Jews were only truly liberated in the summer of 1943, when they were once again considered citizens of France and all anti-Jewish laws were nullified.

The Jews of Algeria were sent to labour and concentration camps throughout Algeria, including Bedeau and Djelfa. I have not managed to find out if any children were sent to these camps, but it is a possibility.

Libya

Libya was under Italian rule and was therefore treated differently to the other North African countries. During the first German invasion of Libya, in spring 1941, although food was not plentiful, they didn't starve. The British managed to push them out at the end of 1941, beginning of 1942, with much rejoicing from the locals. However, the Germans reinvaded, in 1942. At this point, Mussolini ordered all Jews to resettle in Benghazi. The city became very dirty and lice became a problem. In addition, food was even scarcer and children had to go and scrounge around for food, even taking from German leftovers. They would also go into homes that had been emptied of its inhabitants and would find food there.

Libya was liberated around the year 1943.

Entire families, with their children, were sent to the work camp Jado (Giado), where 562 Jews died of starvation, disease and exhaustion.

"There wasn't a family who didn't have someone who had died in the camp."

Russia

Between the years 1941-1942, thousands of Russians were evacuated by the Soviet authorities, from the major cities, due to the war.

Ghettos

The *'Altestenrat'* or *'Judenrat'* was the Jewish council set up in the ghettos. They were the 'middle man,' negotiating with the Nazis, obeying their orders, in exchange for a temporary respite from the Nazi death machine. They were also policemen, in charge of keeping order. The most famous head of the *Judenrat*, was in the Lodz ghetto; Chaim Rumkowski. Rumkowski believed that if he would encourage the ghetto inmates to work productively and cooperate with the Germans, they would be spared from what the Nazis were doing to the rest of the Jews. Thus, he collaborated with the Nazis and was put in charge of creating lists of Jews to be deported. He was also asked to turn over all the children and old people and these too were deported to Chelmno. His efforts however, were in vain, as between June and August 1944, the Lodz ghetto was liquidated and Chaim himself was murdered, with his family, in Auschwitz.

'Selektia' - 'selections,' or *'aktions'* – 'actions,' took place constantly in the ghettos. Children and the elderly were the main targets of deportations. After the ghetto was mainly emptied of its Jews, it would be liquidated and the remaining Jews would be sent to camps across Europe.

Jewish children had to learn to be smart. Even as young as three years old they learnt to fend for themselves. Like little Meierl. Children understood the dangerous situation they were in and under the conditions, were essentially forced to behave like adults. Yet laughter and jokes did not cease. "Humour is the only thing the Nazis cannot understand."

Children continued playing with toys, despite the suffering and death around them. In the Lodz ghetto, children would create cards, using the tops of cigarette boxes.

Young, Jewish children, in the Lvov (Lemberg) ghetto, were handed over to the Hitler youth, to be used as target practice.

In the Sosnowitz ghetto, the Nazis set up an infant's home for children, whose parents were forced to work.

Kovno (Kaunas)

During the first few months of its existence, there were two parts to the Kovno ghetto; the 'small ghetto' and the 'large ghetto.' It was separated by Paneriu Street. In the Kovno ghetto, it was  made compulsory, by the Altestenrat, to attend one of the two schools set up. Despite the fact that many children were being used for hard labour, or had to remain home to watch younger siblings while their parents were conscripted, two schools of 200 children each were set up. This ensured that Judaism would survive at a time when it was being threatened to be completely eradicated. The schools were a form of defiance against the Germans who were not only trying to kill the Jews, but were also trying to remove any vestige of a normal society and culture that humans crave. These efforts were challenged many times. In 1942, pregnancy was an illegal act, instituted by the Nazis; an act punishable by death. This brought to reality the fact that the current children in the ghetto would be the last generation of Kovno Jews. Furthermore, in the 'Book Aktion' of February 1942, all books within the ghetto were confiscated. It was illegal to be found with a book. However, the children continued learning with books that survived the confiscation or without the necessary books. In August of 1942, schools were ordered to shut down and adults were forced to join the labour brigade. Yet, the Jews of the Kovno ghetto refused to be completely stripped of their culture and humanity.

The Kovno Jews were still unaware of the fate of the surviving children. This was until 1 November 1943, when the ghetto became a concentration camp and Jews from the surrounding areas were sent there. Due to this, news of what awaited the children, based on what was told had happened to the children in other ghettos and camps, reached the inhabitants of the Kovno ghetto. This resulted in the smuggling of the Kovno ghetto children to be placed with partisans or hidden with gentile families. Thus, the surviving children of the hidden school of Kovno were saved. For many, this was just in time, as on 27 March 1944, there was a two day Aktion, resulting in the deaths of 1,300 children under the age of 12.

Vilna (Vilnius)

The Vilna ghetto was established on September 10, 1941.

Children were taught in the Vilna ghetto and by September 1941, 2,700 children were enrolled in the ghetto school. However, many did not enrol due to fear, parental negligence or orphaned children having to go to work. In addition, around 200 Orthodox children attended either of the two schools for boys up to twelve, or the Yeshiva, set up for boys aged twelve to sixteen years old.

Compositions were written by the children in these schools. The themes for the compositions chosen, tragically reflected the suffering that had befallen the student's families. Examples included, *"How I Saved Myself from Camp Ponar," "They Led My Parents to Their Death," "I Hid in an Underground Bunker,"* amongst others.

Children enjoyed and momentarily forgot the doom and death awaiting them, with different activities and performing for the adults of the ghetto.

During the Aktions in the ghetto, children would hide. Sometimes the younger children couldn't be controlled and would start crying from fear. The adults, fearing for their lives and the lives of their children, would use sedatives to quiet them down.

When smuggling children out of the ghetto, many times the children would be sedated. Children as young as three or four, realising what was going on, would beg not to be sedated; they promised that they would be good and not cry. Tragically, sometimes the sedatives would kill them.

Warsaw

Children in the Warsaw Ghetto learned how to be extremely resourceful. The smaller children were sent out of the ghetto, to help those trapped within the ghetto. Their small size allowed them to crawl through narrow openings in the ghetto walls and smuggle food to their families and friends. Yet smuggling was a serious offence. If caught, the children would be severely punished. Young people in the Warsaw ghetto wanted to continue their education and so, they would learn in secret, in defiance of the Nazis. Whenever necessary, they would hide their books, as studying was forbidden by the Germans.

Convents

Oftentimes, parents would hand over their children to gentile acquaintances or Christian convents for safekeeping until after the war. There were many gentiles who risked their lives to save Jews.

Yehuditha, a Jewish girl from Milan, Italy, was six when she saw her mother and grandmother for the last time, in 1944. Her Christian neighbour brought her to a convent, where she lived until 1945, when the allies liberated Italy. Yehuditha describes how she was told she was the only Jewish girl in the convent and had to keep her true identity a secret. Being as she was too young to fully understand the danger, the other girls and nuns helped to protect her. Yet sometimes, they would try to instil in her their Christian beliefs. Although she was young, she had difficult choices to make. When one of the nuns covered up for her and saved her life, when soldiers appeared at the convent, Mother Superior decided to change her name to a more Christian sounding name. That night in bed, she resolved to become 'two girls.' During the day, she will be a good, Christian girl, to please those at the convent and at night, she will be her true self, a Jewish girl, to make her mother, grandmother and G-d, happy.

After the war, she was given the choice of staying in the convent or going with the other Jews, to Palestine. She was given half an hour to decide. She chose to go with the Jews, believing that she would find her mother and grandmother there. Mother Superior wasn't happy, but had no choice. She ended her farewell to Yehuditha, by handing her cross chain and whispering Christian words of farewell.

Some Jews, at great risk, escaped over to the Aryan side and lived in constant fear of being recognised and handed over to the Nazis, especially boys and men, who were circumcised.

Ephraim Shtenkler spent five years, from age two until seven, hiding in a cupboard and under beds, with his hosts who wanted him dead. At the war's end, his feet were twisted backwards and he couldn't walk. It took months until he was finally able to walk.

In the Forests

Between the years 1942-1943, survivors of the massacres of western White Russia (Belarus) and western Ukraine, fled to the forests located in Eastern Poland and  Western USSR. These included Jewish men, women and children. The men were well armed against the Germans. However, having women and children to take care of as well, made conditions even harder, considering the harsh and primitive conditions they were forced to live under. In addition, the majority of the Polish and Ukrainian partisans, were hostile to the Jews.

The partisans were sent on dangerous missions, to disturb the enemy, by blowing up trains, headquarters and other strategic places. The children were seen as very useful. And daring. They were seen as the least suspicious looking and could accomplish what others could not. There were children who managed to gain entry into the lion's den itself; Nazi headquarters! They were also very clever and resourceful. They planted themselves as spies within Nazi headquarters and then with their help, they sabotaged them. Twelve-year-old Motele pretended to be a Ukrainian violinist and earned favour in the eyes of the Nazi soldiers. He was invited into the German Soldiers' Home and while there, he discovered a little niche in a wall. With help from his superiors, he planted an explosive inside the niche. At the appointed time, the explosive went off and the entire building blew up, with many soldiers, including even high Nazi officials.

Escape to the Soviet Union

There were some families, who sensing the danger of the approaching Germans, wanted to escape. The most feasible option was to cross, illegally, the newly created border that had been created when Germany and the Soviet Union divided Poland. They crossed from the German controlled portion of Poland, into the Russian section. Most were then sent to labour camps in Siberia.

Camps

Upon arrival in Auschwitz, men and women were separated and waited on the 'ramp,' for the selection. SS men, sometimes Josef Mengele himself, would then inspect each Jew. If the Jew was deemed fit for work, he would be sent to the right, which meant a slow death by harsh labour and starvation. If a Jew were deemed too old, or unfit for work, they would be sent to the left, which meant  instant death in the gas chambers. Young children and their mothers were sent to the left. Sometimes, a camp inmate would manage to inform a young child what fate awaited them and to tell them to lie about their age, for a chance to live. They would lie and say that they are eighteen, so that they would be sent to the right. From 1944, children as young as thirteen or fourteen were chosen for slave labour as well and sent to the right, to help with the war effort.

In Auschwitz, children under sixteen were allowed to accompany their mothers. However, one day, a counter-order was given for all fourteen, fifteen and sixteen year olds to come forward. They would be given double food rations and learn physical cultures with gymnastic teachers. They were to be housed in a separate children's camp. For a few days, they would exercise daily, until one night they were all taken and burned alive in the crematories.

From mid-1943, children suitable for scientific research by Nazi doctors, were selected for life.

The Nazis used trickery and lies to deceive the Jews into trusting them. When the Hungarians arrived in Auschwitz, they were told that all pregnant women should step forward and they would be taken to a better place, with better food, in order to keep them and their future child healthy and well.

However, this was all a hoax. All the women who stepped forward were beaten with clubs and whips by women and men Nazi officers. They also set the dogs upon them, who tore their limbs and dragged them by their hair. These women were then thrown into the crematoria alive. Dr Mengele then announced that women were allowed to have children, however, the babies had to be killed. Many women came to have their children delivered safely. But just then, Mengele walked in and ordered all the women killed. Next, an order was issued allowing the children who would be born to live. But that too was annulled. Thus, a whole generation of babies were not born.

In Majdanek, Auschwitz and other concentration camps, Nazi officers would pick young boys, between the ages of twelve and fifteen, to be their messengers and errand boys. They were known as the *'piepel.'* They were also referred to as 'runners,' as they would run through the camp with messages from the SS. Many *piepels*, wanting to impress their superiors, would cruelly beat the slave labourers. Some *piepels* kept the knowledge of their relatives in the camp a secret, while others found resourceful ways to help their relatives, using their position. Generally speaking, family members of *piepels*, received better treatment.

Despite the ongoing deportations, young adults in the camps made sure to help the children with them. They even established a youth movement. They organised special activities on Jewish holidays, such as lighting the Menorah on Chanukah.

Rena Quint (Frieda Lichtenstein) was born in 1935, in Piotrkow, Poland. She was three when war broke out. Her mother and two brothers were deported to the Treblinka extermination camp and were murdered there. She escaped to her father and pretended to be a boy, working in a glass factory for the Nazis. However, when the entire factory was deported, she had no choice but to separate from her father. She was sent on a death march to Bergen-Belsen, when she was only 6 years old! While undressing for the showers, upon arrival at the camp, she held family pictures in her hand, the only memento of her murdered family. A Nazi officer saw her clutching something and went over to her. Seeing as it was just photographs, he tore them and scattered them to the wind. Rena has no memory of what her father, mother or brothers looked like.

In the camp, she caught typhoid. She was liberated by the British in 1945.

The Tehran Children

The Tehran children were a group of Jewish, Polish orphans, who came to Palestine via Iran, in February 1943. When it was known that they would be coming, quarrels broke out between the secular and Orthodox communities, regarding where the children would be placed. In the end, less than 45% of the children were sent to religious institutions.

When the second group of Tehran children arrived, in September 1943, approximately 83% of the 108 children were sent to the religious institutions. This was done after research into the children's backgrounds, so as to provide them with the traditions similar to their homes.

These divisions caused an uproar by the Orthodox leaders, and rabbis from across the US and UK, including Rabbi Yosef Yitzchak Schneersohn, responded sharply against the secular leaders, calling on American Jews to intervene. Many rabbis in Britain also called to boycott secular Zionist organisations.

Diaries

Every child who went through the war had different perspectives and outlooks on the experiences that were thrust upon them so suddenly. Some children described how they are "tired of this life. A quick death would be a relief for us." However, there were also those children who felt scared, and felt they had not yet lived and wished to survive at all costs. Others, like Anne Frank, constantly saw the beauty, good, and sunshine; imagining freedom and knowing that everything and everyone is good. There were children, like Moshe Flinker, who, living in relative peace, longed to share the suffering of their brethren in Eastern Europe and found that any source of enjoyment that came their way made them feel guilty. Ironically and tragically, Moshe Flinker suffered the same fate as his brethren, as he perished in the Holocaust.

The Boys

Leonard Montefiore received permission from the British government to bring in 1,000 child survivors to England. However, the British economy  was not in a very good state after World War II and despite their promise, the CBF (Central British Fund for German Jewry, now known as World Jewish Relief) could only finance 732 children. Most of the children were survivors from Theresienstadt. They were brought over in five groups.

Theresienstadt was a city converted into a ghetto by the Nazis. The ghetto had a significant number of surviving inmates at the time of liberation. The ghetto was used to fool the Red Cross, when the Scandinavians made an uproar when 481 Dutch citizens were deported there in October 1943, before they could escape to neutral Sweden. Schools, theatres, libraries and other 'normal' activities were run within this ghetto city. Families with children lived in the ghetto. There were barracks for 'unaccompanied children,' children who were living there with no parents. On the 8th May 1945, the Red Cross liberated Theresienstadt, where 'The Boys' were officially formed.

Three brothers, who miraculously survived, wanted to try to get the other teenage orphans, many of whom were sole survivors, to bond and unify as a group, so they requested and received permission for them to stay in the same barracks, while still being housed in Theresienstadt.

Of the 12,000 children who had passed through Theresienstadt during the war, 1,600 were left to be liberated and of the thousands who had been sent eastwards, to the camps, from Theresienstadt, under the age of fifteen, only 142 survived.

Post War
The Red Army

Unfortunately, after surviving tremendous persecution, Jews who had survived the ghettos and camps of Transnistria were often drafted into the Red Army. Even orphans as young as 13 years old were forced to serve. Some were taken for forced labour in Soviet labour camps, deep in the Soviet Union.

Liberation Becomes War

For most child survivors, the moment of liberation was the beginning of their war. The youngest survivors had grown up in an environment where they had to constantly change their identities and living facilities. For them, this was normal. Came the end of the war, many couldn't even remember their original names and who they were. There were legal wars. Different organisations and people wanted them for different reasons. It was a hard decision for care workers to decide where the 'unaccompanied children' should go. Most psychologists and psychoanalysts agreed that returning the children to living parents was the best option. However, in majority of these cases, the ideal reunions envisioned by those carers never came about. Tensions were stiff in these family reunions. The youngest amongst the children did not remember their parents after being separated, for some, almost six years! In addition, even in the case of a child who could remember their parents, the six years of harsh conditions, starvation and forced labour changed many adults almost beyond recognition.

Preconceived Ideas

People were concerned that, although perhaps the bodies of the children could be preserved, their psyches couldn't. These children were considered abnormal and psychologically damaged from their experiences during the war.

In the Homes

After the war, children's homes were set up to assist the many orphaned children from Europe. These homes consisted of children who had survived ghettos, concentration camps and children who had lived out the war years hiding with non-Jewish families or in monasteries.

One of the main disagreements among those running these homes, was concerning those children who were still stubbornly clinging to their wartime host's way of life. Many children still wore crucifixes and insisted on praying the Christian prayers at night. Rabbi Winkelstein and similarly others, believed that no leniency should be allowed in regard to Jewish customs and practices. Whereas others, like Mrs Lederman, believed that these children, who had lost out on years of Jewish religious learning, should be allowed time to slowly readjust to a Jewish lifestyle. They overlooked these children's habits and felt that after some time and gentle prodding, these children would understand and give them up.

Family Reunions

Another tragic consequence of the Holocaust, that caused family reunions to be fraught with such difficulties, was the language barrier. A child from Poland may have found themselves being sheltered and hidden in Hungary and being young, had picked up the Hungarian language, forgetting their native tongue of Polish and/or Yiddish. After the war, the parent, speaking no Hungarian, now had no verbal form of communication with their child. Or if a child from Germany or Austria was sent on the Kindertransport to England and forgot their German, they too would have a hard time communicating with their surviving parent or living relative.

Even if they were lucky enough to find a surviving relative and could communicate, there were generally two extremes of the situations. Some families would maintain silence; no one would speak about their experiences during the war. Children were thought to be young enough to forget and were therefore told to forget the past and move on. However, children, especially children who have gone through and witnessed such harrowing and horrific scenes, can't just forget these things so easily. They had seen friends and family murdered before their eyes. But the adults themselves had also gone through tremendous, unspeakable suffering and they didn't know any better. They wanted to move on and forget as well. They didn't want to live in the past either. In addition, they felt that 'child survivors' didn't count as real survivors. They had experienced the war in different settings, which compared to the adults, did not seem as dangerous and as terrifying as the situations they were thrust into.

On the other hand, there were also the families in which the surviving parent or parents would continuously talk about their experiences.

Both settings were the unfortunate situations that care workers found when fighting for reunions between lost and separated families.

In some cases, reunited families splintered and broke apart again.

In contrast, there were also those psychologists and psychoanalysts who believed that it would be better for the children not to be returned to the families. They thought it to be better for rich families who could afford to, adopt them. Ironically, children from affluent backgrounds were sent to wealthy people. Yet the fact that the child's family was rich didn't help when the surviving relative tried to demand their child back. They were now in a situation where they could not afford their own child back, and in this instance, their former financial standing meant nothing.

There were also the unfortunate situations where the parent did not want to reclaim their child, or felt that they were unable to care for them. There were also situations where a child refused to go back to the relative they did not know, or preferred their adoptive or foster family. Sometimes the child himself would fight the battle against their biological family claiming them.

Children were very good at withholding information or lying to get the result they wanted.

Returning of the Hidden Children

Clifford argues that the claim that hundreds or thousands of Jewish children were being withheld by their war host families has been found to be an exaggeration. After the war, the families, monasteries and convents returned their charges, albeit sometimes reluctantly and if necessary, with force, but most Jewish children were returned at the war's end. However, Clifford does not make any mention of the book '*L'Eglise de France et les enfants juifs*' – 'the French Church and Jewish children,' by Catherine Poujol. In this book, the author, Catherine, talks about the letter that was sent out by the Vatican to the Catholic Church, saying that any child that has been baptised by the Church should not be returned to the Jewish people. The document says, *"Children who have been baptised must not be entrusted to institutions that would not be in a position to guarantee their Christian upbringing. For children who no longer have their parents, given the fact that the Church is responsible for them, it is not acceptable for them to be abandoned by the Church or entrusted to any persons who have no rights over them, at least until they are in a position to choose themselves."* This is clear evidence that many Jewish children were withheld and were not handed back at the war's end.

The Finaly children affair, emphasises that the view of Catherine Poujol, that there were many Jewish children who were withheld from being returned to the Jewish people, including surviving relatives, is more accurate than Clifford's view.

Two Jewish children, who had fled with their parents from Austria to Grenoble, France in 1939, Robert and Gerald Finaly, aged three and two respectively, were handed over to the Catholic nursery of Saint Vincent de Paul, in January 1944. Shortly after that, both parents were deported and were not heard from again. After the war, in 1945, their father's sister, Mrs Fischel, from New Zealand, with the backing of their other sisters, tried to get their nephews back. However, the woman who had been entrusted with the two boys, refused to hand them over. It wasn't until eight years later, 26 June 1953, and countless court cases, kidnappings and false leads, that the boys were finally returned to France, to their families and their faith.

Acceptance

Child survivors weren't really accepted as 'survivors' by adult survivors until almost 40 or 50 years after the Holocaust. Until the 1980's, the term 'survivor' was only used in conjunction with someone who had survived the camps. The children felt lost, unsure where they belonged. The adult survivors, the 'real' survivors, didn't accept them, yet, they also didn't belong to the second-generation survivors, because they had gone through the war.

In The Dark About Their Past

Child survivors who were adopted and were too young to remember their war experiences, were oftentimes kept in the dark. Many would have recurring dreams in which they were lying 'on wooden bunks' and 'on a table,' or where they saw an estate with trees and they felt that these dreams had meaning. However, their adoptive parents, worried about their relationship, or wanting their adoptive child to fit into society, would push away their concerns. Some were worried about providing the children with nightmares or robbing them of their newfound sense of security after years of upheaval and danger. "Everyone has dreams like that."

Children who were adopted as young toddlers sometimes didn't even know they were adopted or that they had gone through the war! Most frequently, it happened that they found this out when they needed proof of their parents Jewishness to get married in an Orthodox synagogue. There was little information on the Holocaust in the decades following the destruction of European Jewry.

Who Am I?

Unfortunately, there were some cases of child survivors who forgot who they were. Some were either too young to remember and during the war, they were living under assumed names anyway. In some cases, the children had been changing their names and stories constantly during the years of the war and so by the time the war ended, they couldn't discern reality from fantasy. However, after the war, this proved to be tragic. They didn't know who they were. They didn't remember any information, their names, birthdates, places of birth; nothing. They were thus unable to look for any surviving relatives and if any relatives did survive, they wouldn't be able to know. Their guardians couldn't write their names on any lists, send out letters or send the children to relatives. These children had to rebuild themselves from scratch. With no identities. They had to move on, while starting again.

Infantile Amnesia

Anna Freud, daughter of Sigmund Freud, used the term 'infantile amnesia' to refer to the forgetting of our childhood memories up until age three. Actually, Freud believed that children do have memories of their early childhood. However, these memories are so overwhelming that over time, they are repressed and forgotten. Hence, Freudian psychoanalysts and other child psychologists believed that the children who had experienced the war as young children would have no memories of the persecution and suffering and therefore, would have no lasting psychological effects. Based on this conclusion, mental health experts in Britain and North America, when dealing with a large number of cases of Holocaust survivors, did not immediately draw a parallel between their wartime experiences and their current symptoms. Even if the survivors themselves suggested the possible correlation, "the professionals generally paid little heed." Eventually, however, largely through the discoveries of William Niederland, a German-born, New York-based psychiatrist and psychoanalyst, it was found that most survivors had common symptoms. Niederland argued that these symptoms were caused by the trauma suffered during the war. This proved groundbreaking in the works of psychic trauma.

How Children Affected Those Around Them

Unfortunately, during the Holocaust, many Jews had to resort to 'murder' in order to save. There were various reasons for this.

Many people felt that it was better to die, than to be killed by the Nazi's. They would therefore poison themselves, or people in their care. Like in the Sosnowitz ghetto. Fredka Mazia, who was a governess in an infants' home, had no rest. What to do if the Nazis come? The reply she received, from Dr Lieberman, emphasises the tragic situation. They were to put the children to 'sleep' quietly, to spare them torture by the

Germans. But this was only done as a last resort. "… But remember: *only at the very last moment; only if there is no way out, when all is lost… Your loving hands.* Not the brutal hands of barbarians…"

In Auschwitz, Giselle Perl was assigned to work in the hospital, by Josef Mengele. She started by treating wounds, but was then told to inform Dr Mengele when a woman was pregnant. The women themselves would go over to inform him about their pregnancy, due to the promise of relocation to a better camp with better nutrition. However, when Dr Perl found out that these women were being used as guinea pigs and then gassed with their babies, she resolved to prevent pregnancies and births, so as to save the women's lives and enable them to have more children when the war ended. Dr Perl performed abortions and killed the babies that were born, in the dead of night, thereby saving the mothers lives. These procedures were performed in the barracks on the dirty, soiled floors and bunks, with no instruments, anaesthetics, bandages or antibiotics.

Conclusion

During the Holocaust, over 6 million Jews were murdered, including more than 1.5 million children. They died by starvation, torture, or cold-blooded murder by the Nazis and their collaborators. They suffered in ghettos, camps and hiding their identities in convents or Christian homes. Yet the end of the war itself did not mean the end of all problems. Many children suffered afterwards, psychologically, physically, spiritually and some were scarred completely for life. Some may have had surviving relatives, yet this did not always mean a happy conclusion. Whether it was the social workers, preventing reunions, or the parents or children themselves, many issues prevented families from reuniting properly and kept families torn apart forever. There were also the cases of children who couldn't remember who they were and were thus unable to look for relatives.

The effects of the Holocaust lasted for decades after, many times passing on to the next generations.

ABOUT THE WRITER

Sorale Labkowski enjoys reading, drawing, knitting, singing and playing musical instruments. She chose to do EPQ, because it gave her the opportunity to research any topic she wanted to explore more about. Sorale chose to do her EPQ about children and the Holocaust. She has always been very into the Holocaust and doing this EPQ gave her the opportunity to learn more about it in a structured framework and it also gave her a chance to research more into her own family history during the Holocaust..

She really enjoyed doing EPQ and she would 100% recommend it to anyone who wants to learn more about something that interests them!

CHAPTER ELEVEN

INVESTIGATING THE PLACE OF TRADITIONAL JUDAISM IN RUSSIA/USSR

Chaya Lewis

Jews have lived in Eastern Europe, in the lands that would later on form Czarist and then Soviet Russia, since the 12th Century. Some of the greatest movements within Judaism, most notably that of Chassidism, were born in that land, and grew out of its unique environment. Over the centuries, they faced many hardships and were forced to adapt, but they always maintained their identity. One of the greatest threats to their existence was the violent change from Czarist to Communist rule. In this essay, we will explore the historical background and foundations to Jewish life that enabled them to survive and even thrive through this change. Communist Russia was arguably one of the biggest threats to Judaism in thousands of years, as it attacked the very nature of the religion and its practices: How did Traditional Judaism survive and outlive it? In this essay, we will be focusing mainly on the Chabad response to this threat.

1905-1917
Life in the Shtetl

Russia during Czarism was a difficult time for the Jews. Czar Nicholas who ruled in the early 20th century was an anti-Semite, and new decrees against the Jews were continuously put in place. Despite the difficulties, Jewish life in Russia flourished.

Jews lived in little villages, known in Yiddish, as Shtetls. The Shtetl was sheltered, and there were minimal interruptions or distractions from the outside world. Although modernity was slowly making inroads into Russia, with the revolutionary movements, and the advent of the railroads; it was taking much longer to seep into the cloistered life of the Shtetl.

Life was idyllic with religion at the forefront of their every action. From the time they were very small, children were educated in the ways of the Torah. Young boys learnt in a Cheder, which usually consisted of a small table, with boys sitting together on a bench, listening to the Melamed, the teacher. The girl's education was in the home. The mother taught her daughter all that she needed to know; but her learning was mainly practical, in the kitchen.

The Haskalah movement started in the late 18th century. Often referred to as the Enlightenment, because it's adherents, the Maskilim, endeavoured to revolutionise Judaism, and bring Jews closer to the way of life of their 'enlightened' countrymen. Their attempts often ended in assimilation of dress and language, and in some cases, even conversion.

When the Haskalah movement arrived in the Shtetl, it was the girls who were affected the most at first. There are several reasons for this, chief amongst them was that the boys had a strong foundation in Jewish learning, with a more rigid structure to their day and less free time to get caught up with these new ideas, whereas the girls learnt at home, and had more free time in their day. As a result, they lacked the knowledge to be able to defend themselves and Judaism to the Maskilim, and were thus more susceptible to their arguments.

Revolutionary Winds- the 1905 Revolution: Hopes Built Up and Dashed

The revolution of 1905 was a pivotal changing point for Jews in Russia. The shifting political climate and the creation of a State Duma, brought hope to the Jews of Russia. There was hope that the new, more conservative government led by Piotr Stolypin, would be more tolerant to Orthodox Jews.

Since the emergence of the Haskalah, which began in Germany and Central Europe, then making its way eastwards to Russia, Orthodox Judaism had not had any connection with the Russian Government. However, the Orthodox Jewish leaders now saw an opportunity to recreate that connection, and hoped to take advantage of it. They would argue that the Jews were loyal to the Regime, and Orthodoxy could be a faithful ally in preventing young Jews from joining the revolutionaries. In this way, it was hoped to create new channels through which Orthodox Jews could have connections with the Government. Concerning this attempt at rapprochement, Vladimir Levin wrote:

Orthodox leaders hoped that a rapprochement with the conservative, but society-oriented government of Piotr Stolypin would be possible and desirable. With government support, they believed that they could successfully fight against the revolutionary-minded Jewish youth.

Through the Conference of Rabbis in 1908, the Orthodox leaders asked the government to not hinder religious observance, and to strengthen the position of the "spiritual" Rabbis, who were thus far, not recognised by the government.

At first, it seemed that the Government was agreeable to the proposition put forth by the Conference of Rabbis. But during a talk at that conference, Stolypin showed his true feelings, saying: "Jews ruined their chances of having laws helping them, by taking part in the revolution."

Even though only a small percentage of Jews were revolutionaries, because a large number of the revolutionaries were Jews; the Jews were judged as one complete unit and considered a dangerous enemy of the Regime. This was not the case with other religions, like Islam, where the different factions were considered separate. With the Jews however, all the different factions, even those who opposed the revolution, were considered enemies of the Regime.

In spite of this, Jewish life continued on, but the difficulties began to worsen. Pogroms were occurring with a terrifying frequency, many of them perpetuated by the Black Hundreds, who were secretly supported by Stolypin. Indeed, there was no love lost between the Jews and the Regime. It was with an ironic sense of relief that the Jews welcomed the second round of revolutions in 1917.

Activism and Activists

Although there were all different kinds of forces of assimilation at work; religion and the Torah was the way of life for a sizable number of Jews. For some of the younger generation, the winds of reform and revolution were too enticing; an adventure compared to the staid, stable environment of the Shtetl. With the pogroms so harsh and terrifying, they were desperate for a chance to better themselves and their lot. Soon, youths became enamoured with, and joined in, all different movements. The Zionist and Bund movements saw significant growth in numbers, and a high proportion of revolutionaries were Jews.

Young Jews joined the socialist revolutionary movements for a number of reasons. There were those who joined out of ideological reasons; after the pogroms that rampaged like a storm through Russia following the October Manifesto, they choose not to emigrate, but to stay and change the country from its anti-Semitic stance, to one that was more welcoming of Jews. There were others who joined out of a sense of rebellion. Some wanted to break free from the strict, rigid atmosphere of a traditional Jewish home. Still others wanted to rebel against the Regime that restricted their right to live as observant Jews.

With all the influences from the outside penetrating into traditional Jewish life, there was a need for Religious Judaism to put up a united front. As David E. Fishman notes; with the rise of Communism, most of the Rabbinic leadership fled from the USSR, with the notable exception of Rabbi Sholom Dovber of Lubavitch and his son and successor Rabbi Yosef Yitzchok.

Rabbi Sholom Dovber was the fifth leader of the Chabad Chassidic movement, which had begun in 1772 under his great, great grandfather Rabbi Schneur Zalman of Liadi. By this time, the movement's headquarters were in the city of Lubavitch, in what is now Belarus, and its adherents numbered in the tens of thousands, spread across much of the Pale of Settlement. Under Czarism, Rabbi Sholom Dovber had battled against the Maskilim and their interference in the Cheder educational system, and then in 1908 when the Government (then known as the "Third Duma") called the above-mentioned Conference of Rabbis to decide wide ranging changes to the structure of the Jewish Community, it was Rabbi Sholom Dovber who gathered together the Rabbis from across Russia to present a united front. Rabbi Schneersohn's goal was to strengthen Religious Judaism across Russia. Chief Rabbi Lord Jonathan Sacks explains this drive to activism as inner directedness.

> *Societies on the brink of growth... produce inner directed types. Culture is in a state of change. There is a high personal mobility. There is a mood of invention and exploration. This means that people have to constantly adapt to new challenges without losing a sense of where they are going and why. This means facing the future whilst keeping faith with the past. Such societies pay great attention to education. The young internalise the values of the group, which stay with them through life as a way of navigating change without disorientation or dislocation. They carry their inner world with them whatever they do and wherever they go.*

Rabbi Sholom Dovber was determined that whatever challenges that Traditional Judaism faced, they would be able to combat it by educating the younger generation to stand strong in their own Judaism. This approach was reinforced and perpetuated by Rabbi Sholom Dovber's son and successor, Rabbi Yosef Yitzchak, when Russia became a Communist State.

Rabbi Sholom Dovber's public stance was so vital. As due to the many different organisations vying for dominance, everyone was looking for direction and leadership, and Rabbi Sholom Dovber's clear message became the clarion call that was then adopted, to great effect, by his son.

1917-1929

After the October Revolution, with the outbreak of the Civil War, the condition of the Jews deteriorated. All the different opposing sides used the Jews as a scapegoat; and wherever their armies went, a trail of murder and pogroms followed.

During the first years of Bolshevik rule, the condition of the Jews fluctuated. At first, even amidst all the anarchy, it seemed that it would be possible to live a traditional Jewish life. However, events later proved this wrong, as the Yevsektzia hounded away at the religious Jews, making traditional Jewish life almost impossible.

It was not only the Yevsektzia that was tearing at the foundations of Jewish life. Although the New Economic Policy - NEP established by Lenin, to boost the economy after the civil war was making life easier, this furlough did not last long. Lenin himself described it as a 'temporary expedient' and when Stalin abolished the NEP in 1928, all private business and enterprises were banned. This hit traditional Jews particularly hard and many lost their source of livelihood. In search of work, Jews migrated away from the Shtetls to the big cities. There, in an attempt to be successful, certain religious customs started falling by the wayside. The whole infrastructure of the Shtetl, of a sheltered life with no distractions from the outside world, crumbled, and in its place were the big cities, where the hardships and distractions were making it much harder to live a traditional Jewish life.

The Yevsektzia

When the Bolsheviks took over, all Jewish organisations of any kind were outlawed and both the Bund and Zionist movements were closed. Those young Jews who had joined these movements, throwing off their religious identities, naturally found themselves aligned with the Bolshevik socialist ideology.

Determined to show that the Jews were loyal to the revolution, these Jews formed the Jewish section of the party. To prove that they were better than their religious brethren, these communist ideologists, ably assisted by the Bolshevik party, waged a concentrated war against religion. In fact, they were so zealous in their work that one non-Jewish communist wrote in a Soviet paper, "I would be delighted if only I could see the Russian communists bursting their way into the churches on the major festivals just as their Jewish comrades do in their places of worship on the Day of Atonement."

Unsurprisingly, given their education and background, even these hardened socialists still possessed a Jewish spark inside them, no matter how small it may have been. When the inevitable happened, and that Jewish spark broke through, the Soviet newspapers would pounce on the exposes, unmasking supposedly loyal members of the party, and showing their true colours.

One such incident happened after a member of the Yevsektzia addressed a rally regarding the law of circumcision. After spending hours denouncing the laws and practices of circumcision, he returned to his home. Participants from the rally were walking past his home, when they heard a child's cries, and came to help, where much to their surprise they saw this member of the Yevsektzia holding a baby, whilst a Rabbi performed the circumcision.

Unfortunately, the Yesvetzika's sacrifice of themselves for their leaders was worth nothing, when the inevitable happened and they were almost all liquidated during the purges of the 1930's.

The Cheder Trials

One infamous war of the Yevsektzia against Traditional Judaism was the Cheder trials. In this series of trials, which lasted from 1921 until 1928, the accused were not only the different religious institutions but also the actual specific commandments, such as that of circumcision.

The first Cheder trial was held in Vitebsk in 1921. No matter what the prosecution had to say, the defence were not intimidated, upholding the values of the Cheder educational system, demonstrating the falsehood of the Yesvetzika's claims. After an hour of consultation, the judges returned with the verdict that the Cheder infringed on section 6 of the Soviet Constitution, which outlawed religious teaching to children and youth under the age of eighteen.

It was clear to everyone that these trials were all staged, with the verdicts written even before they began. These trials did not put an end to the Cheder, on the contrary, a fierce resistance started, with the Cheder system going underground, and continuing their work.

Rabbi Yosef Yitzchok Schneerson

Rabbi Sholom Dovber had passed away in 1920, and his son Rabbi Yosef Yitzchok took on the mantle of leadership. During this time of hostilities towards Judaism, Rabbi Yosef Yitzchok tirelessly continued his father's work, strengthening Judaism throughout Russia. He sent emissaries to cities throughout Russia, wherever there were Jews. These emissaries ensured that each city had everything they needed to enable them to live a Traditional Jewish life. They found teachers, and opened Chadorim, to ensure that the boys were able to learn. They built Mikvaos, ritual baths in each city. They performed circumcision on the baby boys. These emissaries were also shochtim, ritual slaughterers, and they made sure that all the Jewish community had access to kosher meat.

Writing about this in a letter at a later point, Rabbi Yosef Yitzchok explains how he took a map of Russia, and divided it up into ten sections and gathered ten idealistic young them, assigning them each an area of Russia. He made them swear that they would dedicate themselves to strengthening Judaism in their area, even to the point of self-sacrifice.

The Yevsektzia kept a close eye on his activities, angry at this obstruction to their goal of eradicating Judaism. But the net was tightening around his neck. On the night of 14th/15th June 1927, the GPU burst into Rabbi Yosef Yitzchok's house. Arrested and imprisoned in the notorious Spalerno prison, he was charged with counter-revolutionary activities, the Soviet

Union's label for all religious activities. This prison was only for hardened criminals, enemies of the regime, yet this peace-loving man had been sent there for the sole reason of keeping the flame of Judaism alive in what was quickly becoming an atheist State.

The government decided that for such a 'serious' crime, Rabbi Yosef Yitzchok should be sentenced to death. Through the help of activists, in and out of the Soviet Union, particularly Madam Ekaterina Peshokva, president of the Red Cross in the Soviet Union, this sentence was commuted, initially to five years of hard labour in the Solovaki Islands, then to three years exile in Kastroma. After much political manoeuvring, he was eventually released after only 19 days exile.

With his life still very much in danger, Rabbi Yosef Yitzchok left the Soviet Union on 20th October 1927, but he still wielded tremendous influence over Jewish life in the Soviet Union. This led to many people being arrested during the purges on the charges of being a 'Schneersoniski': someone who fights to keep Traditional Judaism alive.

1929- 1941

In the early 1930s, after Stalin's ascension to power, the Communist Party's hostile attitude towards religion deepened. Judaism, the only religion still publicly functioning in the Soviet Union, received special attention.

Industrialisation

Stalin's move in 1928 from Lenin's NEP to industrialisation was a vital turning point in the situation of religious Jews.

Private businesses were previously allowed under the NEP and many religious families ran these businesses from their homes. However, once Stalin collectivised all businesses and placed them all under the State, this set-up was no longer available. Religious Jews had to figure out how to work, whilst adhering to traditional Judaism, in this purely atheistic, anti-religious environment.

With Stalin's new Nepreryvka (Непрерывка): "a continuous working week," Jews were now forced to work on Shabbos, otherwise they would be labelled as enemies of the State. They could stick to their values and risk being arrested and sent to Siberia or worse, executed; or they could abandon their ideals, and embrace Communism, which would enable them to live without fear. This choice was not easy to make, especially as it was now more common to live in the big cities rather than the Shtetls. The Communist ideology was filtering into their homes, making the second option much more alluring. How could a person stick to his ideals, when he faced the ridicule of everyone around him, from the State, to his own family?

Concerning this difficult decision, Zvi Gitelman wrote:

It seemed that only some of those who had come to maturity before the revolution were preserving the religious traditions. They found it increasingly difficult to do so, not only because of repression and the constant ridicule of the "League of the G-dless," but also because their own children often regarded them as relics of an age that had passed. Even those who respected their elders and their ways rarely followed them. How could one keep the Sabbath and the holidays when these were workdays and the penalties for absence were severe?

The Great Purge

The purges in the later half of the 1930's, gave Stalin the ability to really hammer the nails into the coffin of Judaism in the USSR. Thousands of Religious Jews were arrested on trumped up charges of espionage, or counter-revolutionary activity; sometimes called Trotskyism. Thousands of them were executed, and many were sent to the gulags, never to be seen or heard of again. Those who did survive were broken, both physically, and in spirit.

An especially heartrending case is that of the Ten Martyrs: ten especially gifted young men, who had dedicated their lives to revitalising Judaism in the USSR. All ten were arrested on the same night for opening Cheders and collecting funds to support Religious Jews who were not working on Shabbos. Although they were executed a few weeks after their arrest, their families were only told of their death 16 years later, after being lied to by the authorities that they had been sentenced to ten years exile and hard labour in Siberia.

All these arrests should have been a deathblow to the few surviving traditional Jewish communities in the USSR, especially with the majority of their community leaders being arrested one after the other. However, the resilience of the religious Jews is remarkable; for every Rabbi or community activist arrested, five more came in their place. For every underground religious institution discovered and closed down by the NKVD, a new one was quickly set up in a new secret location.

The hunters became the hunted, as Yevsektzia was also purged, with almost every single member 'getting the beans' a NKVD slang for being executed. Those that were lucky enough to avoid the firing squad were exiled to remote labour camps in Siberia, from where they never returned.

The Gulags

The labour camps in Siberia were freezing cold, and the prisoners were housed in subhuman conditions. Forced to work from early in the morning to really late at night, and sometimes even through the night whilst constantly being harassed by the guards, it was not easy for a person to keep to his ideals in this environment. But this is exactly what Religious Jews did. As Avraham Netzach writes in his memoires, when refusing to work on Shabbos he was put in solitary confinement, thus earning him the nickname, Subbota, meaning one who keeps Shabbos. Avraham was one of the early emissaries of Rabbi Sholom Dovber, and later on was a devoted disciple of Rabbi Yosef Yitzchok, and was arrested for his activities, with letters sent to him by the Rabbi forming part of the evidence against him. However, it was precisely this connection that gave him the strength to stand up against the severity of the Gulag and the brutality of his guards for twenty years, never once violating the Shabbos.

1941-1953
The War

When the Soviet Union joined World War Two, the relentless persecution against Traditional Judaism eased a little bit. Because the State was now focused on the war, and pushing back the German's advance, they were not focusing on the war against religion at the moment. This unexpected boon was a great benefit, enabling all the different religious institutions to come out from underground for a short while. They still had to be very careful, but life was much easier.

Fleeing the German advance, many traditional Jewish families fled to Central Asia, mainly to Samarkand and Tashkent. There, away from the Front, and the worry of the constant surveillance of the KGB, a flourishing religious community, albeit mostly underground, flourished.

Samarkand

In 1945, at the end of the war, most adherents of Traditional Judaism had moved to Central Asia, with Samarkand becoming the headquarters for all underground Jewish oriented activities. In order to make sure that everything was running smoothly, a secret organisation called Chamah (חמה) was set up. The members of this organisation, all young Chassidic Jews, travelled the length and breadth of the Soviet Union, collecting funds for secret underground Cheders and Yeshivos, and teaching far-flung, lonely families about Judaism.

This fight for children to have a Jewish education was not only for the Cheders and the Yeshivos, sometimes it was a fight for the children themselves. By law, all children were required to attend the Russian public school, where they were indoctrinated against religion with Communist ideology. If a parent did not send their child to school, their rights as a parent could be taken away, and their child sent away to an orphanage to be re-educated. In order to prevent their children from going to school, or at least to stop them going on Shabbos, parents often had to hide their children, or come up with ingenious excuses as to why they were absent all the time. In his memoirs, Rabbi Hillel Zaltzman writes what happened to him when the school discovered he was staying home and not coming to school on Shabbos for religious reasons.

When my father appeared in school, they warned him that if he continued to prevent his son from going to school on Shabbos for religious reasons, he would be in trouble. They threatened that his parental rights could be rescinded and I would be re-educated in a State school where I would be forced to stay in a dormitory. My father denied responsibility for my absences, and maintained that it was only a matter of my health. They demanded that if it was so, I had better appear in school the following Saturday.

When neighbours discovered school-age children, and reported them to the principal of the school, the pressure to send the children increased tenfold. Many families decided that it would be better to send the girls to school, as traditionally, they did not usually receive an education. In this way, with at least some children going to school, none of the children will be sent to a government orphanage to be re-educated. Although the girls were sent to the public schools, their parents spent hours with them at home, trying their hardest to undo all the damage done in school.

The majority of religious parents tried to make sure that their children had a Jewish education, but the great lengths that the Chassidic families went to were noticeable. It was not just formal education, but it was ensuring that their children were not corrupted by the atheist regime. Young children were sent to far away cities to avoid the KGB and to be able to learn with peace. This entailed a tremendous sacrifice on behalf of both the parents and the child, as it was extremely difficult, and the punishment for participation in this kind of activity usually resulted in arrest and exile or death.

Mass Arrests

1948-1953 were terrifying times for all Jews living in the Soviet Union, regardless if they were religious or not, as purges against Jews were carried out. Unlike the purges before World War Two, which were directed at the general population, these purges specifically targeted Jews. Many Jews were arrested for wanting to immigrate to the newly established State of Israel, but many more were arrested just because they were religious Jews, as such they were considered counter revolutionary and no other proof was needed.

The Doctors Plot

The situation only got worse. In the beginning of January 1953, the official Communist newspaper, the Pravda, ran an article entitled *"Vicious Spies and Murderers Under the Mask of Academic Physicians."*

> *A terrorist group of doctors, uncovered some time ago by organs of State security, had the murderous goal of shortening the lives of leaders of the Soviet Union- the Politburo- by means of medical sabotage...*

> *The majority of the participants of this terrorist group... were bought by American intelligence. They were recruited by a branch-office of American intelligence- the international Jewish bourgeois-nationalist organisation called the "Joint." The filthy*

face of this Zionist spy organisation, covering up their vicious actions under the mask of charity, is now completely revealed.

Of the nine doctors who were arrested, six of them were Jewish, and all of them were the top doctors in the Soviet Union at that time.

The arrests aroused a great furor in the Soviet Union, people became suspicious of every Jew that they met, especially doctors, and anti-Semitism once again reared its ugly head. Jews were fired from their jobs, and beaten in the streets. Religious Jews were at an even greater risk, as they were easy to distinguish because they looked Jewish. The fear pervading the streets was tremendous, Jews were afraid to step out of their houses, lest they be beaten up, or killed.

The pogroms that would undoubtedly have broken out after the verdict would have destroyed Russian Jewry, but the plot was stopped in its tracks by Stalin's death. On 4th March, 1953, an announcement came over the radio that the 'mighty Stalin had fallen seriously ill and lost consciousness.' A few days later, on 9th March 1953, Yuri Levitan the top Government broadcaster announced, "On the 9th of March at 10:50pm Moscow time, the heart of the First Secretary of the Communist Party, of the Soviet Union, Chairman of the Supreme Soviet Council, the Generalissimo Iosif Vissarionovich Stalin stopped beating."

Shortly afterwards, when it was realised that the evidence against the doctors had been fabricated, they were released, and the false witnesses were either put to death or imprisoned.

The death of Stalin didn't just end the Doctor's Plot, it also changed the whole focus of Communism. Whilst Jews were still under surveillance by the KGB, especially with the advent of the Cold War and the emergence of the United States as an ally to the State of Israel, they were "officially" free to practise Judaism. Whilst there were no specific anti-Jewish laws, it would take many years of struggles before the Iron Curtain fell and Jews once again felt safe to openly practice their religion. Over ten years after the death of Stalin, Elie Wiesel was sent by the Haaretz newspaper to Russia in 1965. In his book *The Jews of Silence*, he describes the oppressive environment that pervaded every Jewish community he visited there. The worst of Communism may have been over, yet the Jews of Russia still felt imprisoned and not truly free.

Conclusion

So how were Traditional Jews able to survive, and in the case of the Chabad Chassidim in Samarkand, even thrive in these challenging times, when everyone around them was integrating into Soviet Society?

My research has shown me that there was a three-pronged approach to their survival: Education, Leadership and Dedication.

Under the leadership of Rabbi Sholom Dovber during the Czarist Regime and later his son and successor Rabbi Yosef Yitzchok with the advent of Communist rule there was an emphasis on authentic and sustained Jewish education. The education the children received, both in their homes and also in the Chadorim, equipped the children and thus the future generations, with the tools needed to be able to withstand the Communist onslaught. This education was not just theoretical and academic, it was supported by a real sense of leadership and personal dedication. The children saw how important this was to their parents, they saw the reality of living a Jewish life and were immersed in it on a daily basis.

From the Shtetls, the vibrant, all-encompassing Jewish education gave them the strength to not only stand strong, but to also raise the next generation as well. The emphasis placed on the education even whilst under Communist rule, the self-sacrifice of the parents to give their children a Jewish education and not send them to the public schools, imprinted in the minds and hearts of all the children the importance of Traditional Judaism, and helped them pass the torch to the next generation growing up behind this Iron Curtain, even when they themselves had never experienced what it was like to live freely as Religious Jews.

Education without leadership would not have survived the onslaught. Leadership without education would not have survived the move from one generation to the next. However, there still required that third pillar that supported the education and leadership: that percularlity of Chabad Chassidus; the dedication of the Chossid to his Rebbe.

ABOUT THE WRITER

Chaya Lewis is currently in seminary in Beis Chana Tzafat, in Israel. She enjoys reading, writing and learning. Her favorite subjects are Chassidus subjects and Jewish history. In particular, she really enjoys learning about the times of the Spanish Inquisition and Russia under Communism. The lengths the Jews had to go to, to keep Judaism during those times, and their richness of life despite all their hardships really inspires her to overcome her own bumps in the road of life. This is why she was so excited to write about this topic for her EPQ, being that it's one of her favourites to learn. She had studied this time-period for her GCSE, but this particular subject was just touched upon lightly, and she wanted to expand her knowledge of this fascinating time period. Also, as a Lubavitcher chosid, this was part of her history, so it held a special interest for her.

CHAPTER TWELVE

CAN THE MODERN STATE OF ISRAEL AND TRADITIONAL JUDAISM COEXIST?

Chassia Pruss

Since the birth of Zionism, this question had been a prime source of controversy between the many factions in European Jewry from the late 1800's. The explosion of modern ideologies, such as socialism, nationalism, post-religionism and other revolutionary ideas, stirred up a desperate feeling of necessity to create a homeland, a safe haven to unite the Jewish people. Despite its popularity and success, it created and continues to create a deep chasm among the Jewish People. One of the practical manifestations of this dream is to determine if the modern state of Israel and traditional Judaism can, indeed, coexist.

Throughout this thesis I will consider the different ideological camps, and whether the Modern State of Israel comes into the framework of traditional Judaism. This will be presented through the lens of different ideas and realities, prevalent in Israel today, which have multifaceted arguments, comprising Zionism, nationalism and traditional Judaism.

Ideological Camps

In the past century, there have been several, different opinions on the Modern State, as well as the varied views within Zionism itself. In the following section, I will outline some of the main schools of thought including; Religious-Zionists, Secular-Zionists, Anti-Zionists and Non-Zionists.

Religious-Zionists

Religious-Zionism, the earliest founded Zionist movement, believed in creating a coexistence between the two faculties, as depicted in its very name. The foundation of their dogma, originally articulated by one of the forerunners to Zionism, Yehuda Alkalai, is that the physical in-gathering of exile will prompt the arrival of the Messiah, known in the vernacular as *aschalta d'geulah.* This means that the literal immigration of all Jews to Israel will practically begin the ultimate redemption. It can be summed up in Rabbi Z. H. Kalischer's statement, "The redemption will begin by… gaining consent of the nations to the gathering of some of the scattered of Israel into the Holy Land." After being subjected to incessant anti-Semitism, the resolve was to act on bringing it to an end conclusively and once and for all.

A primary founder of religious-Zionism was HaRav Abraham Isaac HaCohen Kook. An initial objective of his was to re-establish Judaism in Israel. Relocating was intended to redesign Judaism with a nationalistic spin. As Chief Rabbi

Sacks put it, "a Jew strives for harmony with himself, his people, his Torah and his land." Within this, the Zionist idea is prominent: In order to connect to oneself as a Jew, one must connect to all the other three factors, including 'his land.' This alludes to their ideology of *chibbat ha'aretz* - a love of the Land of Israel, to such an extent that immigrating there and devoting oneself to it, is part of the fundamentals of Judaism. Feeling that staying in the Diaspora is of no benefit as, "the nation itself is in a state of decadence in the Diaspora."

Moreover, they were keen on ingratiating all Zionists - secular and religious alike - saying that those workers who were cultivating the land were on a higher level than that of the Jewish, rabbinic giants in Europe. He claimed that, although they were religiously deficient, they were the emissaries of G-d as part of bringing the Messiah. This alludes to the religious-Zionist notion of fusing the secular with the religious in order to achieve one goal, as seen in statement that Rav Kook laid down, "an ethos of traditional Judaism engaged with Zionism and with modernity."

Nonetheless, the religious-Zionists still appreciated their secularity and understood it to be unsustainable, long term. Ultimately, this merging was intended to achieve the final redemption where a completely religious society will prevail. While the role of the secular people in the Divine plan was settling the land, the religious-Zionists saw their role as the ambassadors for religion. Perhaps this is why the religious-Zionists did not want to lose touch from the modern, universal society. As mentioned before, they were keen on gaining consent from the nations of the world, to legitimise their State. In doing so, a State could be established and settled, but be one "in which religious law will prevail and whose mission would include service of Judaism."

Thus, Religious Zionism presents a nuanced ideology, one that is not compatible with secularity, yet combines the two for their ultimate mission.

Another complexity occurs when one parallels the above, to HaRav Kook's model for the Chief Rabbinate in Israel. He asserted that, being in a new era, there must be a Jewish renaissance. Kook thought Judaism was dying out in the Diaspora as it relies on "memory and hope... [which]... cannot last forever." Thus justifying his theory that the Torah in the Diaspora is limited to the pious, intellectual people of the generation. Hence, Religious Zionism intended for Judaism to become experiential for every Jew, regardless of mental capacity, achieving this through reinventing the archaic texts of Halakhah to suit this generation. From here was conceived the idea of a Chief Rabbinate modelled off the pre-exilic Sanhedrin. This was the leading Jewish institution, which had jurisdiction over many aspects of a Jews life. It was also in their capacity to enact new laws. Kook sought to recreate this system, to establish a space where the reestablishment of Judaism - and Halakhah - could be enacted with genuine authority, as well as act as a precursor to the Messianic reality. Yet, the original Sanhedrin's authority came to an end in the 5th Century, and will only be reinstated by G-d Himself; "I will restore your magistrates as of old, and your counsellors as of yore," delegitimising Kook's Jewish redefinition and renaissance. This points to Kook's messianic outlook, and his desire to restore the redemption as stipulated by the prophets.

Many Ultra-Orthodox sects, specifically Haredi, interpret this to mean a fusion of the secular and the sacred, professing this as a negative innovation as it grants religious legitimacy to this illegitimate cause. Rabbi Arhon Feldman typifies this idea, "Religious Zionism must make an abject soul-reckoning… open its windows to spiritual leadership of *Gedolei Yisrael*… [or] to divorce itself from its disastrous marriage with secular Zionism."

However, Rav Kook's line of reasoning defines religious-Zionism on a superficial level. Their inherent goal is to bring religion into all levels of belief, including the level of non-religious Zionists.

Secular-Zionist: Cultural and Political

The most non-religious of the ideologies, secular-Zionists represent the nationalists of the Jewish world. Fundamentally, they support only the rational aspects of Judaism, and the features that help present Israel as a 'Jewish State.' Or as some put it, creating a State for Jews, as opposed to a State for Judaism.

From when Jews began leaving the Ghettos, and the Enlightenment movement began to take form, Jews became exposed to the secular world of intellect, providing a solid grounding - both in terms of popularity and ideology - for the 'new Jew.' With more exciting innovations, modern society presented a wealth of change to the face of the religious world.

Originally, Theodor Herzl envisioned a haven to protect Jews from the anti-Semitism they faced in Europe, while offering everything of the secular world. Being secular himself, Theodor Herzl had thought one simply had to assimilate to European culture in order to avoid anti-

Semitism. However, upon his arrival in France he was proven wrong. After witnessing the Dreyfus Affair, where an assimilated Jewish captain was framed for treason, Herzl discovered that a Jew is targeted for anti-Semitism, because of his/her intrinsic Jewish identity and not based on his external practices. In order to counter this anti-Semitism, he founded a place that the said *Jew* would be freed from this discrimination, and, still live a life of an accomplished European i.e. an assimilated Jew. In doing so, creating the same opportunities as the rest of the world, only without the pressure of anti-Semitic attitudes. This was Herzl's dream.

Herzl emphasised the political dimension of Zionism. Wanting to establish a safe society for *Jews*. Being ignorant in Jewish observance, he failed to notice a place for religion in the management of the State. So, a coexistence of law and religion wasn't part of the framework of political Zionism, at all.

Yet, in spite of the aforementioned claim, the Zionists are still keen on representing the face of Judaism to the world, or in the jargon 'Jewish character.' Meaning that, however secular they may be, Israel represented the image of Judaism on a global scale. It is for this reason that Israel strategically chose certain aspects of Judaism, mainly the rational, to retain.

But, 'the secular parties' quandary is how to fashion a modern liberal and tolerant State without losing its declared Jewish character." The ambiguity of their standing is so blaring, it challenges the validity of the whole school of thought. Is it a contemporary minded ideology, tolerant and liberal, or is it religious and steadfast?

There is another sect of secular-Zionism, known as cultural-Zionism, which focuses on the importance of the Jewish heritage, and the revival of the Jewish Culture, but still poses similar contradictions.

A main spear-header of the cultural-Zionist philosophy was Asher Zvi Hirsch Ginsberg, more commonly known as Ah'ad Ha'am. His theory was to remodel Judaism based on Jewish culture, but to "accommodate the regnant scientific perceptions," as Paul Mendes-Flohr put it.

One notion, which became fundamental in cultural-Zionism, and specifically for Ah'ad Ha'am, was the *ruach ha'am - spirit of the nation*. He was vehement that the *ruach ha'am* be preserved and anyone who violated it was "perhaps a perfectly good human, but a national Jew he is not." Clearly, this aligns with the basic idea that being a patriotic Israeli is crucial to a Jew's identity. An example of this is the idea that the national feature, Hebrew was a key part of the Israeli culture, "some even held that speaking Hebrew would place the Jew, no matter how assimilated." Essentially, this means that a person who fits into the Israeli culture, Jewish or not, holds the legal status of Jew.

Another such person who subscribed to this idea was poet Chaim Nachman Bialik; he believed that Jews must cling to their spiritual sensibilities, as well as, open their minds to other ways of life. As he expressed, "only when the tree begins to shed its old fruit, will it begin to bear new fruit." In other words, it will be fundamentally rooted in the Jewish traditions, but its actual ramifications will slightly differ.

One can see this play out in Zionism's relationship with the Bible. Considering it an intellectual text, secular-Zionists perceive the Bible as both a historical textbook as well as an outline to create a 'new Jew.' Through picking out key, national aspects of the Bible, such as the Hebrew Language, adapting and evolving it into Modern Hebrew, and the Jewish right to the land of Israel, they desanctify the text, diminishing it to a history book. As Yitzchak Conforti put it, "To him [Ben-Gurion], the Bible was a national text, not a religious one."

It could be suggested that the romantic concepts of spirit and culture appear to be a method to win the popularity of the masses. This was expressed by the Zionist politician Gershon Scholem, who bemoaned to a close friend Franz Rosenweig that the "Hebrew of the Yishuv have taken on the vulgarities of any other mundane vernacular" The unfortunate degradation of the Hebrew of the Old Yishuv, mirrors the corruption of traditional Judaism into nationalist, Zionist thought. In truth, it is a secular ideology with a Jewish name.

To sum it up, neither Aḥad Haʿam's "Jewish State" nor Herzl's "Jews' State" claims to be motivated by "religious" or theological considerations, and both visions are explicitly committed to what may be very crudely described as the (secular) tradition of the European Enlightenment, justifying it by claiming that due to a Jewish sovereignty, assimilation was no longer a threat. Hence, the function of religion - which they saw as protection against assimilation - becomes redundant.

Anti-Zionists

The anti-Zionist belief was a response to the rising ideas of modern, nationalistic views that threatened to ostracize many traditional orthodox Jews. Mainly, this group comprised the

Haredim of Eastern Europe, including the fifth Chabad Rebbe and other Hasidic leaders.

Relocating Jewish identity to the Middle East, without the guidance of traditional Jewish beliefs, posed a huge risk to the fundamentals of Judaism. Deriving from authentic sources (Talmud), coupled with the fear of potential consequences in establishing a Jewish state, these influential rabbis took a more stringent standing to ensure the endurance of religious Judaism, despite the strong winds of change.

Their fundamental source is the following Talmudic excerpt when the Jewish People took on three oaths:

1) the Jews should not ascend to Eretz Yisrael as a wall, i.e., en masse, whereas individuals may immigrate as they wish.

2) Jews that should not rebel against the rule of the nations of the world.

3) The nations of the world should not oppress the Jews excessively.

There were many leading rabbinical figures in the late 1800's who opposed the idea of Zionism, including the fifth Chabad Rebbe.

The most well-known subscribers to this ideology is a part of the Satmar *Hasidic* group, who named themselves Neturei Karta. Initially founded by Amram Blau, and being strong opponents to the State, they vehemently and sometimes violently claim all Zionists as heretics.

Neturei Karta saw these oaths as equally as binding as Halakhah. Perhaps this explains their adamant position that appears extreme to others. Others argue that because the nations of the world failed to respect their oath all the other oaths are invalid. But, Neturei Karta persists, nonetheless.

Ultimately, Neturei Karta's ideology boils down to four fundamental ideas:

1) **Divine Redemption and Human Passivity:** With regard to Israel and the idea of *aschalta de'geulah*, Jews have no right to initiate, or intervene on G-ds behalf, "here only G-d can act"

2) **Sequence of Redemption:** The key to ultimate redemption is through repenting, and making oneself spiritually fit for the arrival of the Messiah. It is not through practical means.

3) **Agents of Redemption can only be pious:** G-d will not bring the messiah through those who defy Him. Hence, "Zionists - who they claim to be heretical - and the State of Israel are, in effect, obstacles of the true redemption"

4) **The Messianic state a complete theocracy:** Jews can never be governed by a democracy. Rather, they must be ruled by G-d's law alone.

Based on the above, it can be extrapolated that, based on anti-Zionism, the State and religion cannot only not coexist, but the very state undermines the entirety of traditional Judaism. It contradicts the whole idea of ultimate redemption, a crucial part of Judaism. Anti-Zionists go so far as to say that the whole modern history of Israel, beginning with the end of the 19th century, is 'demonological' and it is forbidden to associate with anything that the Zionists were involved in. This prohibition extends to visiting the holy sites rescued by Israel. Notwithstanding the extremity, this is not the most outrageous of their views; being that Zionism was a product of the European enlightenment, the Neturei Karta hold the Zionists responsible for the atrocities of the Holocaust. This outlandish blame was not for the physical ramifications of the

Holocaust, but rather, their ideas and notions angered G-d so, it led to a severe punishment, which manifest itself in a Holocaust.

While their ideology may be completely legitimate, its manifestation, coupled with them being few in number - which requires more effort to be noticed - creates an extremism and a deep discord of the highest order.

Another form of anti-Zionism is represented by secular groups. Their idea of post-Zionism leads them to believe that Israel should be a democratic state like any other, devoid of Jewish character and identity. Here the two groups, of conflicting worlds, join forces against Israel.

Non-Zionists: Chabad

Non-Zionism is the common ideology among Ultra Orthodox Jews. For them, their main objective was to avoid rifts among the Jewish people, while still, unwaveringly maintaining their perspective on the matter. "From the *Ultra-Orthodox* point of view, the State is a religious neutral entity, part of the secular realm still belonging to the age of exile," Chabad remained opposed to Zionism's notion, but were not opposed to the Zionists themselves. They recognized that a Jew is a Jew and they have to be tolerated despite their differing views. Throughout this section I will focus on Chabad and their non-Zionist objective.

Unlike anti-Zionists, the seventh Chabad Rebbe, Rabbi Menachem Mendel Schneerson, does not demonstrate a vehemence against the attainment of the Land. It is recorded that the Rebbe refers to the UN vote of partition, in 1947, as a tremendous opportunity to observe the Torah and Mitzvot with autonomy. Perhaps he derived this from Maimonides interpretation, "the object of legislation in the ideal state is the perfection of the body and soul... [which] can only be achieved through the Divinely revealed law," portraying the Chabad view that a Jewish state is not essentially wrong, as perceived by anti-Zionists, but the State should be governed in accordance with Judaism. Upon the failure to form a fully religious autonomy the Lubavitcher Rebbe lamented, in a private audience, to Rabbi Chaim Gutnik, "In 1948 it was a time of opportunity. But Jewish leaders stood by and debated whether or not to make mention of G-ds name in the 'Declaration of Establishment.'" The Rebbe was inferring from here that the State has become nothing more than "gentile codes of living and gentile form of government... adopted by Jews... bringing *galut* into Tel Aviv and Jerusalem.... This is not the Zion we yearned for."

Further, in emphasis of the above, the Lubavitcher Rebbe made sure to only refer to Israel as Eretz Yisrael; the Holy Land, and not Medinat Yisrael; the Jewish State, claiming that a Jewish State can be in any location, whereas Eretz Yisrael is the physical Land promised to the Jews by G-d. For the Lubavitcher Rebbe, the Jews right to the land was Biblical, not based on political considerations.

An additional notion that Chabad was extremely against was the religious-Zionist *aschalta de'geula.* While the Lubavitcher Rebbe does say that the Messiah is imminent, he affirms that making *aliyah* will not bring the Messiah quicker, very much dissuading mass *aliyah.* Further, 15th century Spanish kabbalist Isaac de Leon explains, in Biblical Scripture it mentions the fact that, "you will dwell in it." The use of the affirmative 'will' as opposed to the request 'shall' depicts that the Jews will be returned to the Land and should not try to intervene.

Still, Chabad does not deny the many assets a Jewish State brings to the table. It acts as a place of refuge. Protecting Jews against foreign oppression, as well as absorbing holocaust survivors and refugees, allowing them settle and earn a living. Yet this position is in no way support of the Zionist, nationalist mindset. It is the simple recognition of the safe space Israel has created.

Moreover, Chabad was sure to emphasise that Jews must seek out that which unifies the Jewish people and not what sets them apart. This mentality is embodied in Rabbi Yoel Kahn's response to a disciple Rabbi Mendel Vechter when asked what the Chabad view is on Zionism. Kahn replied that Chassidic teachings explain that anything that happens comes from G-d, it is up to us to utilise It in the best way we can. Ideologically there is disagreements, but with a sovereign Zionist state in place, one should move away from that which sets us apart.

Hence, Chabad's gradual move from anti-Zionist to non-Zionist is not hypocritical. In ever changing times, modern day events elicit different reactions then that of the pre-state period. Now, Chabad has appreciated the beneficial aspects of the state, as well as focusing on the Zionists as individuals, not in the context of their ideology. Thus, without attempting to create a coexistence, non-Zionists managed to live in harmony with the modern State.

Democracy vs. Theocracy

This topic is one that has perplexed the State for some seventy years. At the birth of the State, the Supreme Court pronounced the values of the state as those of a "Jewish and Democratic State." Contradicting or complementary? Some have perceived this as intentional ambiguity, so as not to attack either camp. Or as Rabbi Yaron Catane coined, it's the "indecisive model."

In this section, I will go through some key areas of tension within the dispute between democracy and theocracy.

Israel's Character and Jewish Identity

The theme at issue here is the question of whether Israel is essentially Jewish or merely represents a Jewish character.

It appears as though the secular-Zionists have adopted their idea in order to appease the religious-Zionists, as well as sustain themselves against the Ultra-Orthodox opposition, irrespective of their true religious intent. Moreover, if they truly attest to a 'State for Jews,' then there is no basis for a Jewish character, as it is not about Judaism, rather another civilization that is made up of Jews. Perhaps the secular-Zionists designed this concept to present a coexistence between the modern State and religion on the surface due to their recognition of the Jewish face Israel presents to the world. Yet, as history has proven, religious influence in the State is not desired.

The foremost secular opinion, based on Ah'ad Ha'am cultural-Zionism, is that regarding the matter from a cultural perspective, they wish to see Israel having a national identity. This was what the President of the Supreme Court in Israel, Aaron Barak meant when he said that the Jewishness of the state is "its Jewish heritage, symbols, holidays, language, and other indicators." Note; *indicators,* inferring things that merely point to a Jewishness in a realm of nationalism, as opposed to intrinsic Jewishness. This is practically seen in the idea behind the Law of Return. Identifying the Jew as having a national right to the Land, due to their status as the people of the State, Jews can return to Israel on the basis of national identity. To emphasise, the Law of Return does not delineate that a Jew is someone who converted according to Jewish law, but merely one who converted, leaving the definition of conversion up to interpretation as to whether it is based on religious or national concept. For instance, religious-Zionist Rabbi Chaim Amsalem, held that if one is dedicated to the responsibilities of an Israeli, such as serving in the IDF, they should be accepted for conversion. Whereas, the Seventh Chabad Rebbe stressed that conversion is only that based on Jewish law.

Another Israeli value, that complements the previous point, is national unity. This is a major factor in the secular-Zionists reluctance to cause division between differing religious demographics. On the one hand, they don't want to upset the religious faction, yet they also don't want to impose religious, theocratic principles, which will upset the non-religious citizens. Therefore, the government balances the authority of the chief rabbinate, while emphasising democratic values. In other words, through recognizing the Jewish peoplehood they create a national identity in Israel. Practically this is presented through the, previously mentioned, law of return. In recognizing a Jews tie to his land, they present no religious character, but rather a national one.

Furthermore, as noted previously, secular-Zionists claim that essential Judaism is unnecessary. Due to Jewish majority in the State, there is far less of a risk of assimilation into other religions, as would be the case in the Diaspora. Hence, the redundancy of the strict laws protecting Jews against assimilation, such as conversion according to Halakha.

Non-Zionists strongly oppose this notion, claiming that they are just as much subject to these laws of conversion, if not more so. The Lubavitcher Rebbe held that a person who resided in the holy Land of Israel must be holy himself. Thus, strongly campaigning that Israel's character should be an essentially Jewish one.

Continuing, secular-Zionists claim that the State of Israel was intended to have a national identity, as opposed to a religious one: "...The Balfour Declaration promised a national home, not a religious one. On Israeli identity cards, "Jewish" describes a nationality (that is, not a religion)." To highlight this, one professor pointed out that, Aharon Barak, former President of the Supreme Court in Israel, made clear that the phrase 'Jewish State' should be understood at a high level of abstraction so that it can coincide with the democratic nature of the State. To which Joseph Raz responded that France could also be the said 'Jewish State.'

To reconcile the secular view with the religious, the government draws on Biblical debates and style to present a Jewish flair. This is noted in a couple of places. Ben-Gurion's response at the Peel Commission of 1973, in which he was said to have claimed that the Bible is the Jewish people's title deed and right to the Land, clearly depicts the secular approach to employ the Bible only where it is seen necessary. Another example of this is the implementation of Shabbat. According to Professor Yedidia Z. Stern, Shabbat took on social character, facilitating the need for the Hours of Work and Rest Law. So, it is not about the religious aspect, but it is drawn on Biblical concepts.

Novak disproves the sincere intent of a 'Jewish Character,' saying that it's "an association of like-minded individuals living in someone else's society." That is, Zionists have created another Western-liberal society with a different name.

In my opinion, by defining the State with this ambiguous definition, it misleads many people regarding their Jewish status. Hence, it would be better to identify as another democratic state, than present a 'Jewish Character' and jeopardise the Jewish people with illegitimate, national Jews.

Religious-Zionists hold a different position. Their main objective is to attain religious autonomy on a public level, wanting it to be seen as a 'Jewish State,' based on Halakhah. For example the prohibition against public transport on Shabbat, or raising pigs, which has been implemented. This is also Chabad's position on the Jewish identity of Israel.

However, religious-Zionism also assigns Israel with a national identity, one that integrates religion and State, as perceived through the establishment of the religious-Zionist *hesder yeshivot*. Perhaps derived from the notion of *chibbat ha'aretz* or Rav Kook's idea of "marrying Torah study to Zionism," these *yeshivot* were designed to be half a day of learning, and the other half of military service. Thus blending the two; religion and Zionism, into one force highlighting the religious-Zionists interpretation of a national identity.

But this is where non-Zionists differ, claiming their students of traditional, full-time *yeshivot* to be 'other-worldly soldiers.' As Meir Z. Maor defines, "the real striving that makes a difference in Israel's wars with the gentiles is that of the study of Torah," objecting to the identity which seeks to blend religion with the State.

In spite of this disagreement, Religious-Zionists also give Israel a spiritual, messianic identity, which, on some level, both Religious-Zionists and religious non-Zionists agree. This can be noted in the Religious-Zionist's reaction to the Six Day War, 1967, defining the expansion of Israel was Divinely ordained, and another milestone towards the Messiah's arrival.

Here both parties affirm that giving back these so-called 'occupied territories' is completely heretical. For the religious-Zionists, the expansion of Israel constitutes *aschalta d'geula,* and settling these areas was driven by *chibbat ha'aretz.* Therefore giving away land was a harsh as "committing the sin of profaning the Name of G-d.'" Similarly, to the Chabad Rebbe, Israel is G-d's capital, it is a holy land and cannot be given away at whim. To add, it is G-d who protects the land and its inhabitants, therefore no human endeavour will increase or diminish this security. Thus, to religious-Zionists the character of Israel is a spiritual one, yet to Chabad, the unbending fact is that Israel has a spiritual identity, an identity that they need not aspire for, but is continually there, which is beyond human definition.

The Balance between Halakhah and Democratic Values

"In order to correlate these two 'values,' one must decide which value is primary, and which value is secondary." As each camp has its own primary value, the other value is often undermined when there is opposing pressure.

Due to there being a religious minority, religion wields less power, so there is already an imbalance of Jewish and democratic values. In addition, the fact that the chief rabbinate is financed by the secular government means that the religious authority in Israel is under the auspices of the government and, consequently, answerable to the secular mindset.

Secular-Zionist's standing are clear, their essential goal is to govern a democratic state, and it is part of the concept of 'the will to be integrated.' To add, the prime issue that secular Jews have with religion, is the spirituality, and G-d given aspect of it. The fact that they lack the sensitivity to the spirituality of traditions, explains why they think religion is limited to the past and therefore, doesn't apply nowadays. In truth, in the original conception of the state and how it would run, it was never the plan to create a theocratic entity, as mentioned before. In essence, the secular-Zionists are more focused on the democratic values, proven in the fact that 89% of secular Jews will give precedence to democratic principles over Halakhah.

Nonetheless, in their idea of national unity, there is an attempt to align religious and secular thought. When laying out the legislation in 1958, Prime Minister David Ben-Gurion sent out letters to various different rabbis and religious leaders to hear their take on "Who is a Jew," seeking advice that would be "accepted by all religious and secular streams of Judaism." But once the strong religious opinions came to the fore, the legislators were less sympathetic to each, respective point of view and the law was formulated as inclusive as possible. Ultimately, the desire for a coexistence turned into a desire for a unilateral acceptance of the secular objective. On this premise, there is no balance between religion and democratic values.

An example of this is the terrible situation surrounding the Tehran children. These children were refugees from Eastern Europe who were sent to Tehran and later taken into

Israel. The secular-Zionists did everything in their power to try to rid these children of their Jewish past. Thereby integrating them into the secular Israeli society and reducing the potential opposition to a secular, democratic state.

The government also implemented many other laws to minimise the influence of religion in Israel. In 2010, a law was passed that one can by-pass the Chief Rabbinate, and in 2023 a bill is to be passed, transfering Kashrut licensing from the chief rabbinate to any private company. The above points to the secularists' utter undermining of halakhic values in the State.

Yet, within the religious-Zionist groups, there is a strong desire to create a coexistence. For instance, Rabbi Chaim David Halevi, chief rabbi of Tel Aviv, 1973-1998, claims that Israel is run on a "secular legislation that is based on Halakhah," inferring from here that Halakhah adapts to the current times and trends.

The religious-Zionist community hold a position that possibly contributes to the State of Israel undermining Halakhah. Perhaps, because religious-Zionists see secular-Zionism as the unconscious expression of the Divine spark of the Jewish soul, or because of the religious-Zionist and secular-Zionism shares similar goals to religious-Zionism - cultivating the land - it attempts to find a balance between the two aspects. One can venture to say that because religious-Zionists don't adamantly reject the secular notion of prioritising democratic principles over Jewish law, the secular sects are now at liberty to implement all kinds of acts that diminish the halakhic values of the State further.

On the other hand, while the secular government doesn't give the chief rabbinate much power, the religious-Zionists still think that they have a religious monopoly, which causes clashes in practical dealings. As Ben-Gurion stated "rabbis have no authority except what the state gives them." Plus, he mentions that religion is by no means a priority, emphasising that "according to the Declaration of Independence, the State is a democracy," and the many areas of Judaism, such as marriage, conversion, Shabbat and so on, gives the sense that they do have autonomous religious authority. This friction confuses the primary value of the State.

Therefore, religious authority in Israel attempts to find the balance between religious and secular values, while the secular government, who have ultimate authority in Israel, design a society in favour of democratic values.

Ultra-Orthodox groups take the position that Israel should be based solely on halakhic values, and religious-Zionists are causing the undermining of Halakhah. As represented in their response to national conversions; annulling negligible conversions carried out by the Zionist rabbis in their communities. This is the root of the rift between religious-Zionists and the non-Zionists; the view that religion and state are separated. The Ultra-Orthodox define the current position of the State, as functional and completely devoid of religious meaning, and not a place to meddle religious practices with political affairs. To this group, there can be no equal balance, it's all or nothing.

In spite of this, the one thing that all the groups have in common is their Jewishness. This, says Professor Yedidah Z. Stern, is the secret behind Israel's resilience, which can mobilise a majority to support national missions by virtue of Jewish solidarity, which is stronger than disagreements.

Conclusion

The consensus is that the two notions cannot coexist, and no group strives for a coexistence. While the secular-Zionists want to see a primarily secular, democratic state, the non-Zionists campaign for a Jewish, halakhic autonomy. As for anti-Zionists, the whole notion of Zionism is heretical, and religious-Zionists seek to utilise secular-Zionism to achieve their own ultimate goal of a religious, halakhic sovereignty. The only factor that rises beyond these conflicting beliefs is authentic, unchanged Judaism as it has lasted throughout the centuries. Being that Israel represents the Jewish image globally it is vital that it be presented correctly, based on traditional, authentic Judaism. Through recognizing that G-d has granted us the sacred gift of His Divine law and not being selective with the Bible, one can rise beyond the limited ideological thought and create an unequivocal Jewish State in line with His Will.

ABOUT THE WRITER

Chassia Pruss is eighteen years old. She is keen to pursue the truth about the deeper meaning of things and likes to read a variety of books on all different matters. Particularly interested in history, especially Jewish history, she enjoys understanding how it has affected current life. Her hope is to share this truth with those around her in the future.

Chapter Thirteen

How a Leader can Build Effective Leadership?

Leah Pruss

"Leadership is one of the most observed and least understood phenomena on earth," according to James MacGregor Burns. In this paper, I attempt to provide a guide for leaders to build effective leadership with their followers. First, I elaborate on the four characteristics Shlomo Ben-Hur and Karsten Jonsen bring in their treatment of Moses. Then, using his model, I explore the leadership of Moses, Rabbi M M Schneersohn and Winston Churchill. Based on my findings, I then propose a developed model of leadership.

Four Roles of a Leader

Ben-Hur and Jonsen present Moses' leadership as balancing the four characteristics: visionary, shepherd, servant and teacher. However, because an effective leader cannot be defined by a simple list of traits - as previously thought in the Trait Theory (1930's-1940's), but later dismissed by 1950, after a conclusive list had not been reached - I would like to preface my explanation with the 'three fundamental axioms about leadership' Goffee and Jones propose. These are: leadership is situational, nonhierarchical and relational.

As explored in the Situational and Contingency theories of leadership, theorised in the 1960s, where the leader must assess the situation and adapt their style to it, it is important for a leader to recognise the context of their leadership. This can apply in the broader context, the circumstances of their leadership role, influencing their vision and strategy, but it is also relevant on a smaller scale. Meaning, a leader must be able to assess any given situation - even daily interactions - and decide on which aspect (visionary, shepherd, servant or teacher) is the most suitable response.

Furthermore, contrary to common conception, leadership is nonhierarchical. While power, when shared, divides, influence multiplies. Therefore when operating through influence rather than authority, the organisation will grow far stronger. Rost views leadership as a relationship that has a multi-directional flow of influence, perhaps evident when the followers influence the leader's decisions and the leader influences the followers to action. The theory of Servant Leadership further challenges the conception of leadership equating a hierarchy, as will later be explored.

Most importantly, a leader needs to understand that leadership is a relationship that both leaders and followers actively engage in, as expressed by Joseph C. Rost (1993), thus distinguishing between a leader (the person) and leadership (the process). Therefore, these elements are not characteristics that equate effective leadership, but are rather tools for leaders to build an effective relationship with their followers.

Visionary

Simon Sinek theorised the Golden Circle of Leadership: All organisations operate through a concentric circle containing three parts, the outermost is 'what,' closer is 'how,' and the innermost is 'why.' He believes every company knows 'what' they do, their results. Most organisations know how they do that, the process, but very few know why they do it; what their purpose and belief is. Most commonly, people function from the outside-in, starting with 'what' and eventually reaching their 'why.' But inspired leaders need to think, act and communicate from the inside-out; they must 'start with why.'

This will inspire their followers to devote themselves entirely to the movement at all costs because they understand the purpose. Otherwise, the follower's loyalty might be contingent upon peripheral results or benefits and, as soon as those conditions are absent, they will disengage, weakening the movement. He emphasises the importance of the vision being something tangible, not just a superlative, so people can realistically identify with it. It is termed vision precisely because it must be possible to see. To cultivate a relevant vision, a leader must be able to blend their understanding of the past with the possibility of the future.

Shepherd

Another imperative to building a relationship with one's followers is creating a safe environment for them, one that

Sinek labels the 'Circle of Safety'. He believes it is the leader's "primary role…to look out for those inside their Circle." Once a leader exhibits authentic care for their followers, they will reciprocate, thus fortifying a strong bond of devotion between each other, so they needn't protect themselves from each other, but work together against external challenges. A leader should also maintain a profound awareness of their followers' needs and capabilities and lead them accordingly, ensuring the relationship remains compatible with their followers.

Servant

With all this, a leader must remain a servant as conceptualised by Greenleaf in his theory, Servant Leadership. In his essay, he writes:

"It begins with the natural feeling one wants to serve, to serve first. Then conscious choice brings one to aspire to lead. That person is sharply different from one who is leader first."

Interestingly, he theorises not that the leader must act as a servant, but that the person, by nature, is servant *first*. Not only should the leader be a servant to their followers, but also a steward for the vision of the organisation, their function being, to facilitate that vision. When the leader is servant first, it ensures the vision is for a mutual purpose. If the leader's motivation is for self-advancement, it will result in the corruption of power. In many cases, even if the leader has good intentions, once they are suddenly given access to so much power, they may become corrupted. Because of this, often, true leaders are reluctant to accept leadership, but their sense of duty, driven by courage, motivates them to do so.

Hence, their role in this relationship is, primarily, to serve others.

Teacher

The role of teacher is a pivotal aspect of leadership because it distinguishes a leader's role from that of a manager's. A manager holds an authority-relationship with their subordinates, establishes detailed steps to achieve a goal, and ensures it is achieved through controlling the situation. A leader, on the other hand, has an influence-relationship with their followers, establishes a vision and inspires their followers to overcome obstacles and achieve it. The manager situation produces results without bringing about drastic change to the organisation because the followers remain subordinates occupied with filling out their task. Rather than subjugating one's followers to control, in which the capabilities and contributions of the followers are subdued, a leader should teach them how to uphold the vision and achieve the objective on their own, empowering them to become leaders in their own right. With this in place, the vision of the movement will endure past the leader's term, indicating that the leadership has been effective since it hasn't crippled the followers to being dependent on their leader.

Using this model, I have investigated the leadership of Moses, Rabbi Menachem Mendel Schneersohn and Winston Churchill and how they each achieved these four components of visionary, shepherd, servant and teacher.

Moses

I have chosen to explore Moses because he is, arguably, the greatest Biblical leader. He took out the Israelites from slavery in Egypt to Mount Sinai, where they became a nation, a task requiring changing a state of mind, not only a location (from victimhood to freedom), and then led them through the desert for forty years, tending to them the entire time.

Before investigating his leadership, it is important to note, first, how he gained his leadership. There are four biblical stories preceding his leadership that help shed light on why G-d chose him to be the leader of the Jewish nation.

In the first three episodes, Moses is referred to as *'ish,'* the Hebrew word for 'man' as a result of his courageous behaviour. Interestingly, in *Pirkei Avot,* Ethics of the Fathers, Hillel declares, "In a place where there is no man *(ish)*, strive to be a man." Moses' description as 'man' is not a mere title but an illumination of the moral courage he possessed. A vital precedent to being a successful leader, is having the courage to act when it is required, regardless of other people's lack thereof.

However, courage independently is not sufficient. The Midrash describes how, once, while tending to his father-in-law's (Jethro) flock, one lamb ran away. Moses pursued the single lamb and found it drinking from a pool of water. Recognising its thirst and exhaustion, Moses picked up the lamb and carried it on his shoulder, back to the rest of the flock. With this activity, G-d saw Moses was genuinely empathic and only then bestowed the task of leadership upon him by the burning bush. One acting with courage alone, without taking the needs of their followers into account, may more accurately be described as a hero - defined in the Merriam-Webster dictionary as 'one who shows great courage' or 'admired for achievements and noble qualities' - but not a leader. Both elements, courage and empathy, are necessary.

Moses as Visionary

Moses received a mission from the L-rd at the burning bush - to redeem the Israelites from their slavery in Egypt and bring them to the Land of Israel. With moral courage, he confronted Pharaoh, a powerful king, despite his fears. Moses remained focused on this vision throughout his leadership, as depicted by the verse describing the end of his life: "his eyes were undimmed and his vigour unabated." Despite his demanding role, Moses remained strong in spirit because he kept sight of his goal. With this idealism, he was able to inspire an entire nation to follow him, wandering through the wilderness for forty years.

Moses as Shepherd

Moses, in recognition of epitomising empathy, is termed *Raaya Meheimna*, a faithful shepherd. As previously mentioned, a strong indication of Moses as Shepherd, was the episode of his care for the lamb in Midian, upon which G-d found it suitable to appoint him as leader. There are other such instances where Moses displays authentic concern for his followers, such as after the Israelites sinned with the Golden Calf, when G-d wanted to destroy the Israelites and start a new nation from Moses. However, Moses did not accept this resolution and declared, "if You forgive their sin [do not erase me] but if not, erase me now from Your book, which You have written." Moses possessed the moral courage to refuse the opportunity to have a nation stem from him, in favour of the survival of his followers, concerned not for himself, but for them. This episode exhibits the *Circle of Safety* Moses cultivated, giving his followers the confidence that he would protect them at all costs.

When asking G-d to appoint a successor, he requests: "L-rd…appoint someone over the community, who shall go out before them and come in before them, and who shall take them out and bring them in, so that the L-rd's community may not be like sheep that have no shepherd." The ostensible repetition indicates an important element of effective leadership. While a leader must be courageous in leading from the front, confronting the unknown, they cannot only 'go out,' but also 'take them out.' They should not mistake their role for a hero, leading too far in front, only to turn around and find no one is following them. While courage is essential, a leader must remain cognizant of their follower's condition and lead them according to their capacity.

Moses as Servant

Humble by nature, Moses did not pursue power, indicated by his reluctance to lead. At first objecting to his appointment, pleading with the L-rd to 'send [Your message] with whom You would [usually] send' and appoint someone else as leader. His humility is explicitly mentioned in the Bible: 'Moses himself was very humble, more so than any other human being on earth.' This underscores his nature to 'serve first,' only after rising to the role of leadership.

Furthermore, one of Moses' titles is *Eved Hashem,* a servant of the L-rd. After one of the greatest miracles in the Jewish history, the splitting of the Red Sea, the Israelites 'had faith in the L-rd and in Moses, His servant.' On his deathbed, Moses is again labelled with this term - 'Moses, the servant of the L-rd, died there.' Throughout all his activities, it was clear to his followers that he was not motivated by self-interest, but was acting as a steward for his mission.

Yet, the challenge arises when a leader's commitment to their vision is set against the loyalty to their followers. Tasked with bringing down the Tablets to the Israelites on Mount Sinai, Moses descended the mountain to find the Israelites dancing around the Golden Calf. In spite of his own distress, destroying 'Bible of Moses, My servant,' as well as betraying the mission of the L-rd, to whom 'the death of the righteous is as tragic to the Almighty as the day on which the Tablets were broken,' Moses courageously broke the Tablets. In so doing, he symbolised his defense of his followers above all else, even over the fulfilment of the L-rd's instruction, exhibiting his absolute loyalty to the relationship with his followers. Ultimately, he is praised for this courageous act as the entire Pentateuch ends with this episode:

'And for the mighty hand and great power Moses performed before all the eyes of Israel.'

Rashi, in his commentary on the verse, clarifies the event that Moses 'performed before all Israel' was the shattering of the Tablets.

This demonstrates the ultimate servitude of Moses and, when he courageously put aside himself and his mission for the sake of his followers, unabashedly - 'before the eyes of all Israel' - G-d praises him for having reached the ultimate level of an authentic leader.

Moses as Teacher

Moses is primarily referred to by Jews as, *Moshe Rabbeinu,* Moses our teacher. Forty days prior to his passing, he gathered the Israelites together, and 'began to expound this Law,' recounting all the commandments given to them at Mount Sinai and after. The entire book of Deuteronomy describes this act. His last role and legacy was as a teacher, ensuring the principles he transmitted would continue beyond his life. Although he physically did not enter the Land of Israel with his people, they carried his lessons with them emotionally. Yet he urged them not only to absorb these principles, but also to perpetuate the vision and be leaders as well, 'make known to your children and children's children: The day you stood before the L-rd [at Mount Sinai]'; 'Teach them to your children.' Thus transforming them from passive participants to actively preserving their relationship.

Rabbi Menachem Mendel Schneersohn: The Lubavitcher Rebbe

I have also chosen to investigate Rabbi M M Schneersohn's leadership of the Chabad-Lubavitch Hasidic Movement. Emerging from the Holocaust, he is viewed as a pioneer in introducing campaigns to counter the negative effects it had on Judaism. Yet, he also had a wider impact on society, awarded a Congressional Gold Medal in "recognition of his outstanding and enduring contributions toward world education, morality, and acts of charity." Margaret Thatcher assesses the "greatest quality of a person like that is fearless leadership."

The Lubavitcher Rebbe as Visionary

Rabbi M M Schneersohn held the Messianic aspect to be of primary importance, as expressed in the first Hasidic discourse he delivered during his inaugural address in 1951, entitled *Bati L'gani*, and believed that through outreach and encouraging Jews to return to orthodoxy, it would lead to the Messianic Redemption. Although this polarised the attitude of Orthodox Jewish communities towards Chabad, receiving public disapproval from figures such as Rabbi Yoel Teitelbaum (leader of the *Samar Hasidic* sect) and Rabbi Shach, the Lubavitcher Rebbe remained firm in his vision, displaying the courage necessary for a leader to defend their organisation's principles despite opposition.

Indeed, the Chabad-Lubavitch followers still devote themselves to Rabbi M M Schneersohn's mission until today. As Professor Elie Wiesel shared in a 2013 interview, "One of the greatest achievements of the *Rebbe* is the *Shluchim* [emissaries]...they are the carriers of his vision." These *shluchim,* (Hebrew for emissaries), were sent to many distant locations, such as France, Morocco, Vietnam and Thailand, to name only a few. They would engage in communal affairs regarding religious Judaism and general humanitarian aid. This may include synagogue services, building schools, hosting events and providing food. It often meant sacrificing their personal comforts, such as their preferred childrens' education and ease of access to *Kosher* food. Nonetheless, Chabad Hasidim still sacrificed these personal comforts for the sake of an ideal engraved into them by Rabbi M M Schneersohn.

For many Hasidim, the potency of his vision did not end with his term. After his passing (11th June 1994), despite the tremendous loss and mourning felt by the movement, it did not hinder their growth. While, during his lifetime, 1181 families moved as emissaries to different locations, after his passing, this number multiplied to 4203 new emissaries, as recorded in the roll call of the International Conference of Emissaries, 2021. Some regard this as the greatest proof that Rabbi M M Schneersohn was successful in communicating his vision.

Another aspect of his vision laid out at his inaugural address in 1951 was: "Here in America, it's customary to begin with a statement…My father-in-law, the [*Frierdiker*] *Rebbe* [the sixth Lubavitcher Rebbe, Rabbi Joseph Isaac Schneersohn], said that there are three things: love of G-d, love of *Torah* [Bible] and love of every Jew, and all three are one." Through continually communicating this objective to his followers, he ensured they would adopt it as their own, evidenced when the Hasidim viewed his second stroke in March 1992, as a time for intensification of his vision - love of G-d and love of one's fellow- even though it was a time of crisis for them.

The Lubavitcher Rebbe as Shepherd

In many instances, Rabbi M M Schneersohn displayed deep care and concern for his followers. Primarily seen in the private audiences he held with his followers, known as *Yehidot*, or the letters he sent in response to individuals - now published in over 30 volumes, called *Igrot Kodesh* - where he would offer individual advice and encouragement to people. After a decline in his health, when he was unable to continue holding private audiences in the traditional way and answering the many letters, he instituted Sunday Dollars as a method to continue interacting with his followers. This began in 1986, where his followers would queue up outside 770 Eastern Parkway, Crown Heights, Brooklyn - referred to as Chabad-Lubavitch's headquarters for in it contained a synagogue and the Lubavitcher Rebbe's office - and wait to receive a dollar from the Lubavitcher Rebbe, meant to encourage the giving of charity. Many used this opportunity to exchange a few words with him, such as sharing their problems and asking for advice to which he would offer support in return. Every Sunday, approximately five thousand men, women and children would pass by him, and Rabbi M M Schneersohn would stand, for sometimes seven hours straight, about which, many followers considered exhibited his authentic concern for each of them. From commenting to a man recently released from jail that it is time to forget his bondage just as the Jews forgot their Egyptian bondage, to Senator Joe Lieberman's daughter, Rebecca, who had feminist leanings: "Very often a daughter can do more to carry out a parent's ideals than a son can." This strengthened the impact of his leadership since, as Israeli scholar Adin Steinsaltz proposes, one of Rabbi M M Schneersohn's leadership strategies was to begin by allowing his followers to forge an emotional bond with him, which would develop into their adherence to his ideology.

The Lubavitcher Rebbe as Servant

Many of the Lubavitcher Rebbe's followers maintained that his activism was in service of others, proven in his reluctance to accept the leadership, clearly not seeking power. Rabbi M M Schneersohn adamantly opposed any suggestion of his candidacy following Rabbi Joseph Isaac Schneersohn's (Sixth *Rebbe* of the Chabad-Lubavitch movement) passing. For example, in response to Rabbi Yitzchak Dubov's request, on 31st January 1950 (three days after Rabbi Joseph Isaac's passing), that he accept the leadership of the Chabad-Lubavitch movement, Rabbi M M Schneersohn responded, "What are you thinking? That Mendel Schneersohn is a *Rebbe*?" Despite his initial rejection, Rabbi M M Schneersohn ultimately accepted the position as the Lubavitcher Rebbe on January 17th 1951, since, as he commented in an interview with Reform Rabbi, Herbert Weiner, "It is always pleasant to run away from responsibility, but what if one's running might destroy the congregation?" demonstrating his courage in taking action despite his discomfort.

Another element which presents Rabbi M M Schneersohn's attitude as servant, was the immense quantity of mail he received on a daily basis. Although there is no record of an exact amount, Rabbi Leibel Groner (one of the Lubavitcher Rebbe's secretaries) estimated it to number 250 to 300 letters daily. However, despite his followers' desire to ease his load through purchasing an automated letter opener, The Lubavitcher Rebbe objected to its use, claiming, 'A machine does not feel what is in the soul of a person.' Not only did the Lubavitcher Rebbe insist on hand opening every article of mail addressed to him, when suggested to use a rubber stamp to sign routine letters, such as well wishes on the occasions of weddings, birthdays and other such occasions, he outright refused the idea; "How can I send prayerful wishes to someone in such an artificial manner, and how would anyone feel, receiving from his *Rebbe* good wishes in a letter that is signed with a rubber stamp?" This expression of devotion stimulated his followers to reciprocate with their own commitment to his movement.

For his followers, his servant leadership was summed up by Rebbetzin Chaya Mushka's (Rabbi M M Schneersohn's wife) testimony during the legal case pertaining to the incident where valuable archive books began to go missing from the Chabad-Lubavitch library. On the last day of the trial, in December 1985, Judge Sifton viewed her deposition. In it, she stated: "The books belong to the Hasidim because my father [Rabbi Joseph Isaac] belonged to the Hasidim." With Rabbi M M Schneersohn's utter dedication and subscription to his father-in-law and predecessor, Rabbi Joseph Isaac Schneersohn in mind, many of Rabbi M M Schneersohn's followers felt he adopted a similar model of leadership and so would act in accordance with this statement. They viewed it as indicating Rabbi M M Schneersohn's belief that his leadership role required him to belong to his followers rather than his followers belonging to him. This nurtured the movement's trust that he contained moral courage, leading them in their best interest rather than vice versa, fortifying the effectiveness of his leadership.

The Rebbe as Teacher

Again, we look to his inaugural speech to investigate Rabbi Menachem Mendel Schneersohn's leadership style. During his address, he declared: "The *Rebbes* of Chabad demanded that their Hasidim take personal action - not to rely on the *Rebbe*…it's in your hands alone." Rather than binding his followers to be codependent on him, many felt he taught them to actualise their own potential, transforming each one into a leader, as Rabbi Lord Jonathan Sacks observed.

An incident which some feel typifies his role as an empowering teacher occurred in a private audience with

Yehuda Avner, former ambassador of the State of Israel to Britain, in 1977. Avner remarked how the Lubavitcher Rebbe does not recognise the powers others recognise in him. Rabbi M M Schneersohn turned serious and responded by explaining what he attempts to do - to ignite people's souls, like a flame to a candle. As he was about to exit the room, Yehuda Avner asked, "Has the *Rebbe* lit my candle?"

"No," replied Rabbi M M Schneersohn, "I have given you the match. Only you can light your own candle."

Rabbi M M Schneersohn, as a true teacher, did not complete the task for his followers. Rather, many Hasidim felt he equipped them with the skills, through his many teachings now published in hundreds of volumes, but they ultimately had to achieve it themselves.

Although past his lifetime, many followers still identify strongly with the Chabad-Lubavitch movement, as Israeli scholar, Adin Steinsaltz notes, "The *Rebbe* did not leave a legacy, he left marching orders." The fact that the Chabad-Lubavitch organisation has grown exponentially since its leader's passing, is tribute to the success of his leadership.

Winston Churchill

Finally, I will explore Winston Churchill. He is viewed as a leader who held a vision formed by knowledge of past and present to anticipate the future, and who contained moral courage to implement that vision in the face of adversity. Despite personal and political cost, he acted upon principle, not popularity.

Churchill as Visionary

Following the First World War, in the early to mid-1930's, pacifism and disarmament reached its peak in Britain. This was reflected in the Oxford Union vote (February 9, 1933), the result being 275 to 153, to pass the resolution "that this House will in no circumstance fight for King and Country." Despite the country's strong anti-war sentiment, Churchill, using knowledge of past and present (having read Mein Kampf), foresaw the looming threat of Hitler's rise to power and future conflict as early as 1931, before Hitler even came to power. He continually attempted to warn the nation of the impending disaster, and while Germany was swiftly re-arming, he begged Parliament to build up Britain's military strength. In a speech presented in the House of Commons on 8 March 1934, Churchill warned: "Germany is… rapidly arming…we must act in accordance with the new situation."

However, of over six hundred Members of the House of Commons, only five members supported him. He was fighting the opposition party, his own party members and leaders. Many came out harshly against Churchill. Most often, he spoke to 'empty seats, dozing MPs, and disapproving frowns…he was largely ignored.' Still more, he was ridiculed and mocked by many, labelled by Lord Maugham as an 'agitator' who should be 'shot or hanged.' Despite the lack of interest and antagonism, Churchill had courage in adhering steadfastly to his principles, despite these setbacks.

He clearly communicated his vision, 'in one word: It is victory, victory at all costs.' Churchill remained unbending in maintaining this vision and communicating it to others even in the most dire situations. From when David Lloyd George (Churchill's close personal friend and the victorious prime minister of World War One) refused to accept a cabinet position, since he believed Britain's stand to be hopeless; to 16 June 1940, which brought a French surrender to Germany, a little over a month after he gained office. Britain was facing Germany alone, without allies. When Lord Halifax, among others, wanted to open negotiations with Hitler, Churchill categorically refused, even threatening the stability of the national unity he had formed. The commitment displayed, through making sacrifices for his ideals, strengthened his leadership since, once the British people accepted his ideology, they felt they could trust him in delivering without compromising in the face of opposition.

Churchill as Shepherd

He also acted as the shepherd, an empathizer, treating each loss as his own. Rather than leave London during the bombings and find safety, he attempted to develop a relationship with the public and visited many damaged sites, as a close advisor to Churchill, Major-General Hastings Ismay, recounted: 'Churchill lost no opportunity of visiting the stricken areas…as Churchill got out of his car they literally mobbed him…Churchill broke down…I heard an old woman say, "You see, he really cares; he's crying."' The British victims felt Churchill truly valued them, causing them to value his leadership in return.

Churchill as Servant

In his famous accession speech, delivered on 13 May, 1940, in front of the House of Commons, Winston Churchill uttered the unforgettable words: "I have nothing to offer but blood, toil, tears and sweat," portraying absolute Servant Leadership.

At a time where the overwhelming majority were unwilling to adopt his vision, he declared himself to be a Servant Leader. Perhaps through impressing upon the British people that he contained the moral courage to serve them, and was not concerned for himself, he succeeded in convincing them to enter into the relationship of his leadership.

Indeed, he was not concerned about himself, jeopardising his position in Parliament as representative of Epping, as a result of his stand. He even went so far as to sacrifice his personal situation, placing the nation before himself. Even though he was under financial strain and was forced to place his family home in Chartwell for sale, he refused a speaking tour offer in the United States, which would have greatly relieved his economic burden since he felt bound to stay in Britain as the crisis was deepening. With loyalty and courage, Winston Churchill risked his political career, popularity and personal situation in order to stand by his principles for the best interests of the British nation. With these acts, he was able to secure the support of his followers so they could work together in achieving their mutual purpose.

Churchill as Teacher

Nevertheless, Churchill was well aware of the difficult reality the British people faced. Therefore, he empowered them through his oratory, from his cabinet ministers - as Leo Amery noted, "No-one ever left his cabinet meetings without feeling himself a braver man,"- to the front line soldiers, as one recalled, "all of us were scared and dazed…Then he got on the wireless and said we'd fight…that we'd never surrender. I cried when I heard him…WE'RE GOING TO WIN!" He equipped the British nation to rise above themselves and continue the fight for the greater good.

Most importantly, "Churchill was putting into words what the majority of us instinctively assumed - that, being British, we could not be defeated." Rather than imposing his principles on his followers, he taught them to see what they thought impossible, to be possible.

Conclusion - My Leadership Model

Based on my investigation of these three leaders, Moses, Rabbi M M Schneersohn and Winston Churchill, I have identified a primary characteristic that is necessary for leaders to build effective leadership. In addition to the four elements of visionary, shepherd, servant and teacher, there is another component required of the leader: courage. With courage, a leader is able to confront external and internal challenges, in order to defend their vision in the face of adversity; make sacrifices out of care for their followers; overcome their egoism to serve others; and allow their followers to be leaders without feeling threatened. In Robert W. Terry's view (1993), 'courage ignites leadership.' Possibly, all other leadership characteristics fail to matter in the absence of the quality of courage, as Aristotle asserts. Thus, I extend Ben-Hur and Jonsen's model to include the quality of courage at its core. Essentially, courage is the component vital for the implementation of the aforementioned four qualities.

But, first, it is necessary to define courage. Rather than being the absence of fear, which would more accurately be termed fearlessness, courage is taking action *despite* the presence of fears. It is further defined, by Kidder, to be the 'bridge between talking ethics and doing ethics.' According to Breeding, courageous leadership is 'about serving others and not about concern for oneself,' iterating the concept of Servant Leadership.

However, it is important to note that courageous leadership does not mean blind adherence to an initial path, regardless of all circumstances, which may be the less complex option. Instead, a courageous leader, while still having strong beliefs, must have an acute understanding of their situation and be able to adapt to meet the changing needs. Through this, the leader will remain relevant to their followers, cultivating an effective leadership.

As Ben-Hur and Jonsen put it, a leader should strive to have their head facing up, open to the future, as a visionary, while their feet are rooted firmly on the ground with their flock, as a shepherd. Simultaneously, combining the roles of teacher and servant. Graphically illustrated with visionary and shepherd on the y-axis, and teacher and servant along the x-axis. I propose to develop this model to include courage at the centre, with 'relationship' overarching the graph, since an effective leader cannot be defined by a mere list of traits. Rather, this is intended as a guide for leaders on how to build an effective relationship with their followers.

Appendix 1. Moses's Leadership: Managing Creative Tensions

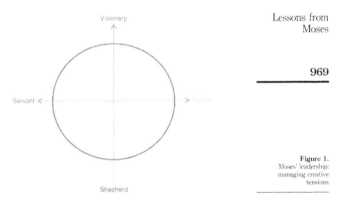

Lessons from
Moses

969

Figure 1.
Moses' leadership:
managing creative
tensions

Source: Shlomo Ben-Hur and Karsten Jonsen, 'Ethical Leadership: Lessons from Moses', *Journal of Management Development* (2012), vol. 31, no. 9, pp. 962-973, see p. 969

Appendix 2. My Guide for Leaders on How to Build Effective Leadership

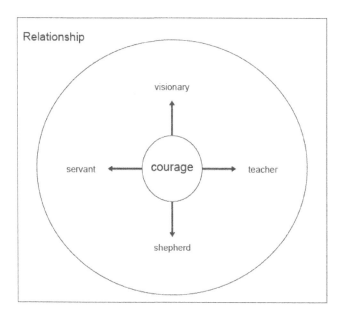

ABOUT THE WRITER

Leah Pruss is sixteen years old and has dedicated her EPQ to her father. He was an individual who interacted and related to a wide range of people, thus leaving Leah with the desire to uncover the key to effective leadership, such he possessed. As his daughter, Leah also enjoys influencing other people for the better and hopes that through this project, more people will be inspired to have a positive effect on their personal circles of influence.

CHAPTER FOURTEEN

WHAT WILL LIFE BE LIKE IN THE MESSIANIC ERA?

Draizy Raskin

I am investigating what life will be like in the Messianic Era, analysing the Halachic, Aggadic, and Chabad Chassidic dimensions of this time. I am going to look at Maimonides's twelfth Principle of Faith, where he discusses how central the Messiah is to a Jew's faith and defines the Messianic Era. Then, I will bring Biblical passages prophesying about the Redemption and Messianic Era; the explanations that the Midrash and Talmud give on them, followed by Chabad Chassidic texts' perspective of understanding Maimonides, the prophecies and the Aggadah.

I am not investigating who the Messiah is, when he will come and the stages before his arrival, or how to hasten the Messiah's arrival, because I feel these topics are explored in other works at length, such as Dr Naftali Loewenthal's book *'Hasidism Beyond Modernity'* (London: The Littman Library of Jewish Civilisation, 2020), in chapters 9 and 11, which discuss various aspects of ideas about the Messiah, but not what life will be like in the time of the Messiah.

The sources I will use are Maimonides' book *'Commentary on the Mishnah;'* the Babylonian Talmud, specifically Chapter Eleven of Sanhedrin as it speaks a lot about the Messiah; various Midrashim; Rabbi Shneur Zalman of Liadi's book *'Tanya;'* talks of Rabbi Menachem Mendel Schneerson of Lubavitch, as recorded in *'Likutei Sichot,'* *'Torah Menachem'* and *'Sichot Kodesh'* and first-hand interviews. I used Rafael Patai's book *'The Messiah Texts'* to access many of the Midrashim, the websites sefaria.org and chabad.org for much of the Talmudical and Biblical references and translations, Rabbi Menachem Brod's book *'Yemot HaMashiach'* for references to Chassidic ideas and I used copies of the individual Chassidic works in the full original text.

Twelfth Principle of Faith

Maimonides' twelfth Principle of Faith is about the Messianic Era. He says:

> *"We are to believe as a fact that the Messiah will come and not consider him late. If he delays, wait for him; set no time limit for his coming. One must not make conjectures based on Scripture to conclude when the Messiah will come... The Messiah will have more honour than all the kings who ever lived... The King of Israel must come only from the house of David and the seed of Solomon. Anyone who rejects this family denies G-d and the words of His prophets."*

Before discussing the Messianic Era, the term 'Messiah' must be defined.

The Hebrew word for the Messiah, 'Moshiach,' literally translates as 'anointed one.' He is the one who is anointed to bring the redemption of the Jews from exile. It is the generally accepted Jewish view that the Messiah will be a human of flesh and blood, descending from the tribe of Judah, through the royal line from King David. He must be a man who is more than the average man - he must have the spirit of G-d resting on him, the spirit of wisdom and understanding, and the spirit of knowledge and of the fear of the L-rd. He must also delight in the fear of G-d, which is explained as the ability to sense what is true and rule on that basis. The Messiah will have G-dly qualities, as signified by G-d giving him His crown and the royal purple garments.

Haftarah of the Last Day of Passover

Isaiah describes many aspects of the Messianic Era:

He starts by describing the Messiah as coming from King David, son of Jesse, and he will be a righteous, holy, and fair man:

> *''And a shoot shall spring forth from the stem of Jesse, and a twig shall sprout from his roots. And the spirit of the L-rd shall rest upon him, a spirit of wisdom and understanding, a spirit of counsel and heroism, a spirit of knowledge and fear of the L-rd. And he shall be animated by the fear of the L-rd, and neither with the sight of his eyes shall he judge, nor with the hearing of his ears shall he chastise. And he shall judge the poor justly, and he shall chastise with equity the humble of the earth, and he shall smite the*

earth with the rod of his mouth and with the breath of his lips he shall put the wicked to death. And righteousness shall be the girdle of his loins, and faith the girdle of his loins."

He then describes the peace between species of creations:

"And a wolf shall live with a lamb, and a leopard shall lie with a kid; and a calf and a lion cub and a fatling [shall lie] together, and a small child shall lead them. And a cow and a bear shall graze together, their children shall lie; and a lion, like cattle, shall eat straw. And an infant shall play over the hole of an old snake and over the eyeball of an adder, a weaned child shall stretch forth his hand. They shall neither harm nor destroy on all My holy mount..."

The reason for this peace will be the recognition of the L-rd as G-d:

"...for the land shall be full of knowledge of the L-rd as water covers the seabed."

The nations of the world will respect and honour him, not only the Jews whom he came to redeem:

"And it shall come to pass on that day, that the root of Jesse, which stands as a banner for peoples, to him shall the nations inquire, and his peace shall be [with] honour."

G-d will also gather all the Jews from their exiles in all the corners of the earth to come home to their Land of Israel:

"And it shall come to pass that on that day, the L-rd shall continue to apply His hand a second time to acquire the rest of His people, that will remain from Assyria and from Egypt and from Pathros and from

> *Cush and from Elam and from Sumeria and from*
> *Hamath and from the islands of the sea. And He shall*
> *raise a banner to the nations, and He shall gather the*
> *lost of Israel, and the scattered ones of Judah He shall*
> *gather from the four corners of the earth.''*

There will be unity between the Jews as they get rid of their enemies:

> *''And the envy of Ephraim shall cease, and the*
> *adversaries of Judah shall be cut off; Ephraim shall*
> *not envy Judah, nor shall Judah vex Ephraim. And*
> *they shall fly of one accord against the Philistines in*
> *the west, together they shall plunder the children of*
> *the East; upon Edom and Moab shall they stretch*
> *forth their hand, and the children of Ammon shall*
> *obey them.''*

G-d will make it the routes easier to travel for the Jews returning from exile:

> *''And the L-rd shall dry up the tongue of the*
> *Egyptian Sea, and He shall lift His hand over the river*
> *with the strength of His wind, and He shall beat it into*
> *seven streams, and He shall lead [the exiles] with*
> *shoes. And there shall be a highway for the remnant*
> *of His people who remain from Assyria, as there was*
> *for Israel on the day they went up from the land of*
> *Egypt.''*

When the Jews are gathered in the Land of Israel, in this peaceful time, they will praise G-d and thank Him for redeeming them:

> *''And you shall say on that day, 'I will thank You, O L-*
> *rd, for You were wroth with me; may Your wrath turn away*
> *and may You comfort me. Here is the G-d of my salvation, I*

shall trust and not fear; for the strength and praise of the Eternal the L-rd was my salvation.' And you shall draw water with joy from the fountains of salvation. And you shall say on that day, 'Thank the L-rd, call in His Name, publicise His deeds among the peoples; keep it in remembrance, for His Name is exalted. Sing to the L-rd for He has performed mighty deeds; this is known throughout the land. Sing to the L-rd for He has performed mighty deeds; this is known throughout the land.' ''

Halachic Dimension - Maimonides

Maimonides set out the criteria for the Messianic Era. Although there are many miracles described in the prophecies of the later prophets and the sages of the Mishnah and Talmud, Maimonides holds that from the perspective of Jewish Law, none of them need to occur literally, and can be fulfilled metaphorically. This is in line with what the sages taught:

''The only difference between this world and the days of the Messiah is that the oppression by the other kingdoms will be abolished.''

    i.   Messiah will reveal himself

    ii.   Messiah will re-establish the monarchy of the Davidic dynasty

    iii.   Messiah will build the Holy Temple

    iv.   Messiah will gather the Jewish exiles

    v.   Messiah will clarify everyone's lineage and tribe

    vi.   All Commandments will then be able to be performed

    vii.   This is not necessarily the final Messiah. This Messiah - or his descendant - will deliver Israel from its enemies.

This may sound relatively simple, but even this, without all the miracles changing nature, is an extraordinary life, different from any time in history or the present.

Following these criteria, the Jews will all be in Israel, instead of scattered all over the world. Each Jew will know their exact lineage and live in their tribe's allotments. Everyone will know who their family is, even if they had never known of their family before.

The government will be a fully religious body, staffed with Torah scholars and led by the righteous King Messiah, who will be working to fulfil G-d's commands, instead of his own agenda.

The centre of all Jewish life will be the Holy Temple, serving as the central place of worship, and the centre of Jewish Law, due to the Sanhedrin being situated there. Jews will all stream to Jerusalem three times a year, for the festivals of Passover, Shavuot and Sukkot, with their families and many sacrifices. Practically, imagine the traffic jams at the major intersections across Israel as the Jews drive to Jerusalem for the pilgrimages, which turn into dance fests from the joy of the upcoming festival and the joy of being with so many other Jews. There will be many herds of animals coming in to serve as sacrifices in the Temple, decorated to celebrate their honour and sanctity. The whole country will smell aromatic as the incense burns.

All the commandments and laws regarding agriculture will resume. The whole land - all the farms, fields, vineyards and orchards - will have to rest every seven years, during the Shemitah year, as part of the Shemitah cycle. This will allow the farmers a whole year to focus on studying Torah, rather than working the land.

The year after every Shemitah will be a 'Hakhel,' where every single Jew - men, women, children, the sick, the blind, the mute, the pregnant, the nursing women, and the proselyte living amongst them - will gather in the Holy Temple to hear the king read from the Torah, to inspire them to fear G-d. Even the largest stadium in the world at the time of writing - the Rungrado 1st of May Stadium in Pyongyang, North Korea, with a capacity of 150,000 - will not be big enough to contain the entire Jewish population of over 15 million people.

Aggadic Dimension - Talmud and Midrash

Within the Messianic Era, there seems to be two stages. The first stage will be that all the criteria for being able to do all the commandments will fall into place - the Messiah revealing himself, the Holy Temple being built and the Jews gathering - without nature changing in any way. This is the lifestyle I briefly described above in the Halachic dimension. This stage will be necessary to show that all commandments can be done, and life can be lived, in this world, the way G-d wants, without extreme miracles. Through the application of the teachings of the Messiah, this will morph into a time in which all the prophecies will be fulfilled in a more literal sense than that Maimonides holds in his introduction to Chapter Eleven of Sanhedrin, in his Commentary on the Mishnah. This includes, but is not limited to, Isaiah's prophecies in the passage above.

The Midrashim and commentaries elaborate on the various verses about the ingathering of exiles in the first stage:

The Midrash says that the Jews were exiled due to their sins, yet they are still promised to be redeemed.

G-d said He will gather the Jews ''even if your exiles are at the end of the heavens.'' The commentators interpret these words differently, showing the scope and totality of the Jews that will be gathered.

Rabbi Yoseph Karo (c.1475 - c.1535) explains even the lost Ten Tribes who are so lost in exile that it is not even known where or who they are nowadays. Rabbi Meir Leibush ben Yehiel Michel Weisser (1809-1879) writes that even a person who is so distant from G-d, that there is no further away to go, even these people, G-d will gather them, not in a way of judgement, but in a way of taking them each lovingly, individually, Nachmanides (1194 -1270) understands it allegorically to mean that even the being most distant from G-d, namely, the Evil Inclination, will be brought over to G-d's side, the side of goodness and holiness, so that it will no longer be evil and people will no longer have to choose between good and bad.

The day of the ingathering of exiles will be as great as the day of the Giving of the Torah. Procession coming into the Land of Israel will be a massive ceremony: The Shechinah will come at the head, then the nations of the world, the prophets at the sides of the nations of the world, the Ark and the Torah with the prophets, and lasts, after all these forerunners, the nation of Israel returning home, radiating honour and splendour from one end of the world to the other. All the other nations will become weakened upon seeing this, to the extent that no warrior will be capable of holding a weapon. All weapons and idols will be destroyed and thrown away. All this is to ''remove impurity from the world'' so that G-d can finally rule the world completely from one end to the other.

G-d will make it the routes easier to travel for the Jews returning from exile.

In addition to Isaiah's prophetic passage above, he prophecies to the Jews, that G-d will make the roads as pleasant as possible to travel over - raising rivers to make them easy to cross, and making highways for smoother walking, and the travellers will never be hungry or thirsty or be bothered by the heat, as G-d will direct them along routes that have water. They will not even have to walk, as the winds will carry them.

In the second stage, the Jews will eat and enjoy the tremendous physical bounty of the Messianic Era. The Jerusalem Talmud says that produce will ripen much faster then. In this world, crops take around six months to ripen, and trees take around twelve months. In the Future to Come, the produce will ripen much faster: it will take even a twelfth of the time (fifteen days for crops and one month for trees).

Although the crops will grow fast, it will not cause additional work to harvest - the wheat will shoot up like a date palm and be higher than the peaks of the mountains, yet it will be reaped by G-d: He will bring a wind to harvest. This wind will induce the flour to fall from the stalks of wheat, and a person will go out to the field and bring back a palmful of flour, from which he will provide his livelihood and the livelihood of the members of his household.

The Book of Elijah writes that what nowadays yields 1 *kor* (a Hebrew measurement equivalent to about 230 litres) of produce - be it wheat, wine or oil - will yield 900 kors (207000 litres) in the future! Moreover, each tree will be loaded with fruits and delicacies, even trees that were not fruit-bearing trees until then.

As tall as the wheat stalks will be, the kernels themselves will also be huge - each as big as the two kidneys of a large ox. The grapes will be so giant, that only one grape will fit in each wagon. With this one grape, one will be able to fill at least thirty full jugs of wine, each a Se'ah (six litres, totalling 180 litres of wine from one grape), and light a fire from the wood of this grape.

The grape harvest will be so plentiful, that every grapevine you have in the Land of Israel, requires a foal to carry the load of its harvest. Every barren tree you have in the Land of Israel will produce sufficient fruit in the future to load upon two donkeys. This wine will be flavourful, red wine that will inebriate those who drink it. It will be good for both the young and old.

The Talmud depicts further ways the world will be different in the Messianic Era: People will be two hundred cubits tall (300 feet), the equivalent of twice the height of Adam, the first man, who was one hundred cubits tall (150 feet). The third and final treasure buried by Joseph in Egypt that he accumulated from the sales of grains in the years of famine will be revealed. (The location of one was revealed to Korah, the other to Antoninus, son of Asveirus, emperor of Rome, and one is for the righteous in the Messianic Era.)

Rabbi Gamliel taught that in the future, a woman will give birth every day, spared from the nine-month journey of painful pregnancy; trees will produce fruit every day and the Land of Israel will produce ready-made cakes and garments of fine wool.

Isaiah prophesies a world wherein G-d will give forth (new) teachings emanating from Jerusalem to the whole world and all the nations in it. The Midrash teaches that the Torah that a person studies in this world, in physical exile, is vanity relative to the Torah of the Messiah.

G-d and His Torah are eternal and will not change, so although there will not be another Torah, there will be a revelation of the hidden secrets of the Torah, giving a new understanding and perspective on it, hinted to as the blank spaces between words that will be revealed to contain meaning and messages given with the rest of the Torah on Sinai but are not currently visible.

Midrash Talpiyot points out that this will be important then, as the practical application of some commandments will no longer apply, such as those of punishments for sinning, because no one will sin.

He continues, saying, the reason this new understanding of the Torah can come is that since the sin of the Tree of Knowledge, the letters in the Torah are bound into specific patterns, forming specific words and commands, whereas the letters were in a random, unspecified order before then. In the Future, the Torah will return to its original, unlimited state, with the possibility to form other words.

Rabbi Avraham Azulai (1570–1643) says that the world then will not be characterised by its bodily aspect, so people will no longer be bound to the physical body, and therefore the Torah itself will divest itself of its bodily aspect so that the hidden will be revealed, and the righteous will understand the hidden combinations and will become more adept in the Mysteries of Torah. But the Torah itself is the same for all of eternity and will not, G-d forbid, ever change.

Isaiah prophesied:

''for the land shall be full of knowledge of the L-rd as water covers the seabed:''

The Yemenite Midrash explains this to mean that everyone - all Jews and all gentiles - will be cognizant of G-d as the one, true Master of the World, the Torah will be learned everywhere, both from the Messiah, as well as in their own personal Study Hall at home.

Rabbi Azulai continues: Everyone - Jew and Gentile alike - will flock to hear the Messiah teaching the commandments and deep wisdom that he will teach Israel. The Study Hall that this teacher will teach in will be vast - 18,000 parasangs (54,000 miles) - yet when he teaches, his voice will go from one end of the world to the other. He will be a brilliant and clear teacher - everyone will understand whatever he teaches, be it Law, Midrash, Traditions, Aggadah or any other part of Torah, and no one will forget anything they learned from the Messiah because G-d will reveal Himself in the Study Hall and pour Holy Spirit on everyone.

The Midrash Alpha Betot elaborates on Isaiah's prophecy of the nations honouring the Messiah: nations of the world will admire the Jews and cleave to them. The kings of the various nations will bring gifts to the Messiah, acknowledging him as king of the world, and their subjects will lick the dust from under the Israelites' feet, and seek them to influence their children as much as possible, by hiring the Jews to be their tutors and wet-nurses.

Chabad Chassidic Dimension

Although there will be physical bounty as was and will be described, the main difference and the change that will be most important to those alive then will be the revelation of G-d's glory.

The Midrash Tanchumah states:

''When the Holy One, blessed be He, created the world, He desired for Himself a dwelling place in the lower realms like there is in the upper realms.''

Rabbi Shneur Zalman of Liadi (1745–1812), in his book Tanya, expounds upon this by explaining that before Creation, nothing existed except G-d. G-d desired to create a world that was so distant from infinity, that His light and truth would be (almost) fully concealed, and although it is patently obvious that He is the Creator in the upper worlds, there would be a possibility in this world to deny His existence. G-d's intent in creating this lowly world is so that He should be revealed in the physical world, too. He gets pleasure from the transformation of darkness to light - when He is discovered in the most hidden places, meaning that it is recognised that He is the Creator and Life Giver, even in the places that are the most physical. When the Messiah arrives, G-d will be revealed in all His glory everywhere, even the places that until then were un-G-dly.

Later in the book, he explains further that just like nothing existed besides G-d before the world was created, so too, nothing truly exists besides Him even after the world was created, because He is constantly reciting the Ten Utterances, constantly commanding the world into existence. If He would stop commanding something to exist, it would cease to exist and there would be no memory of it ever existing. (Even though most things in the world are not explicitly commanded into existence in the Ten Utterances, there is a version of a combination of the letters within the Utterances that spells out the object's name in Hebrew. This Hebrew name for something is its soul - its life force because the object is only kept in existence by G-d repeating the name.)

Isaiah prophesied:

"And the glory of the L-rd shall be revealed, and all flesh together shall see that the mouth of the L-rd spoke."

When the Messiah comes, the world will be seen as constantly being kept in existence by G-d and therefore everyone will realise that everything in the world was created by G-d and it contains holiness.

His son, Rabbi Dovber of Lubavitch (1773-1827), explains what it means that G-the glory of the L-rd will be revealed:

When one sees a king, not only does one see the king's ornate clothing and carriage, but one also sees and senses the power of the king from the aura and majesty surrounding the king. With their physical eyes, they see power and they see the essence of the man before them - kingship. When G-d created the world, He did so to be recognised, perceived and grasped. Through hard internal work and the refinement of the world that will take place, this will be possible to be seen with physical eyes in the Future to Come, as Job says, ''I will behold G-d from my flesh [i.e., whilst alive].''

He brings a parable of a rainbow: When the sun is blocked by clouds after rain, it appears as a rainbow. By hiding the sun, it is seen completely differently from how it really is. So too with G-d's Infinite Light. G-d's name, Elokim, is explained Kabalistically as the name that veils G-d's true greatness and limits it to be able to be expressed and to form worlds. The Tetragrammaton, G-d's name of YKVK, relates more to the Infinite Light than to the finite, physical world so it is hidden from mortals. It is the name that translates the Infinite Light into relatable light, and the name Elokim translates the relatable light into the finite letters that form the souls of creation to keep it in existence (See above). Humans cannot relate to the YKVK name of G-d, and in fact, are not even sure how to pronounce it. In the Messianic Era, the veil of Elokim over YKVK will be removed, so people with human intellect can see the glory of YKVK, seeing with human's physical sight that it is the Divine Power in existing things that keep them existing, ex nihilo. This is what Isaiah refers to when talking of people hiding in caves and hollows of the earth out of fear for G-d - they will be so overcome with awe for G-d's glory, that they will not be able to face it.

Even animals will be able to perceive the glory of G-d, as the verse says "all flesh" will be able to, because they will be refined enough to also be able to sense G-dliness and know their Creator.

Rabbi Menachem Mendel Schneerson of Lubavitch (1902-1994) taught:

''All flesh will see together'' - the Hebrew word for 'together' is 'יחדו' (read: Yachdav) can also be translated as 'His Oneness.' When the Messiah arrives and teaches the new kind of Torah, everyone will see that G-d is One - nothing else exists or has any power other than G-d. The people will see that the mouth of G-d spoke - that it is Ten Utterances that G-d continually recites that is the Divine Power which makes every existing thing exist.

In the Messianic Era, the essence of everything will be revealed. The essence of everything is in the Torah of G-d, as he ''looked into the Torah and created the world.'' Isaiah prophecies that in the future, the lion will act tame, like a domesticated animal, and eat hay.

The source of lions in the physical world of Asiyah is the face of a lion in Ezekiel's vision of the Heavenly Chariot in the supernal world of Beriah. Being that the lion was on the right side, the source for the lion in the Chariot, is the attribute of Kindness in Atzilut, as the right side is connected with Kindness. The source for the lion in the attribute of Kindness in Atzlilut is in the Wisdom in Atzilut, because the Hebrew word for lion (Aryeh) has the same letters as the Hebrew word for seeing (Re'iyah) and Wisdom is having an entire idea in one flash, similar to seeing whole scenes in one glance. The source for the lion in the Wisdom in Atzilut is in the Heavenly Crown. Although each layer is only a parable for its source, as in truth, the source and its fruit of entirely different intrinsic value to the point of no actual comparison, we can thus see that everything in the physical world, like the lion, has a parable of a source in supernal worlds.

With the coming of Redemption and the arrival of the Messiah, as mentioned, the essence of everything will be revealed. For the lion, its essence as emanating from the Kindness of Atzilut will be revealed, and so it will lose its aggressive nature to one of benevolence, as befits its source. This is the Chassidic interpretation of how many of the prophecies regarding the Messianic Era will be fulfilled: as a direct extension of G-d's glory being revealed to all and the recognition of the Divine Power causing all existence to exist, rather than as a fantastic reward for good behaviour during exile.

The Mechilta relates that ''one cannot compare hearing to seeing,'' since one can mishear something, but one cannot refute what another person saw with their own eyes. According to this prophecy of Isiah, in the Messianic Era, ''all flesh will see G-d's Oneness'' as an undeniable fact that will be internalised as truth. Once people live with this perspective on life - that life is all about G-d because life only exists because of G-d and is an expression of G-d - then by extension, all the other prophecies will be fulfilled. For example, Isaiah prophesied that there will be peace in the Messianic Era - no war. It is not that there will be a big bash, and boom, suddenly everyone is friends. Rather, once people realise that G-d is everything, war will seem foolish and pointless because if G-d is true, then the Torah He wrote is true, too, and the Torah commands offering a peaceful negotiation before waging war. Furthermore, wars started for political gain generally stem from arrogance or jealousy, which will seem foolish because it will be realised that the whole world is G-d and belongs to G-d and not to them to rule.

This is the opinion of Touger:

''The world will not change. Man will.''

The prophecy of beating swords into ploughshares can be fulfilled as ''peace through prosperity.'' An intimation is the unlikelihood of war between the USA and Western Europe because the stakes are too high and it would ruin the global economy they both rely on.

According to Rabbi M. M. Schneerson, by inculcating oneself with this perspective of G-d being the life force behind the world, one is bringing the Messiah closer practically, as one will be living in that fully positive reality.

Conclusion

From my research, I have found that there are many ways of understanding the Messianic Era. They differ on the details but have the same overarching message: a better, complete world. This may start as a very basic completion of the commandments of the Torah, as Maimonides outlines and it may be a miraculous era, very different to the world, as we know it today, as the Talmud and Midrash foretell. Chassidic texts synthesise these two approaches by explaining how a world where all the commandments are fulfilled is an era different to the current one, where miracles can take place on a constant basis.

About the Writer

Draizy Raskin decided to write an EPQ on the topic of 'What Life Will Be Like In The Messianic Era' because she felt that as a Chabad girl, she heard very often of the urgency to bring Moshiach, but she heard a lot of the abstract elements to it that she didn't relate to and wanted to know exactly what it is that we are all working towards. So, she set out to understand this time period and why it is exciting even though it is so foreign to us. She found the journey fascinating, and she hopes you enjoy her findings as much as she did.

CHAPTER FIFTEEN

HOW ARE THE CONCEPTS OF MASCULINITY AND FEMININITY DISCUSSED IN TRADITIONAL JEWISH THOUGHT?

Chana Vogel

As society has evolved, the traditional view on the roles of Man and Woman have become increasingly modernised. Often, in an earnest attempt for equality and societal acceptance, man and woman have sacrificed their uniqueness. Although these changes have been celebrated amongst the secular society, Judaism retains the idea that rather than engage in "the battle of the sexes," Jewish traditional thought emphasises "the dance of the sexes," how within the roles of Men and Woman, there is room for both. In order to better understand, it is important to first look at the Masculine and Feminine energies separately.

Men and Woman: Equal but different

"Toward a Meaningful Life" is a book authored by Chabad-Chassidic writer, Rabbi Simon Jacobson (1956). Rabbi Jacobson is responsible for publishing the talks and exploring and elucidating the ideas of Rabbi Menachem M. Schneerson, (1902-1994), famously referred to as "The Lubavitcher Rebbe" or simply "The Rebbe," who was the most recent leader of the Chabad-Chassidic Dynasty. He is the founder of the Meaningful Life Centre, whose core aim is to build bridges between the secular and the spiritual and helps to discover the deeper meaning of life based on the three-thousand-year-old wisdom of the Jewish sages.

In his book, Rabbi Simon Jacobson writes, 'G-d is neither masculine nor feminine, but has two forms of emanation: the masculine form, which is more aggressive, and the feminine, which is more subtle. For a human being to lead a total life, he or she just must have both forms of energy: the power of expression and the power of deliberation; the power of strength and the power of subtlety; the power of giving and the power of receiving. And, ideally, these energies are merged seamlessly.'

A strongly reiterated term within Jewish teachings is the idea of "Mashpia" and "Mekabel"- Giving and Receiving. Within a relationship that consists of two individual entities, you will often find one taking the role of the provider, mainstay and source of what is needed, wanted or important to the recipient. The recipient in a relationship is who takes from what is provided, the beneficiary and receiver. The way that this 'Provider and Recipient' relationship manifests itself within human beings is called Masculinity and Femininity.

'The heavens kiss the earth with rays of sunlight; they awaken her with droplets of rain. Impregnated, she delivers life, she nurtures life, she sustains life. The most spiritual heavens, the worlds of angels and souls, they do not have this power – to create being out of nothingness, to transform death into life. For the earth, in her source, is beyond the heavens. They are of G-ds light, but she extends from His very Essence. And from His Essence comes this power to cause being.'

The masculine energy represents one's interactions with others, whilst the feminine energy represents one's interactions with oneself. The introvert versus the extrovert. To better appreciate, one can use the analogy of a garden. In this case, the feminine energy would illustrate the nurturing of the garden, the watering and the growing, the same attributes as one might recognise in a mother; soft, tender and subtle. In contrast, the masculine energy can be depicted through the weeding of the garden. This is the role of the man and the woman.

"The man "goes out" in search of G-dliness; the woman absorbs G-dliness. The man provides the seed to create life; the woman bears life. The man teaches his children how to live; the woman is life. The man gives love; the woman is love.' By affirming the energies of both genders, by accepting the masculine within the feminine and vice versa, man and woman cultivate the forces with which they can have a profound effect on the world."

Man and Woman represent these two energies, the masculine, and the feminine from which the whole world is created and is kept alive. When balanced, these energies can complement each other to the point where the entire environment is affected, for within the man exists the feminine, just as within the woman exists the masculine. Although one is usually dominant within a person, both coexist within him.

This idea is discussed at length by Carl Gustav Jung (1875-1961) a Swiss psychiatrist and psychoanalyst who founded analytical psychology. He proposed the "Anima" and "Animus" theory, describing the "animus" as the unconscious masculine side of a woman and the "anima" as the unconscious feminine side of a man, each transcending the personal psyche.

Jung's theory regarding masculinity and femininity is highly applicable to our current society. In a society where gender roles are highly defined, it's common for men to suppress qualities such as compassion and vulnerability that are traditionally considered feminine, and for women to struggle with developing and expressing traits that are perceived as masculine, such as dominance and assertiveness. According to Jung, understanding the innate temperamental differences between men and women can help men tap into their suppressed compassionate side, and give women the ability to assert themselves, despite having cancelled out the possibility of these traits during their course of development because of the stereotypical categorisation of inappropriate behaviour. The feminine approach can often be more effective than the masculine approach, which often hinges on confrontation. So, the man must access his sensitivity and subtlety, while a woman must access her assertion when necessary. By doing so, individuals can unlock their true potential and achieve greater personal fulfilment.

Jung's perspective was not that individuals should be raised without a solid gender identity, but rather that once a person has established a sufficiently mature personality that is socially acceptable and functional on an individual level, they have the opportunity to expand their personality and incorporate elements of perception, behaviour, and thought that may not have been manageable at an earlier stage of development. Jung believed that for males, developing masculinity may precede the development of femininity, while for females, the opposite may be true. However, if one's character development culminates in a limited and rigid gender identity, one may miss out on other essential aspects that could contribute to their growth and well-being. Such limitations can result in weaknesses that need to be addressed.

Masculinity and Femininity within Time

Time is an organising principle within the physical, the progression of events from the past to the present into the future. The earliest recollection of time, from the traditional Jewish point of view was, of course when it all began, at the beginning of creation: The six days of creation and the seventh day of rest, the Sabbath.

To further explore masculinity and femininity within the context of time, it is important to understand, what the relationship is between the six days and the seventh.

"One who toils before the Sabbath," the Jewish Sages explain, "will have what to eat on Sabbath." The relationship between the six days of work and the seventh day of rest shows us another dimension of a provider and recipient. The Sabbath cannot provide her own work and is therefore the recipient in this relationship.

Even though the concept of a Provider and a Recipient might insinuate a stereotype of dependence and helplessness on the feminine, it is only one half of a broader equation. The six days of toil during the week ultimately provide for the Sabbath, but it is the seventh day that is the rebirth of the following six days, the nourishment and a blessing for it to continue providing and bring forth what is needed. A real provider and recipient is not a one-way relationship but rather a reciprocating correspondence.

Masculinity and Femininity within Nature

Furthermore, the idea that everything within the universe was created through the prism of Masculinity and Femininity, is apparent within the world around us, within the everyday, observable natural order of things.

Third Day of Creation

On the third day of creation, G-d said, "Let the earth sprout vegetation: seed-bearing plants, fruit trees of every kind on earth that bear fruit with the seed in it."

"The earth brought forth vegetation: seed-bearing plants of every kind, and trees of every kind bearing fruit with the seed in it."

Among the various aspects of plant life, reproduction through sexual means, plays a crucial role in their survival and evolution. Plant sexual reproduction is a biological process by which plants produce offspring with genetic diversity. It involves the fusion of gametes, specialised reproductive cells produces by male and female organs of the plant. In flowering plants, the male gamete is produced in the pollen grains, while the female gamete is produced in the ovules located in the pistil.

The process of the plant's reproduction involves pollination, fertilisation and seed development. Pollination is the transfer of pollen from the male to the female's reproductive structures, which can be achieved through wind, water, or insects such as butterflies and bees. Again, a model of the male provider and its female recipient. Fertilization occurs when the male gamete fuses with the female gamete inside the ovule, which leads to the development of an embryo. After fertilisation, the ovule develops into a seed, which contains the embryo and nutrients for its growth. The seed is dispersed by various means, and when in favourable conditions, it germinates and grows into a new plant. Thus, the cycle begins again.

The process of sexual reproduction within plants can also be mirrored within human biology. When a woman conceives a child, she receives a minuscule piece of DNA, a tiny microscopic droplet of genetic information. What she has received from her provider, she has then turned into a baby - an incomparable upgrade.

Fourth Day of Creation

On the following day, G-d said, "Let there be lights in the expanse of the sky, to separate the day from the night; they shall serve as signs for the set times—the days and the years; this is the birth of the sun, the moon, the stars and all the constellations.

The Torah goes on to state, 'G-d made the two great lights, the greater light to dominate the day and the lesser light to dominate the night, and the stars.' Here we are first introduced to the roles that the sun and the moon will play during the course of nature.

Following this theme, this big ball of fire represents the masculine and the moon, feminine. This idea of associating genders with these celestial bodies might prompt someone to ask, what were people noticing about the sun and moon that led them to personify these celestial bodies this way?

The sun is considered masculine, because it penetrates. The light of the sun radiates outwards from space and into the Earth. This light provides the conditions that are necessary for creating life, just as a man provides what is necessary for a woman to conceive. Another way this similarity portrays itself is through the Sun's twenty-four-hour cycle, which echoes the twenty-four-hour hormonal cycle in men. Additionally, the sun embodies such energy associated with the man, that of strength and dependability.

Counter to this dominating star, we have the moon, which does not make its own light, but rather receives and reflects that of the sun. This symbolises the idea of a provider and a recipient (*"Mashpia"* and *"Mekabel"*); where a woman receives and amplifies what is given to her by a man, just as the moon continues to magnify the light of the sun even after it has set. The moon is Feminine, similar to a woman's alluring, mysterious and mercurial nature. The moon's gravitational pull, moves the tides of the ocean often associated with the realms of emotions. Another way we can see this sameness is during a woman's twenty-eight-day menstrual cycle, which echoes the moon's phase cycle, during which the moon waxes and wanes.

This idea that the Male and Female elements exist within the course of nature is also a renowned concept in Chinese Philosophy. Notably "Yin-Yang," a Chinese philosophical concept that describes opposite but interconnected forces. These polar forces could be specified in many ways—heaven and earth, hot and cold, dry and moist and the sun and moon, but the pair that came to dominate is yin and yang. 'Yang originally referred to the south side of a mountain, which received the sun, while yin referred to the north side. Ultimately, yang was associated with the masculine, the forceful, and the bright, while yin was associated with the feminine, the yielding, and the obscure. Creativity followed from the interaction of yin and yang."

Sixth Day of Creation

The progression of days leads to the sixth and final day of creation where G-d blesses the earth with Man. "And G-d created man in His image; in the Divine image of G-d He created him; male and female He created them." G-d created the first human- "Adam," Hebrew for "man"- who was formed by the dust of the earth. When G-d blew life through his nostrils, "the human became a living being." Jewish mysticism teaches that when one blows out air, the breath comes directly from one's essence. This breath is internal and unchanged. When the Torah states that G-d "breathed into Adam's nostrils the soul of life," it is insinuating that G-d imparted His "essence" into man, unlike all the other creations, which were brought into being "externally" through His speech (G-d "said" let there be…)

Wanting to instil the desire for a spouse in Adam, G-d brought forth all the male and female animals he had created previously and instructed him to name them. Seeing that all the animals had a mate but himself, Adam then desired for himself a spouse.

Masculinity and Femininity within Marriage

Dissatisfied with only Adam, the Torah states that G-d said, "It is not good that man should be alone; I will make for him a "helper corresponding to him," an "Ezer Kenegdo," "And He took one of his sides, and closed the flesh in its place… (And He made it into a woman) and brought her to the man." A more literal translation is "helper opposite him." G-d then took his rib while he slept and fashioned the side that had been taken from the Human into a Woman. She is called *isha*, "woman," because, the text says, she is formed from ish, "man." We learn from this moment a man will leave his parents to "cling" to a woman, the two becoming one flesh.

It is clear from here that G-d intended a wife to be a companion to her husband. It can be extrapolated from this verse that she is indeed 'corresponding' to him, but such correspondence does not mean similar. On the contrary, if a relationship would consist of two very complementary individuals it would probably be terribly monotonous and hardly an enjoyable companionship.

The Zohar, Hebrew for the word "splendour," is a series of books that contain Jewish mystical thought known as "Kabbalah," including commentary on the mystical aspects of the Torah (the five books of Moses). As Zohar explains, Man and Woman, originally comprising two halves of a single body, likewise share a single soul.

When a child is born and a designated soul descends into the physical body, this is, in fact, half a soul, separated at birth from its mate, embarking on a journey to reunite with its other half. It is only that G-d desired that for a certain portion of its life on this physical earth, the soul should be divided in two, half of it in a male body and the other half in a female body. Each half would perform its mission in life separately, until the time that G-d unites them in marriage. This explains the unparalleled joy that accompanies a wedding, two halves of the same soul, who have been raised separately, find each other, reuniting with their lost half, to become one.

"That is why it is the man who chases after a woman and not the other way around. For the soul of a man sees what he is lacking: the very essence, the core of being. And he sees that only in a woman can that be found."

However, originally, Adam was made up of both male and female before G-d had separated these two entities to create Eve, a wife for Adam. Following this action, G-d then desired for both Adam and Eve to reunite and become one as husband and wife. But initially, Adam was one with the female?

In order to make sense of this we can ask, 'Why do Men and Women need each other?'

According to Jewish traditional thought, it is not natural for a male to be without a female and vice versa. This conclusion stems back to the first man, who was only whole with woman. Adam found himself in an "unnatural" state when divided from an entity that was initially intrinsically a part of him. Only when he took for himself a woman, did Adam return to his whole and natural state. This reiterates the importance of marriage as a fundamental aspect, since in doing so, it enables a person to return to their natural, whole and full state, which can only be achieved by joining with the opposite sex. Without one's other half, it would prove impossible for one to reach his/her Divine potential. This is because without one's soulmate, eternally bonded through marriage, one would not be able to go beyond the individuality into which one was born.

As mentioned previously, when Adam was first fashioned, he was the epitome of all creation, a direct outcome of G-d's handiwork, comprising of both the man and the woman, as they were before the separation.

As mentioned previously, the world is comprised of both masculine and feminine energies, which are represented by the concepts of "Mashpia" and "Mekabel"- giving and receiving. By embodying these qualities, one can attain spiritual purity and holiness, and provide delight to the universe and its attributes. This is known as the male element. Additionally, one can also receive spiritual sustenance from the universe, which is the female element.

The union of the male and female elements results in the transmission of love to the world, giving birth to spiritual flux and affecting future generations. This is exemplified in the story of Adam, where the concept of femininity was taken from him and replaced with a physical form, a real woman.

"Eshet Chayil" - "Woman of Valour" is a multi-layered poem written by King Solomon as part of the book of Proverbs. The poem is acrostic, with each verse beginning with a successive letter of the Hebrew alphabet, for just like the Hebrew alphabet is the building blocks for creation, so too is the woman. This poem is often sung by Jewish families on Friday night as part of the Shabbat celebration, welcoming in the Shabbat Queen.

This poem extols the qualities and virtues of an ideal wife or woman, commending her for her strength, wisdom, hard work, and devotion to both her family and community. In Jewish tradition, women are seen as channels of creation, providing nourishment, sustenance, and generation. As such, the Hebrew letters themselves are said to speak through them, and the poem "Eshet Chayil"- "Woman of Valour" is dedicated to them. It begins with the question, "A Woman of Valour, who can find?" and goes on to assert her worth as being far beyond that of pearls, and the trust and fortune she brings to her husband.

"A king without a queen, the Zohar says, is neither great nor a king. For it is the woman who empowers the man to conquer his space. And it is the man who empowers the woman to penetrate and nurture hers. Then the man will learn from this woman that he, too, can reach within others and provide and nurture. And the woman will learn that she, too, can conquer." Jewish Sages teach, 'A good ("kosher") woman does what her husband wants.'

Upon first glance, it might seem that in order to be a good wife, a woman should follow the will of her husband. However, the Lubavitcher Rebbe adds a spin to the proverb: 'Who is a good ("kosher") woman? She who 'oise'-does the will of her husband. But the Hebrew word "oise"- "does" can also mean, "to rectify" or "create." Hence: 'Who is a good woman? The woman who creates the will of her husband.

It can be understood from this proverb the immense power that a woman holds within a relationship. The power where she can have a profound and influential effect on a man, where she can cultivate through her subtlety and nature the ability to sway and impact the will of her husband.

The Ten Sefirot

Rabbi Isaac Luria, commonly referred to by many as 'The Arizal' was a 16th-century Kabbalist who revolutionized the study of *Kabbalah*, a form of Jewish mysticism. He is considered one of the most important figures in the development of *Kabbalah*, and his teachings have had a significant influence on Jewish thought and practice. Rabbi Isaac Luria is known for his complex teachings on the nature of the Divine, the structure of the universe, and the inner workings of the human soul. His ideas have had a profound impact on Jewish theology and have been studied and debated by scholars and mystics for centuries.

Rabbi Isaac Luria notes that there are two aspects of femininity. These are represented by the two letters *hei* of G-d's name *Havayah*, spelt *yud-hei-vav-hei* (י-ה-ו-ה). He explains that the Hebrew letters *yud* and vav represent the two aspects of masculinity. According to Jewish mystical thought, it is taught that G-d created the world through the means of the Hebrew alphabet. Every form, name and numerical value of a letter embodies different energies, fused together to then create words, through which G-d created the world.

Specifically, it is taught that G-d created the world using the Divine name *"Havayah."* This name reflects the personality and order of its four letters; two aspects of femininity and two aspects of masculinity. "We thus have here a clear indication that the male-female dynamic is the existential underpinning of all reality." The structure and dynamics of the name *"Havayah"* are reflected throughout all of reality since according to traditional thought, the entire world was formed through this name. Furthermore, the name itself represents two levels of unity between male and female – "yud-hei" and "vav-hei."

The Jewish mystical teachings, known as *Kabbalah* are distinguished by their theory on the ten creative forces that mediate between that of the finite and infinite, G-d, who reveals Himself and continuously creates both the physical realm and the chain of higher metaphysical realms. The *sefirot* represent ten ways through which G-d reveals Himself within creation, with each *sefira* representing a different degree of revelation. The term *sefira* itself has the same root as the word 'Sapir', which is the Hebrew word meaning "sapphire" or "radiance," alluding to the Divine light that is contained within the sefirot and illuminates the creation through them. These ten Sefirot are directly associated with the four letters of G-d's name *"Havayah."*

These ten *Sefirot*-emanations include the seven emotional and the three cognitive/intellectual. Those Sefirot that fall under the intellectual/cognitive attributes consist of "Chochmah"-Wisdom, "Binah"-Understanding and "Daat"-Knowledge. The first six emotional attributes or emanations are the following: "Chesed"-Kindness, "Gevurah"-Strength, "Tiferet"-Beauty, "Netzah"-Splendour, Hod- Serenity and "Yesod"-Foundation.

The seventh and final emotional attribute is "Malchut"-sovereignty representing the "hei" of "Havayah." Different from the previous six, it is a state of being rather than activity. The emanation of "Malchut"-sovereignty is receptive to the six emotional attributes, which invest themselves entirely into this emanation. Sovereignty which is susceptible to these six sefirot then turns these energies into something else. This is masculinity and Femininity at their highest level.

In Kabbalistic thought, these ten attributes are often referred to in relation to masculinity and femininity. The first six emotional Sefirot are considered masculine because they are associated with the energies of assertiveness and activeness. While the masculine form represents the flurry of activity "Malchut"-sovereignty and so too the feminine represent that of simply being.

Furthermore, a man accomplishes through his activeness while a woman is in a state of being. Man *does* while a woman *is*. And like the emanation of "Malchut"-sovereignty, it is through the woman's state of being that the Divine light of G-d is expressed.

To better understand this, these ten Sefirot can be divided into three columns: the right column, the left column, and the central column. The right column represents the masculine or active energy, the left column represents the feminine or receptive energy, and the central column represents the balance between the two.

The Rise of the Feminine – Exile and Redemption

Within Chassidic and Kabbalistic literature, it is taught that there will come a time when the feminine consciousness will transcend all that was thought unattainable. She will then hand out this knowledge, to the man who will only be able to receive this wisdom from the woman. This idea can be learnt in the text, "The Voice of the Bride," which was written by Rabbi Shneur Zalman of Liadi, known as the Alter Rebbe (1745-1812) who expounds upon a model from Rabbi Isaac Luria (1534-1572).

During the traditional, Jewish marriage ceremony, there are a total of seven blessings that are recited for the bride and groom as they stand underneath the wedding canopy. The last two of these seven blessings write: "He rejoices the groom *and* the bride"- placing the groom before the bride. But then we conclude, "He rejoices the groom *with* the bride" implying that the groom's joy is of secondary importance to the bride.

This slight change in the wording of the blessings displays that as of now the bride receives from her groom. However, in the time yet to come, the Messianic Redemption, "they will be equal in their stature with a single crown as it was before the moon was diminished."

Following this it is said, "Once again, in the cities of Judah and the streets of Jerusalem, the voice of the groom and the voice of the bride will be heard," approving that in the future the bride will have a voice. The inner feminine light that had been hidden away will come out and be revealed, a concept that is described in great depth in the poem "Eishet Chayil ateret B'aalah,"- "A Woman of Valour is the Crown of her Husband"- referring to the spiritual light of the Infinite that can only be channelled through the woman which will be the crowning glory of the husband, in the ultimate future.

Rabbi Shneur Zalman notices two shifts within the recital of these blessings; firstly, there is an emergence of the bride's voice from passive silence to full expression. Secondly, there is a reversal of polarities between that of the man and the woman. Now when the spiritual consciousness descends from above to below it first passes from the man and then from him to then from him to the woman. However, in the time to come, by the Messianic redemption, these polarities will invert and G-d's consciousness will move in the opposite direction. It will first descend to the woman and then from her to the man.

It is in the Messianic redemption - a Feminine era where she will be "the crown of her husband." Since she now has the ability to access levels that she was not able to beforehand and the man's vessel of consciousness is too little to contain the revelation of G-d's Divine light. It is only through her that the man can receive this transfer of Divine light. She now encircles the man's head as a crown fulfilling the statement as it says, "The Woman of Valour will become a crown to her husband."

As the Messianic Redemption comes closer, we find ourselves slowly advancing into this "Feminine Era." Kabbalistic and Chassidic teachings share a special understanding of the role of the feminine during the Messianic era. Echoing the previous idea on Woman of Valour, "all the "feminine" aspects of the world will emerge from their concealment and diminution in the unredeemed world and rise to the highest stature."

Jewish traditional thought has an enriched, complex and empowering view of the relationship between masculinity and femininity. Throughout the relationship between man and woman, the course of nature, the prism of time, and the observable natural order of things, Jewish thought has recognized the importance of both masculinity and femininity separately and as one unit. How both these energies are vital in the creation and the upkeep of this world? It is mostly through the constant synergy of both the masculine and feminine energies within the framework of "Mashpia" and "Mekabel"- Giving and Receiving where both these energies constantly insert themselves. The masculine energy takes the role of the provider and the feminine is his recipient.

The traditional Jewish point of view explores the concept of masculinity and femininity through ancient texts such as the Bible, Talmud, and Kabbalah. These ideas are retained and remain constant. However, it is through the Chassidic dimension, that describes the evolution of these concepts, both the masculine and feminine energy, as we near the Messianic redemption. The feminine energy will rise to a higher stature and it will be through the woman that the man will receive. Seeing the feminine as higher than the masculine.

Ultimately, the view of masculinity and femininity in Jewish traditional thought reflects a deep appreciation for the diversity and complexity of human experience. By recognizing the importance of both masculinity and femininity, Jewish tradition offers a powerful framework for understanding the rich tapestry of human nature and relationships, and for fostering greater harmony and understanding in our world.

ABOUT THE WRITER

Chana Vogel is a student at Lubavitch senior girls school. She is currently in sixth form, taking her A-levels in English language and Psychology. Chana has recently completed her EPQ on the topic of "Masculinity and Femininity," due to her avid interest in the mystics and her great love of the creative arts.

Chapter Sixteen

What was Spinoza's relationship with Judaism?

Miri Groner

In this essay, I will explore several factors involved in Spinoza's relationship with Judaism such as his Jewish background, his critique and divergence from traditional Jewish thought and his impact on modern Judaism. I will show how his Jewish upbringing inevitably influenced him; and led to his later critique of Judaism in the Theological-Political Treatise.

The Portuguese Jewish community of Amsterdam, the community Spinoza was raised in, was composed of crypto-Jews or their descendants who had fled from the Portuguese Inquisition and had been attracted by the relative tolerance and economic prosperity of the Dutch Republic. He received a traditional Jewish education; studying Bible and Talmud at the community school of the Talmud Torah congregation (the name of the Amsterdam synagogue). He was probably taught by well-known Dutch rabbis such as Menashe ben Israel, Isaac Aboab da Fonseca and Saul Levi Morteira. His education exposed him to many Jewish philosophers, such as Maimonides, Gersonides, Hasdai Crescas and Ibn Ezra; whom he sometimes referenced in his works. He was a bright student; and might have become a rabbi but was forced to cut short his studies at the age of 17 after the death of his half-brother Isaac in order to attend to the family business of importing fruit.

At the age of 23, in 1656, Spinoza was excommunicated by the Talmud Torah congregation. Records show that this was not a rare occurrence; forty people were excommunicated just between the years 1622 and 1683. One of these excommunications was that of Uriel da Costa, probably the most well known case after Spinoza. Da Costa had been excommunicated twice after espousing dissenting views on the Bible's literalism, the origins of the oral law and the immortality of the soul. However, he was soon to recant his views due to the loneliness caused by forced isolation from the Jewish community (which in those days, could comprise one's entire social life). The second time, in 1640, he was forced to confess his sins in front of the congregation, endure 39 lashes and allow the congregation to walk over his body. He committed suicide shortly after. Spinoza may have witnessed that ceremony, but he would have been only seven and it is possible that this incident influenced his later break with the community. Da Costa's views, interestingly enough, were quite similar to Spinoza's.

What was different between Spinoza and all the other individuals who were excommunicated was that most of them recanted shortly afterwards. Plus, the language used in Spinoza's excommunication is unusually harsh. However, it did not specify what exactly Spinoza had done that had led to decision to excommunicate him; referring only to his "abominable heresies." Because of this, scholars have had to second-guess possible reasons. Supposedly, he was expressing the views he would later express in his books.

It is also possible that Spinoza was already distancing himself from the community. He had stopped contributing to the congregation, though that may have been due to financial reasons. He had also filed a suit against his sister over his father's property in a civil court rather than a Jewish one, something that is not looked at kindly in Jewish communities to this day. Spinoza had already been acquainted with Franciscus Van Enden, the freethinking ex-Jesuit who had introduced himself to secular philosophy, for quite some time and had had already begun boarding with him. There is also a recorded incident of him being attacked with a knife on the steps of the synagogue – after which he probably stopped attended services. Upon hearing news of his excommunication, he is reputed to have said, "Very well; this does not force me to do anything I would not do of my accord, had I not been afraid of a scandal."

There may have also been a political dimension to the excommunication –the community, being ex-Marranos who had fled from the Inquisition were wary of anything that may jeopardize their position as tolerated subjects of the Dutch Republic. Spinoza's heterodox views were radical for the overwhelmingly Calvinist society of the 17th century and association with it could cause a scandal.

Another view is that it resulted from his study Descartes – although it's not certain that he had studies Descartes at that time or whether the relatively open-minded Amsterdam community found fault in that. Steven Nadler has suggested it was because he denied the immortality of the soul – although this is not supported by any written records.

Fourteen years after his excommunication, in 1670, Spinoza published his Tractatus Theologico-Politicus (Theological-Political Treatise), in which he expounds on his philosophy, in particular his views on the Bible, Judaism and religion in general. In chapters seven to ten, he presents his views on biblical authorship and hermeneutics; positing that the Bible could not have been written by Moses, as it consistently refers to him in the third person, but was compiled many years after him, by Ezra the Scribe. The Books of Joshua, Judges, Samuel and the Prophets were not written by the individuals for which they were named, but by other people later in the Second Temple period. And the book's format, he claims, was only canonized in the second century BCE by the Pharisees.

This had drastic implications for the interpretation of Scripture and was a direct assault on the medieval Jewish philosopher Maimonides, who had posited that biblical interpretation should be based on what could be demonstrated through reason. For example, Scripture often uses human features to describe G-d. But since we know through reason that G-d is an immaterial being, that should be understood as metaphor. Spinoza, however, argues that biblical hermeneutics should be understood solely on Scripture's historical and linguistic background. Being that, according to Spinoza, Scripture was only a 'work of nature' it should be interpreted like any other natural science.

Although he did not believe the Bible contained absolute truth, Spinoza did think that it contained moral truth. Its moral message was, according to him: Love G-d above all, and love one's neighbour as oneself. Scripture's relevance as a source of practically applicable commandments though, he saw as being only the remnants of the political constitution of Ancient Israel and thus no longer relevant to Jews in the Diaspora.

The third chapter of the TTP is titled "On the election of the Jews" and discusses Spinoza's views on the Jews as the chosen people. In it, he writes that the ancient Hebrews had been chosen only in respect to their political good fortune. Since they were no longer a political entity, they were no longer chosen. He also disputes the idea that the Jews' continued existence is proof of their chosenness. To him, it is because of the hostility engendered by them continuing to keep biblical laws. He particularly attacks circumcision; saying that "it alone will preserve the Jewish people for all time."

His view on G-d also differs significantly from that of Judaism; which he discusses in length in his Ethics. Spinoza was a pantheist, believing that G-d was the universe and not an individual entity. This means it's impossible for G-d to exist and not the world, which contrasts with the Maimonidean position that G-d is independent of the world and chose to create it of his own volition. A pantheistic god can also never break the laws of nature as he essentially is nature; meaning that miracles could not occur.

As a pantheistic god does not have agency or a will, Spinoza's philosophy is incompatible with the idea of free will; instead, he believed in causal determinism. Part of his philosophy of G-d was that everything in nature, including human beings, were just modes of one "substance," whom he identified as G-d. Thus, humans were not autonomous individuals possessing free will and their actions and desires were ruled by the laws of nature. People's belief in free will could be attributed to the true causes being unknown. He wrote in Ethics, "In nature there is nothing contingent, but all things have been determined from the necessity of the Divine nature to exist and operate in a certain way." This conflicts with Maimonides's dictum that "Free will is granted to all men."

As his views on biblical hermeneutics required a thorough understanding of the Bible's linguistics, Spinoza was fascinated by Hebrew grammar. He believed the original Hebrew language had been distorted by centuries of diasporic transmission and dissection. He wanted to free the study of the Hebrew language from the study of the Bible, saying 'There are many who have written a grammar of Scripture, but none of the Hebrew language'. In an attempt at fixing this, he wrote The Compendium of the Grammar of the Hebrew Language; where he attempts a complete revision of the study of Hebrew grammar and routinely criticises many renowned medieval grammarians for their inauthentic view of the subject.

Many scholars have noted the similarity between Spinoza's metaphysics and the Jewish mystical tradition of Kabbalah. Pantheism is similar to the Kabbalistic doctrine of panentheism, which maintains that G-d is nature but not synonymous with it. The two philosophies also concur that G-d is infinite, that it is impossible for anything to exist outside G-d and they both regard the laws of nature as a manifestation of G-d's essence. Spinoza's teacher, Isaac Aboab de Fonseca, was a Kabbalist and might have introduced him to the philosophy. In addition, many Kabbalist works have been found in his library. It is clear, though, that he did not have a high opinion of it, as he writes in the TTP, "I have also read, and for that matter, known personally, certain Kabbalistic triflers. I've never been able to be sufficiently amazed by their madness." He does seem to be aware of the similarities between his own philosophy and Kabbalah, as he wrote in a correspondence to the German natural philosopher Henry Oldenburg that he shared the idea that "all things are in G-d" with certain ancient traditions of the Hebrews, "corrupted as they have been in many ways."

However, it is important to note that though there are some similarities, they are in no way identical or interchangeable. The differences largely outweigh the similarities. For example, Kabbalah maintains that people can affect G-d through their prayers and observance of his commandments. In fact, G-d needs humanity as they play an integral part in the process of creation. However, in Spinoza's metaphysics, people play no part in the natural order and Spinoza's god has no particular interest in people. In addition, Kabbalah sees the world as possessing a purpose while Spinoza maintains that Nature does not have a teleological function.

In the 17th century, religion was the main form of identification. One could either be Jewish, Christian or Muslim but not nothing. Spinoza was unique in that he left

Judaism without converting to Christianity. This makes him significant when answering the question of Jewish identity. Can someone be Jewish if they do not affiliate with the established Jewish community? Although Spinoza himself might not have considered himself Jewish and there is little evidence that he came into contact with Jewish people after his excommunication, the fact that he did not convert to Christianity has earned him the title of "the first secular Jew." After the rise of secular Judaism in the 19th century, he was admired as a cultural icon by many secular Jews. Perhaps the most famous secular Jew, Albert Einstein, declared that he believed in Spinoza's god.

Zionists are another Jewish group who have adopted Spinoza. In the TTP, Spinoza says that he believes the Jews will one day, "establish their state once more, and that G-d will chose them afresh." This line made him the instant icon of the Zionist movement; who considered him a "proto-Zionist." David Ben-Gurion, the first prime minister of Israel, was an avid fan of Spinoza; calling him "the first Zionist of the last 300 years." Ben-Gurion even tried to convince Israel's chief rabbi to rescind Spinoza's excommunication, but without much success. Another such attempt was made in 2012, when the members of Amsterdam's modern-day Jewish community petitioned their rabbi to rescind the ban. A further attempt occurred in 2015, when a symposium was held by the Amsterdam community. However, the rabbi of the community decided to maintain Spinoza's excommunication.

In conclusion, Spinoza had a complex and multifaceted relationship with Judaism. He was born into it and grew up in its shadow, so was inevitably influenced by it. Throughout his later works, we see a common theme of his obsession with

Judaism, particularly in the TTP, where he made his most systematic critique of Judaism. Because of his education, he was familiar with many Jewish philosophers like Maimonides; whom he criticizes frequently. His impact on Judaism after his death was perhaps more significant than during his life. Besides for his influence on the 19th century secular Jewish movements, he has become a household name for many Jews and is mentioned in many Jewish history books.

ABOUT THE WRITER

Miri Groner had a strong interest in Jewish History, and indeed, in all aspects of history, from a young age. When she was in Year 11 it was suggested that she work on an HPQ (Higher Project Qualification). She decided to write about Spinoza's relationship with Judaism, a fascinating topic. In the Sixth Form she studied History and Sociology at A level and is hoping to continue her studies in University.

Printed in Great Britain
by Amazon

23808617R00189